ULTIMATE pasta

ULTIMATE pasta

JULIA DELLA CROCE

Photography by
IAN O'LEARY

BARNES & NOBLE BOOKS NEW YORK

LONDON, NEW YORK, SYDNEY, DELHI
PARIS, MUNICH AND JOHANNESBURG

Project Editor Lorna Damms
Art Editor Helen Diplock
Senior Editor Nicola Graimes
Senior Art Editor Tracey Clarke
US Editor Laaren Brown
Editorial Assistant David Summers
DTP Designers Karen Ruane
Harvey de Roemer
Managing Editor Susannah Marriott
Managing Art Editor Toni Kay
Production Controllers Antony Heller
Manjit Sihra
Production Manager Maryann Rogers
Home Economist Oona van den Berg
Additional Photography Dave King

For my beloved Gabriella Leah and Celina Raffaella, who rejoice in pasta stars, rings, shells, butterflies, and all the rest

All recipes serve 4, unless otherwise indicated.

All nutritional-information figures are approximate and are based on figures from food composition tables with additional data for manufactured products, where appropriate, not on direct analysis of prepared dishes. Nutritional information is given per serving based on the number of servings in parentheses. Use these figures as a guide only. Please note that KCal is an abbreviation for kilocalories, sometimes inaccurately called calories. Parmesan, when used to serve, has not been accounted for. Readers should note the following breakdown for Parmesan (KCal:68 P:6g C:tr Na:290mg SFA:4g UFA:19g). tr = trace, neg = negligible.

First American Edition, 1997
This edition published by Barnes & Noble, Inc., by arrangement with DK Publishing Inc.
2001 Barnes & Noble Books
M 10 9 8 7 6 5 4 3 2 1
ISBN 0-7607-2739-2

Library of Congress Cataloging-in-Publication Data
Della Croce, Julia
Ultimate pasta / by Julia della Croce.--
1st American ed.
p. cm.
Includes index.
1. Cookery (Pasta) 2. Sauces. I. Title.
TX809.M17D27 2001
641.8"22--dc21

97-16375
CIP

Cover reproduced by Oaktree Press, UK
Reproduced by Colourscan (Singapore)
Printed and bound by
L. Rex Printing Company Limited, China

Contents

Introduction

WHEN MY PUBLISHER asked me to write this book, I momentarily wondered what more I could say, for it would be my third book on the subject of pasta. Then the thought vanished almost instantly. I began to feel an enveloping delight in being able to continue my conversation, as it were, on the subject. In attempting to describe my affinity for this wonderful food, my thoughts stray to the words of anthropologist Folco Portinati, at the University of Turin, about the meaning of pasta in Italian life: "Pasta, like wine," he said, "is to the Italians somewhere between a sacrament and a psychotropic drug." The Italian devotion to pasta is perhaps most aptly noted in the designation of St. Stefano as the patron saint of pasta makers. The event preceding his canonization is illustrated in a Renaissance painting now hanging in the Museo Nazionale della Paste Alimentari in Rome: it shows the discovery of the murdered saint lying in a wooden trough of the kind used for kneading pasta dough.

There is evidence that pasta existed in the Italian diet from the time of its earliest inhabitants, the Etruscans, but its real popularity came with the eighteenth and nineteenth centuries, when the development of dried pasta made large-scale production possible. It was made of durum wheat semolina flour rather than refined white flour, and contained no eggs, which rendered it both more viable for mass production and cheaper to make. Manufacturing began first in Sicily, then spread to Liguria through Genoa, an important port in the trade routes. Finally, by the end of the nineteenth century, Naples had become the center of pasta manufacturing due to its climate and port, which could receive shipments of wheat from abroad to supplement native crops. Dried pasta became identified with southern Italian cuisine. *Pastificci*, pasta factories, sprang up all over Naples and along the Amalfi coast, where the hot and breezy climate was ideal for drying the dough outdoors. By the late 1900s, there were as many as 1,500 pasta manufacturers in Naples alone.

PASTA drying out of doors at a spaghetti factory in Naples, c.1900.

Pasta and Myth

Dried pasta became abundant and accessible to even the poorest Italian and a reverence grew for this food that had kept the proverbial wolf from the door. In turn, pasta became part of a new folklore. The Italians began to endow pasta with magical properties. In the *commedia dell'arte*, the popular street theater of the sixteenth to

THREE PULCINELLAS grouped around a simmering pot of *gnocchi*. Giambattista Tiepolo, 1751.

eighteenth centuries, *maccheroni* was a central theme. The Neapolitan love of pasta is played out in the character of Pulcinella, the roguish hunchback who in England and America became Punch of Punch and Judy fame. According to legend, his deformed shape is the result of having been sired by a chicken. His white pantaloons and conical hat (his cooking pot in some drawings) were the customary dress of the southern peasant. In an essay on Pulcinella, Alberto Consiglio describes how traveling troupes of actors, wearing the mask of Pulcinella, spread the clown's popularity throughout Europe, and thus ensured the popularity of macaroni: "... with Pulcinella, macaroni becomes diffused as an instrument of funniness, as a symbol of the grotesque hunger of the Neapolitan people."

For Pulcinella, the mascot of the poor, hunger is a state of mind; *maccheroni*, the dried pasta of the south, an unceasing obsession. The image of Pulcinella gluttonously attacking a plate of pasta was used as a symbol of the Neapolitan appetite for *maccheroni* and appears in the work of popular illustrators and great masters alike, from Pinelli to Giambattista Tiepolo. And what is Pulcinella but an idealized image of people's gratitude for a wonderful invention? To this day, illustrations of Pulcinella eating spaghetti – as often as not with the telltale tomato-sauce stains decorating his white peasant garb – survive on pasta packaging and *spaghetteria* signs throughout Europe and America.

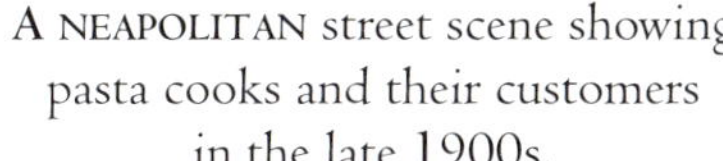

A NEAPOLITAN street scene showing pasta cooks and their customers in the late 1900s.

A Heroic Food

A sketch published in *The Street Lamp Newspaper for Everybody* on September 4, 1860 (three days after Garibaldi, fighting to liberate Italy, entered Naples), portrays a Neapolitan army as a legion of *pulcinellas* armed with chamber pots full of spaghetti. The Neapolitans, reputed to be outlaws and fierce fighters, were, it seems, fueled by the potent properties of pasta, much as Popeye was miraculously endowed with superhuman strength after inhaling his can of spinach.

However, the history of pasta has been a rocky one. Throughout the centuries, popes, philosophers, reformers, dictators, and men of medicine have speculated on the dangers to health and psyche posed by its consumption. The challenge to the Italian gastronomic obsession has persisted even in modern times. In 1932, the futurist artist and social reformer F.T. Marinetti wrote *La Cucina Futuristica*, a manifesto against pasta. He led a crusade to convince Mussolini and the Italians that continued pasta-eating would bring the country to ruin, insisting that pasta addiction had produced a nation of dreamers, not fighters, and that because of its pasta diet, Italy had remained mired in the past. Marinetti devised menus that were designed to prepare the future race for an existence that would be "more aerial and rapid" and conducive to the ideas of the twentieth century. In place of pasta he recommended banana and anchovy sandwiches, and boiled vegetables cut into astrological shapes. But his ideas fell on deaf ears. Mussolini made the new sleek aluminum trains run on time, but he couldn't revolutionize the Italian table.

"MANGIAMACCHERONI" (macaroni eaters) as depicted by the English artist Percival Seaman, Naples, 1843.

A Primal Food

"If you want to live forever and ever, drink wine and eat maccheroni." (Sicilian proverb)

My first introduction to the mysteries of pasta was in my mother's kitchen. She concocted endless innovations of pasta and sauce to tame ferocious appetites. True to the old Italian saying that food is first eaten with the eyes, then the mouth, she transformed flour and eggs into ribbons, curls, butterflies, half-moons, and angel hair. There was also dried pasta, *pasta secca*, encompassing a great assortment of sleek miniature flour and water sculptures, each designed for a different culinary purpose. In accordance with the Italian impulse to delight and divert, there were the absurd and the extravagant, from "flying saucers" to *ave marie*. There were also the superlatives and the diminutives: not only small reeds *(cannelle)*, but tiny reeds and large reeds; and what

A SELECTION of *pasta secca* (dried pasta) shapes, each one designed for a particular culinary application.

child can resist pasta shapes with such beguiling names as clowns' hats and priests' hats, trouts' eyes, wolves' eyes and sparrows' tongues. Until recently, it was difficult to find the more unusual pasta shapes outside Italy. Now that the appetite for pasta has vastly increased worldwide, many previously unknown varieties are sold everywhere.

ULTIMATE PASTA

The title of this book is not put forward without humility. As a serious student of Italian gastronomical habits, I am familiar with the endless beguiling recipes for pasta that exist from one end of the Italian peninsula to the other. No matter where one goes in Italy, wherever one encounters pasta, whether in the superb home cooking of local people or in restaurants, a plate of pasta is almost always delectable. Sauces are inevitably a combination of the season's most glorious ingredients combined simply but adroitly with the theme aromatics of the Italian kitchen. Complex pasta concoctions, *lasagne al forno* and such, or stuffed pasta shapes, are devised with the same fine hand that has made Italian craftsmanship renowned the world over. A plate of pasta is nothing less than a culinary ode to Italy's culturally complex and richly embroidered past of Etruscan and Greek forebears, Saracen invaders, Spanish, Bourbon or Austro-Hungarian kingdoms, and a multiplicity of other foreign influences, wrought with an amalgam of native and New World ingredients.

The title "ultimate" describes what I consider to be the world's best way with pasta, the Italian way. Simply no one cooks pasta like the Italians. The recipes in this book are the result of a lifetime absorbing the Italian way with food. Some are strictly classic dishes, interpreted in my own way, but more are my own innovations. Others came from friends and colleagues. All are based in the classic Italian approach, even if executed with a creative hand. Thus a butter sauce for pumpkin *tortelli* may be infused with cardamom, a most un-Italian flavoring, or saffron may tint a traditional broth.

It is my goal to tempt my readers with delicious recipes, and to teach how to cook pasta properly so that even the most simple dish, prepared the Italian way, can be experienced to its ultimate.

A GALLERY OF PASTA

PASTA HAS BEEN WITH ME all my life. Indeed, in the form of *pastina*, it was the first solid food I was given. Then came the other endless forms I was raised on, combined with so many different sauces, from garlic and field greens to aromatic *ragù*. On holidays, the same pasta was presented in festive form – handmade *tagliatelle* with a sauce of wine and porcini perhaps, or the savory, rosemary-scented drippings from Sunday's roast lamb or pork. From its modest appearance in soups to lavish pasta molds, pasta is a remarkably versatile food – as the extraordinary variety of dishes in this gallery shows.

MINESTRE

SOUPS

Brodo con zafferano e quadrucci

PASTA AND SOUP ARE PERFECT PARTNERS, but the shape and size of the pasta should be matched to the style of the soup. For broths, use only the smallest soup pasta (*pastina*) or fine angel hair pasta. The proportion of pasta to other ingredients should be modest to avoid overcrowding and also prevent the liquid in the soup from being totally absorbed as the pasta swells during cooking.

MINESTRONE ESTIVO CON PROSCIUTTO E PARMIGIANO

Literally "big soup," minestrone *is thick with summer vegetables and beans. This version is enriched with a meaty ham bone and the best extra-virgin olive oil.* *(See page 64 for recipe.)*

BRODO CON ZAFFERANO E QUADRUCCI

This golden, aromatic minestra *is fragrant with saffron. The tiny egg pasta* quadrucci *may be dried or made by hand.* *(See page 68 for recipe.)*

STRACCIATELLA CON POLPETTINE E PASTINA

*Small, light soup pasta (*orzi *here) and beaten egg are added to the broth-based soup. The miniature dumplings are made of turkey and sweet Italian sausage meat.* *(See page 65 for recipe.)*

BRODO CON POLPETTINE DI POLLO E CAPELLI D'ANGELO

The delicate meatballs retain their juiciness as they cook in the broth. Angel hair pasta adds body. *(See page 69 for recipe.)*

MINESTRA DI FAVE CON LINGUINE

Tender green fava beans, linguine *broken into short lengths, chopped fresh basil and mint, and prosciutto characterize this classic Sicilian soup.* *(See page 67 for recipe.)*

PASTA FRESCA

FRESH PASTA DISHES

Tagliatelle di pomodoro con porri e gamberi

NOWHERE IS FRESH PASTA prepared so well and so imaginatively as in the Italian kitchen. While some of the great fresh pasta dishes of Italy are common on restaurant menus abroad, they cannot equal those made in the home kitchen, where they can be timed to the minute, as all good pasta must be. The pasta itself must be incredibly thin so that it stays porous, tender, and able to absorb the delicate sauce.

TAGLIATELLE CON MELANZANE ARROSTO, POMODORO, E MOZZARELLA

The harmonious pairing of bold and delicate flavors stands out in this unusual dish of smoky baked eggplant, melting mozzarella, and luscious plum tomatoes. *(See page 84 for recipe.)*

TAGLIATELLE DI POMODORO CON PORRI E GAMBERI

Leeks and tarragon combine to impart a naturally sweet flavor to this delicate sauce for tagliatelle. *(See page 84 for recipe.)*

FARFALLE CON CARNE DI VITELLO E PINOLI

An inspired original sauce for fresh "butterflies" that brings together savory pieces of sautéed veal, pine nuts, lemon zest, and aromatic rosemary. *(See page 88 for recipe.)*

MALTAGLIATI CON PISELLI, CIPOLLA, E PANCETTA

Tender peas, pancetta, mint, and parsley are the foundation of this springlike, versatile sauce for maltagliati *or other pasta varieties.* *(See page 89 for recipe.)*

TAGLIERINI CON SALSA DI PESCE

Sweet butter is at the base of this refined, saffron-scented seafood sauce for fresh taglierini *noodles.* *(See page 80 for recipe.)*

PASTA SECCA

DRIED PASTA DISHES

Farfalle con peperoni arrostiti

THE ASTOUNDING RANGE of *pasta secca* (dried pasta) lends itself to a variety of dishes. Generally, dried pasta is served with more robust sauces than fresh pasta. Certain shapes combine with sauces in different ways: *spaghetti*, for example, suits cream or olive oil-based sauces; while *penne* (quill-shaped pasta) is perfect for thicker sauces that can nestle in the tunnels and grooves.

PENNE CON BROCCOLI, SALAME, E FAGIOLI

A robust sauce, incorporating creamy cannellini beans, high-quality salame, *and tender broccoli florets, which demands a chunky cut of pasta to accompany it.* *(See page 95 for recipe.)*

FARFALLE CON PEPERONI ARROSTITI

Roasted red and yellow peppers impart a lovely smoky flavor to the sauce, and provide the ideal shape and texture for the pasta "butterflies." *(See page 92 for recipe.)*

SPAGHETTI CON AGLIO, OLIVE, ED ERBETTE

This simple dish - combining humble yet aromatic and delicious ingredients - is widely popular in the southern regions of Italy. *(See page 96 for recipe.)*

NIDI CON CARCIOFI E FINNOCHIO FRESCO

This Sardinian-style dish utilizes the island's favorite vegetables. The assertive flavor of the artichokes is complemented by sweet fennel. Cream and Parmesan unify all. *(See page 101 for recipe.)*

LINGUINE CON CALAMARI E AGLIO

Seafood, chili, white wine, and fresh vine-ripened tomatoes, enlivened with a hint of garlic, are a classic combination. This dish can also be made with spaghetti. *(See page 99 for recipe.)*

PASTA SECCA CON SALSE CRUDE

DRIED PASTA WITH UNCOOKED SAUCES

Fusilli con pomodoro e mozzarella

THE COMBINATION OF STEAMING, piping-hot pasta with a cool, uncooked sauce is a delightful one. However, it is particularly important that only the best ingredients be used. It is this type of light, refreshing pasta dish that is often served in summer on the Italian table, not the cold, so-called pasta salads with vinegar dressings, which are too often catchalls for all manner of discordant ingredients.

CONCHIGLIE CON POMODORO CRUDO, AVOCADO, E GAMBERETTI

The exceptionally well-balanced combination of tastes and textures makes this a delightful fresh, summer dish. *(See page 104 for recipe.)*

FUSILLI CON POMODORO E MOZZARELLA

Cubes of sweet, milky mozzarella transform this classic tomato sauce into an entirely new dish. It is enlivened with aromatic basil and a sprinkling of freshly ground pepper. *(See page 104 for recipe.)*

TRENETTE AL PESTO ALLA SILVANA

Pesto alla genovese *is one of the most beguiling of uncooked pasta sauces with its aroma of ground, fresh, sweet basil, pine nuts, Parmesan, and fruity olive oil.* *(See page 107 for recipe.)*

SPAGHETTINI CON LIMONE, CAPPERI, E OLIVE

The zesty combination of tart green olives, salty capers, lemon, and hot red chili pepper makes a simple yet very appealing dish. *(See page 106 for recipe.)*

SPAGHETTI ALLA PUTTANESCA

A Neapolitan classic, here made with conchiglie, *this chilled variation of the renowned* puttanesca *sauce has the vibrancy and robust flavors of the cooked version.* *(See page 106 for recipe.)*

PASTE RIPIENE

STUFFED PASTA DISHES

Tortellini con salsa di funghi e panna

MELTINGLY THIN SHEETS of handmade egg pasta can be molded or cut to enclose a delectable variety of freshly made fillings. Regional recipes include such delicacies as sweet pumpkin and orange *cappellacci*, classic spinach and ricotta *ravioli* served with fresh tomato sauce, savory stuffed crepes baked with béchamel sauce and Parmesan, and Bolognese *tortellini* gently cooked in broth.

TORTELLONI AL POMODORO RIPIENI CON PESCE E PATATE IN BURRO FUSO

Delicate fish- and potato-filled bundles of egg pasta tinted lightly with tomato need little more than butter and a sprinkling of pecorino at the table. *(See page 116 for recipe.)*

TORTELLINI CON SALSA DI FUNGHI E PANNA

These tortellini *are stuffed with a fragrant, subtly spiced meat filling. The creamy mushroom sauce complements the flavors of the stuffing.* *(See page 118 for recipe.)*

PANSOTTI DI RICOTTA E PROSCIUTTO ALL'AURORA

Prosciutto is added to the classic cheese filling in these versatile stuffed bundles. *(See page 113 for recipe.)*

RAVIOLI DI ZAFFERANO CON SPINACI, RICOTTA, E SALSICCIA

A little saffron adds a burst of sunny color to the pasta dough in these Venetian-inspired ravioli. *(See page 113 for recipe.)*

CARAMELLE DI ZUCCA E MELA IN BURRO FUSO

These candy-shaped bundles stuffed with sweet potato and apple are made slightly exotic by the addition of cardamom pods in the butter sauce. *(See page 118 for recipe.)*

PASTA AL FORNO

BAKED PASTA DISHES

Maccheroni al forno con funghi

HERE IS THE ONE EXCEPTION to the rule that pasta should be cooked just before being sauced and served. Dried or fresh pasta is combined with sausages, ham, vegetables, and cheeses, and as many sauces as the imagination can conjure. The only caveats are that creativity be tempered with a sense of harmony, and that there be plenty of moisture to prevent the pasta from drying as it bakes.

CONCHIGLIONI AL FORNO CON RICOTTA E SPINACI IN SALSA AURORA
Giant pasta shells are receptacles for a creamy ricotta and spinach filling. Chopped pine nuts add a delectable texture. *(See page 127 for recipe.)*

MACCHERONI AL FORNO CON FUNGHI
Pungent porcini, delicate chanterelles, and cultivated mushrooms are tossed with lumache. *Bread crumbs are sprinkled on the top for a crunchy, light topping.* *(See page 125 for recipe.)*

BUCATINI AL FORNO ALL'AMENDOLARA
This is a succulent Apulian one-dish meal in which sweet plum tomatoes, chicken, and a full-bodied tomato sauce are baked under a pecorino-sprinkled bucatini *"crust."* *(See page 126 for recipe.)*

TAGLIATELLE AL FORNO CON TONNO
The light, tomato-based sauce and generous quantities of sour cream keep these fresh tagliatelle *noodles with flaked tuna deliciously moist.* *(See page 129 for recipe.)*

PENNETTE AL FORNO CON CAVOLO E FONTINA
The flavors of cumin and fontina are in the northern Italian tradition, but this warming dish of baked pasta quills with green cabbage is improvisational. *(See page 128 for recipe.)*

PASTA AL FORNO PER LE FESTE

FESTIVE BAKED PASTA DISHES

Lasagne al forno con melanzane e ragù

ELEGANT MOLDS, many-layered *lasagne,* and pastry drums encasing succulent pasta originated in wealthy homes. The foods of the peasant class were characterized by stove-top methods, since many people did not own ovens. Cooks in wealthy households had fairly well-appointed kitchens and the time to prepare elaborate dishes. Thus *timballe,* molds, and other festive pasta dishes came to life.

TIMBALLO DI PASTA CON POLPETTINE
In this timballo, *macaroni is combined with meatballs and two sauces, béchamel and tomato, then encased in shortcrust pastry, keeping it moist and fragrant as it bakes. (See page 137 for recipe.)*

LASAGNE AL FORNO CON MELANZANE E RAGÙ
This sumptuous lasagne, *made with layers of baked eggplant and a rich Bolognese sauce or ragù, is designed for very delicate fresh wide noodles. (See page 136 for recipe.)*

TIMPANO DI TAGLIATELLE CON SALSA DI VITELLO
Fresh egg tagliatelle *noodles are tossed with an onion-enriched béchamel sauce, baked in a ring mold and then served with a sauce of veal, onion, wine, and sage. (See page 138 for recipe.)*

LASAGNE AL FORNO ALLA MARCELLA
Sliced artichoke hearts, spinach, ricotta, and a mellow béchamel sauce are stuffed between layers of the thinnest possible fresh lasagne *noodles. (See page 134 for recipe.)*

CANNELLONI AL FORNO CON POLLO E FUNGHI
Tender pieces of chicken and mushroom in a smooth sauce are encased in fresh or dried cannelloni. *The dish is then baked until bubbly and golden. (See page 140 for recipe.)*

GNOCCHI

GNOCCHI AND DUMPLINGS

Gnocchetti con pomodoro e mozzarella

CLASSIC POTATO *GNOCCHI*, pronounced *"nyo-kee,"* are probably the most familiar form of this dish, but there are *gnocchi* made of bread, and vegetable variations using pumpkin, eggplant, and spinach. Regional recipes also abound – such as the potato *gnocchi* of Istria, stuffed with sweet plums or plum conserve and, after boiling, drizzled with butter and sprinkled with sugar and cinnamon.

GNOCCHI DI SPINACI ALLA MARCELLA

A colorful variation on classic potato gnocchi, served with a delicate butter-based tomato sauce. (See page 147 for recipe.)

GNOCCHETTI CON POMODORO E MOZZARELLA

Miniature potato gnocchi are dressed with a simple sauce of fresh, luscious vine-ripened tomatoes, then barely baked with a scattering of fresh mozzarella. (See page 146 for recipe.)

CANÈDERLI

These delicious bread dumplings, which are cooked and served in a rich meat broth, are a northern Italian specialty. They make an excellent lunch or supper dish. (See page 150 for recipe.)

GNOCCHI DI SEMOLINO ALLA ROMANA

A combination of staple ingredients - semolina, milk, butter, eggs, and cheese - makes up this elegant dish, which is based on a traditional Roman recipe. (See page 149 for recipe.)

GNOCCHI DI RICOTTA

Fresh ricotta gives these gnocchi dumplings a moist, creamy texture that goes very nicely with the sweetly tart flavor of the tomato sauce. (See page 143 for recipe.)

A Catalog of Pasta

ACCORDING TO AN ITALIAN anthropologist, there are an astonishing 2,000 different kinds of pasta to be found throughout Italy. Some 350 of these are the dried, commercially manufactured pasta shapes; the remainder are the many types of fresh, homemade pasta and uncommon regional specialties. In keeping with the Italian predilection to amuse and beguile, there are the fantastical, the hyperbolic and the sublime, from "kisscatchers" to "bridegrooms" and *ave marie*. This chapter presents some of those that are available outside the borders of Italy.

Soup Pasta

There are so many varieties of soup pasta, but many of them are either unknown or ignored outside Italy. They can be a delightful addition to broths and soups. The general rule of thumb is to use the smallest, light *pastina* ("little pasta"), such as *stelline*, *acini di pepe*, and *semi di melone*, in broths. *Pastina* can also be quickly boiled in salted water and dressed with butter. This is typical nursery food in Italy, but it makes a good, simple lunch or breakfast for adults and children, too. Italian pasta manufacturers produce spinach and carrot flavored *pastine*, which contain additional nutrients, as well as egg *pastine*. Larger soup pasta is made for more robust soups, the size of pasta corresponding to the types of ingredients.

ACINI DI PEPE (Peppercorns)
Probably the smallest variety of pastina, acini di pepe *(also called* peperini*) are ideal for broths.*

ORZI (Barley)
Shaped like grains of barley, orzi *are perfect for my version of* stracciatella *(see page 65).*

RISI, RISONI (Rice)
This pasta variety, which is also called pasta a riso, *mimics rice grains very convincingly when cooked.*

ALFABETI (Alphabet pasta)
Minute letters and numbers that are especially appealing to children.

STELLINE (Little stars)
Delicate star shapes are often tossed with butter and hot milk (see page 100).

QUADRUCCI (Squares)
These tiny egg pasta squares are ideal for giving extra body to light broths.

CAPELLINI TAGLIATI (Broken fine hair)
Break up these very fine pasta strands and cook them in broth.

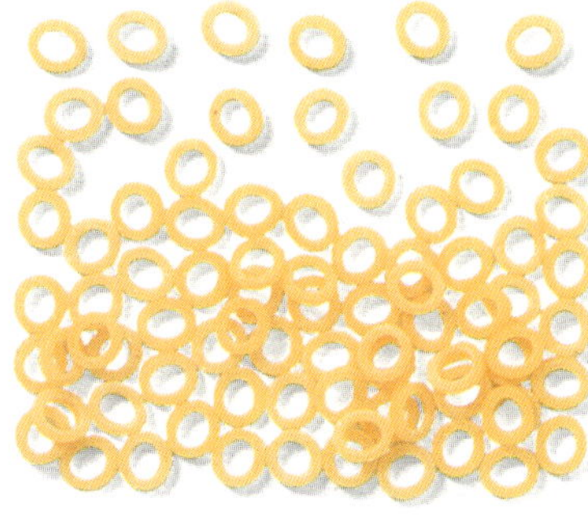

ANELLINI (Little rings)
Select these light anellini *for vegetable and meat broths.*

TUBETTINI (Little tubes)
These tiny macaroni can be used in light soups. The larger tubetti *are perfect for* minestrone.

CONCHIGLIETTE (Little sea shells)
Light soups, perhaps those containing vegetables or lentils, suit these shapes.

FARFALLINE (Little butterflies)
Use this delicate pastina *shape in broths and light soups.*

FUNGHETTI (Little mushrooms)
This quirky mushroom-shaped egg pasta works well in heartier soups.

Long Pasta

Most long pasta *(pasta lunga)* is designed to be served simply with sauces. The very long, wide tubular varieties, such as *zitoni* and *penne di natale* ("Christmas *penne*"), are also meant for baked pasta dishes. I have heard heated debates about whether long pasta should be broken before cooking. Purists believe in keeping it whole; pragmatists feel that cooking and eating is simplified by breaking it. I myself prefer to keep it whole, for why are all these whimsical shapes created if they are then to be broken up before they even hit the pasta pot? Certainly, long tubular shapes are hard to eat in their whole form, but then the skill acquired in keeping one's shirt sauce-free is part of the art of eating it.

CAPELLI D'ANGELO, CAPELLINI
Angel hair, Fine hair
Use capelli d'angelo *in broth;* capellini *in broths, with delicate sieved sauces, or in* pasticci.

Capelli d'angelo ***Capellini***

VERMICELLI / FEDELINI
Little worms, Very fine noodles
Choose fine vermicelli *and* fedelini *noodles, broken up, for broth-based soups. Certain thicker varieties of* vermicelli *are suitable for sauces.*

Vermicelli ***Fedelini***

SPAGHETTI ALLA CHITARRA, SPAGHETTI
Guitar (square-cut) spaghetti, Lengths of cord
Spaghetti alla chitarra *is named after the wire-stringed implement on which it is cut. Use* spaghetti *with tomato or fish sauces, or oil-based sauces.*

Spaghetti alla chitarra ***Spaghetti***

BAVETTINE (MEZZE LINGUINE)
Narrow flat noodles (half linguine)
Use these half-thickness linguine *noodles with seafood sauces and delicate olive oil-based sauces.*

LINGUINE
Little tongues
Traditionally, linguine *are used with "white" clam sauces,* pesto, *and delicate oil-based sauces.*

PERCIATELLI
Small pierced macaroni
Use with ragù, other meat sauces, and baked dishes with eggplant.

BUCATINI
Long "holed" string noodles
These long, thin hollow tubes of pasta are used with pesto *and sauces containing pancetta (such as* bucatini all'amatriciana*), vegetables, and cheeses.*

FUSILLI BUCATI LUNGHI
Long, hollow twists
Springy shapes for meat sauces that are traditionally served with Neapolitan ragù. They can be used in baked pasta dishes.

ZITI
Long bridegrooms
These lengthy tubes are commonly broken into pieces before cooking. Use with ragù and meat and vegetable sauces.

CANDELE
Candles
Traditional with Neapolitan-style ragù, candele *are ideal for all meat sauces.*

TUBES

TUBULAR SHAPES have relatively thick pasta walls, which makes them sturdy enough to support not only tomato-based sauces, but also meat, cheese, and cream preparations. Their shortness, however, also makes them suitable for more simple butter sauces. Tubular shapes with ridged surfaces, such as *penne rigate*, are more successful in holding olive oil-based sauces than those with smooth surfaces. Despite their versatility, the size of ingredients in the accompanying sauces should be kept in mind. For example, wide tubular cuts like *rigatoni* are ideal for *ragù* or broccoli sauce because their cavities are large enough to capture the pieces of meat or vegetables. Tubular shapes are also perfect for baked dishes.

Ditaloni Rigati

Thimbles (ridged)

These "thimbles," which are available in smaller sizes and ridged or smooth, should be used in soups with beans.

Tortiglione

Hollow spirals

Also called "succhietti" *(from the word for a "drill bit"), these short hollow spirals are for use with meat or cheese sauces.*

Fusilli Corti

Short twists

These short, tight twists form hollows that will effectively trap meat, ragù, *and ricotta preparations.*

Sedani Rigati

Striped celery (tomato and plain shapes)

Pair "striped celery" with meat, vegetable, or sausage sauces. Use smooth sedani *as above, or with cheese and egg combinations.*

Elicoidali

Helixes

Use these shapes, which have a spiraling ridged pattern, with tomato, meat, and cheese sauces.

Rigatoni

Large grooved macaroni

Choose this robust shape for meat and sausage sauces, fresh tomato sauces, vegetable sauces, and baked timballi.

Penne Mezzanine

Half quills

These half-thickness penne *are best matched with light vegetable sauces and tomato sauces.*

Penne Rigate

Striped quills

Ridged penne *are designed to take oil- or butter-based sauces, meat or vegetable creations, and unctuous cheese sauces.*

Penne Lisce

Smooth quills

Tomato sauces, including more chunky versions, meat sauces, and cream sauces are compatible with these quills.

Pennotti Tricolori

Large quills

Long durum wheat quills (shown here in tomato, spinach, and plain flavors) are a specialty of Apulia.

Pennette

Little quills

Match these tiny penne *with tomato sauces, meat sauces, and also cream-based concoctions.*

Penne Grandi (Sardi)

Giant quills

These spacious tube shapes are for use with ragù, *meat, and robust vegetable sauces, such as those containing broccoli or cauliflower.*

Ribbon Pasta

Most dried ribbon pasta is interchangeable with fresh pasta, but homemade noodles are designed for use with delicate rather than vigorous sauces. Dried ribbon-type pasta, such as *linguine* and *lasagnette,* has a more rigid texture than fresh ribbon-style egg pasta, which makes it suitable for a wider variety of sauces and uses. For example, *trenette* are the traditional choice for *pesto* because the sturdy, flat strands support the solid ingredients and still absorb the flavors of the unctuous sauce without losing their pleasantly robust texture. Ribbon shapes, whether dried or fresh, should be matched with sauces that cover their surface area from end to end.

TAGLIERINI

These paper-thin, 1/16in (1.5mm) wide strands can be cut on a very narrow pasta machine cutting attachment. They are also known as tagliarini, tagliolini *and* tonnarelli.

Fresh egg taglierini

Dried spinach taglierini

TRENETTE

Traditionally served with pesto, *these 1/8in (2mm) noodles should be slightly thicker than usual (when made fresh, the pasta is rolled up to the penultimate notch of the machine).*

Fresh egg trenette

Dried trenette

FETTUCCINE

Little ribbons

Like trenette, fettuccine *are designed to be slightly thicker than most noodles. They should be cut by hand.*

Fresh spinach fettuccine

TAGLIATELLE

Fresh tagliatelle *are very thin and delicate flat noodles, about 1/4in (5mm) wide, that may be cut on the pasta machine attachment. The dried variety is widely available.*

Fresh egg tagliatelle

FETTUCCIA RICCIA

Rippled ribbons

These wide dried pasta noodles are thicker than tagliatelle. *Use with cream sauces and other sumptuous sauces.*

Dried fettuccia riccia

PAPPARDELLE

The name pappardelle *derives from the verb* "pappare," *to gobble up. The fresh types are 3/4–1in (1.5–2.5cm) wide and have fluted edges. Dried egg* pappardelle *have straight sides.*

Fresh pappardelle

PIZZOCCHERI

Originating in Lombardy in the north of Italy, these flat, thin buckwheat noodles are cut across on the diagonal to make short noodles. They may be purchased dried.

Fresh pizzoccheri

Pasta Shapes

As the consumption of dried pasta has dramatically increased, the varieties of dried pasta shapes have proliferated, especially short pasta, which is easier to cook. In the nineteenth century, pasta producers began a competition of designing ever more imaginative shapes to entice consumers. The goal was to create new types that combined form with utility – interesting shapes that would hold sauce well. Today Italian manufacturers produce some 350 different shapes of dried pasta. With the exceptions of dried egg noodles and whole-wheat pasta, the many varieties available are made from durum wheat flour (semolina) and water. Tomato, spinach, and other ingredients are sometimes added for color.

FUSILLI
Corkscrews
These are suited to ragù and meat and ricotta mixtures that nestle in the twists.

GEMELLI
Twins
Good for picking up meat or vegetable sauces and cheese- or cream-based sauces.

CASARECCIE
Twists
These plain and tinted pasta shapes are perfect for catching tomato, meat, and sausage sauces.

STROZZAPRETTI
Priest stranglers
Handmade shapes to be matched with tomato, meat, and sausage sauces.

RICCIOLI
Curls
Three-color, fluted, trumpet-shaped curls that are excellent for holding tomato and meat sauces.

FARFALLE
Butterflies
Pair these with simple oil-based sauces, butter, tomato, and cheese-based sauces.

CONCHIGLIE, CONCHIGLIONI
Shells, Giant shells
Use medium shells for tomato, meat, and butter sauces. Giant shells may be stuffed and baked.

CAVATELLI (top), ORECCHIETTE (bottom)
Little hollow ones, Little ears (tomato)
Pair with thick, rustic sauces or with sauces made with broccoli rape, vegetable sauces, and ragù.

GNOCCHETTI (top), GNOCCHI (bottom)
Small and large "dumplings"
Use gnocchetti *with meat, tomato, and cheese sauces;* gnocchi *with tomato, butter, or meat sauces.*

RUOTE TRICOLORE
Wheels
The "spokes" of these pasta wheels effectively trap meat and cheese sauces.

RADIATORI
Radiators
Quirky shapes for ragù and meat sauces, as well as ricotta and cream combinations.

LUMACHE, LUMACONI
Snails, Giant snails
Ragù, *tomato, meat, and oil- or butter-based sauces are good with* lumache. *Stuff and bake* lumaconi.

STUFFED PASTA

RAVIOLI, ORIGINALLY CALLED "*RABIOLE,*" seem to have been a precursor to other types of stuffed fresh pasta. According to food historian Waverly Root, *rabiole* were invented by the Genoese, a seafaring people, as a means of recycling leftover food aboard ship: leftovers were ground into fillings and stuffed inside pasta dough. Today, *ravioli* and other stuffed shapes are designed for only high-quality fresh ingredients. *Ravioli* and *tortellini* have become international foods, nearly as well known as *spaghetti* outside the borders of Italy, but there are many other kinds of stuffed fresh pasta in the Italian kitchen. The same egg pasta dough is also made into disks, half-moons, candy-shapes, and other fanciful pasta bundles.

CAPPELLACCI
Made from 3in (7cm) disks (or squares), cappellacci *are often stuffed with a pumpkin filling and dressed simply with butter.*

TORTELLINI *(Little pies)*
Supposedly first fashioned in imitation of Venus's navel, these are made from 2in (5cm) disks of pasta. They are filled with either meat or cheese.

CAPPELLETTI *(Little hats)*
These kerchief-shaped dumplings are made from 2in (5cm) squares and filled with meat or cheese. Serve in broth, or with butter or a cream sauce.

PANSOTTI *(Pot-bellied dumplings)*
Cut from 2in (5cm) squares, pansotti *may have straight or fluted edges. They are typical of the north-west region of Liguria.*

RAVIOLETTI
Tiny versions of ravioli*, usually about 1in (2.5cm) square,* ravioletti *may have cheese, vegetable, or meat fillings, and be made by hand or in molds.*

TORTELLI (ANOLINI)
Cut from 2in (5cm) disks of pasta, these half-moon-shaped bundles may have straight or fluted edges. They usually have cheese or vegetable fillings.

TORTELLONI
These stuffed shapes are usually made from 3in (7cm) squares or disks of fresh pasta. They usually have cheese or vegetable fillings.

CARAMELLE *(Caramels)*
Candy-shaped caramelle *are, appropriately, filled with sweet pumpkin fillings and served with simple butter sauces.*

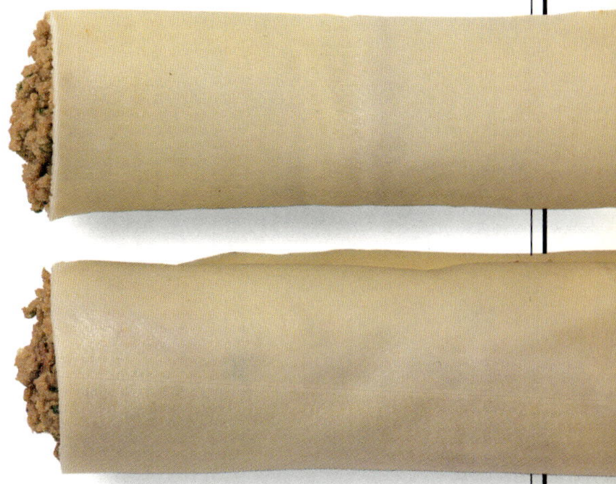

CANNELLONI *(Large reeds)*
The thinnest sheets of pasta are cut into 3½ x 4½in (8 x 11cm) rectangles and stuffed with a variety of fillings. Dried cannelloni *tubes are also available.*

Fresh Colored Pasta

Ingredients as diverse as squid ink, lemon zest, and cocoa powder can be added to pasta dough to impart color. More common, however, are vegetable purées, such as spinach or tomato. Though they give a distinctive tint, their contribution to the flavor is minimal. Egg, which is used in most fresh pasta, imparts a warm straw color, but again its taste is subtle. This is as it should be, for if the pasta is highly flavored it will mask the qualities of the accompanying sauce. It is important to serve colored pasta with a complementary sauce in order to create a harmony of flavors and hues. Recipes for colored fresh doughs can be found on pages 54–55.

PLAIN EGG PASTA

Egg adds extra depth along with a rich color to the dough. In Tuscany oil is also added to the dough, which makes it much easier to work. *(See page 48 for recipe.)*

CHILI PASTA

This pasta has a real sting. When making it, lovers of hot pepper can add more, but the accompanying sauce should not be overshadowed by the fiery pasta. *(See page 55 for recipe.)*

HERB PASTA

It is unusual to find herbs in pasta, but there are some regional specialties – fresh parsley, chives, basil, sage, and rosemary are particular favorites. *(See page 55 for recipe.)*

BEET PASTA

Of all the flavorings added to pasta, beet imparts the most dramatic color, but the intensity of the pink fades into a soft, muted rose tint when cooked. *(See page 54 for recipe.)*

TOMATO PASTA

A little concentrated tomato paste gives pasta dough a warm, pale red blush. It also makes the dough softer and, therefore, slightly trickier to handle. *(See page 55 for recipe.)*

SAFFRON PASTA

Saffron casts a deep golden hue and offers a delicate flavor that is ideal with seafood and tomato sauces. Saffron powder ensures a more even coloring than threads. *(See page 55 for recipe.)*

SPINACH PASTA

Fresh spinach must be cooked, then squeezed dry and chopped before being used in the dough. The added moisture makes the pasta softer and less brittle. *(See page 54 for recipe.)*

MUSHROOM PASTA

I came across this unusual porcini-flavored pasta in Abruzzo. It was served with a tomato sauce, though a meat sauce would also make an excellent partner. *(See page 54 for recipe.)*

BUCKWHEAT PASTA

In traditional Italian cooking pizzoccheri *are a unique specialty of Valtellina in Lombardy. But buckwheat pasta, which has a nutty flavor, suits a range of sauces.* *(See page 55 for recipe.)*

Making and Cooking Pasta

The Italian kitchen is not technique-oriented, and even fresh pasta-making requires only some basic knowledge and the mastering of the pasta machine. This simplicity contributes to the tremendous popularity of Italian home cooking – and the cooking of pasta in particular. Why then is pasta, fresh and dried, rarely cooked properly outside Italy? It is so easy to learn a few techniques that will improve pasta-cooking skills at home and allow you to create many forms of fresh pasta with little effort. This chapter demonstrates the techniques needed to achieve proficiency in cooking pasta.

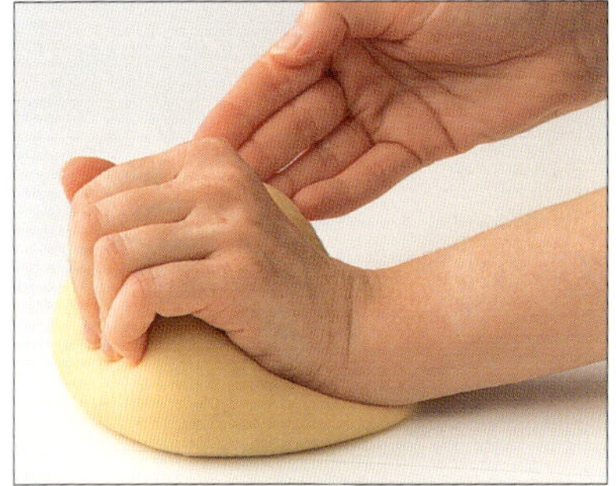

EQUIPMENT

WHILE THE ITALIAN KITCHEN relies very little on equipment, excepting high-quality pots and pans, pasta-making is greatly simplified by using a hand-cranked or electric roller-type pasta machine and supporting supplies and utensils. The primary necessity is a stable work surface that will accommodate the pasta machine, which must be clamped to the edge of the table or counter. If the work surface is too thin to fasten the machine clamp onto, folded dish towels can be wedged between them. A capacious saucepan for cooking the pasta is essential – look for one that will hold 4 quarts (5 liters) of water. A potato ricer is invaluable for making light *gnocchi*.

FORKS: A table fork is needed for working fresh pasta dough, and a wooden fork for stirring pasta and lifting strands out to test for doneness.

DOUGH SCRAPER: In the preliminary stages of working fresh pasta dough, a scraper can be used to clear the work surface of scraps of dough that might otherwise get into the dough ball.

CUTTING WHEELS: Choose a straight-edged wheel (also called a pizza cutter) and a fluted pastry wheel for cutting noodles and stuffed shapes.

KNIFE: Sharp chef's knives are essential for cutting noodles such as *fettuccine* or *lasagne* by hand.

CUTTING BOARD: Select a sturdy wooden board with an even surface (acrylic boards are not resilient).

COOKIE CUTTERS: Straight-edged and fluted cutters are used to press out disks for stuffed pasta. Choose a 2in (5cm) cutter for *tortellini* and a 3in (7cm) cutter for larger shapes.

PIPING BAG AND TEASPOON: Use a teaspoon or a piping bag fitted with a wide nozzle to place mounds of filling along fresh pasta strips to be turned into *ravioli*.

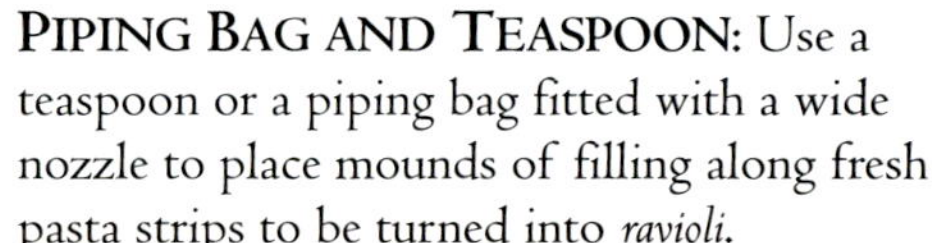

PASTRY BRUSH: Dust the rollers of the pasta machine with a dry brush. Use the brush dipped in water or egg white for sealing *ravioli*.

BUTTER PADDLE: *Gnocchi* are formed on a ridged wooden butter paddle. Ridged wooden boards are also available.

The notches set the width between the rollers

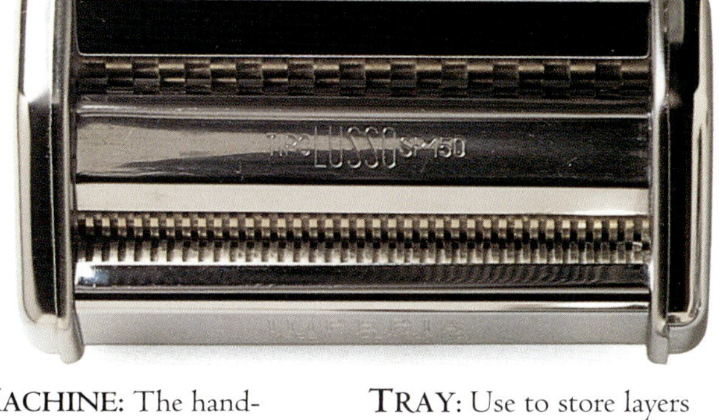

Cutter for making *tagliatelle* and *taglierini*

RAVIOLI MOLDS: *Ravioletti* and *ravioli* molds have raised zigzag markings. The small rolling pin is passed over the top to cut through the dough. The molds allow more filling to be packed in than is possible when cutting the dough by hand.

PASTA MACHINE: The hand-cranked, calibrated roller-type pasta machine is essential for producing good homemade pasta. The rollers both knead the dough and make thin, even sheets of pasta. The model should be sturdy and the rollers precisely aligned to prevent tearing and weaknesses in the dough. An electric motor can be fitted.

TRAY: Use to store layers of fresh pasta that are to be frozen or refrigerated.

COLANDER: A stainless-steel colander with handles and a base is essential. It should have wide holes so that the pasta cooking water drains away rapidly.

FLOUR SHAKER: This is a useful tool for keeping the dough and machine dusted so that the pasta does not stick to the rollers.

PASTA DRAINER: A large slotted spoon allows rapid draining of *gnocchi*, dumplings, and delicate stuffed pasta. A pronged paddle (for lifting noodles out of the cooking water) is also useful.

DISH TOWELS: Leave fresh pasta shapes to dry on towels.

BAKING PARCHMENT: Single layers of fresh pasta noodles or *ravioli* should be stacked between sheets of baking parchment to prevent sticking.

PLASTIC WRAP: Wrap keeps the pasta dough moist so that it does not dry out before rolling.

MAKING FRESH PASTA

ONLY AN EXPERT can successfully produce *pasta fresca*, fresh pasta, by hand. However, a hand-cranked or motorized roller-type pasta machine will produce excellent results. Extrusion machines and pasta attachments on food processors are not suitable as they knead the dough inadequately. For speed, a food processor can be used for the initial mixing of the dough, though it is easily done by hand on a large work surface, or even in a wide-based mixing bowl. Below is the basic recipe for fresh egg pasta. Colored and flavored pasta recipes are given on pages 54–55.

FRESH EGG PASTA

This recipe makes about 1lb (500g) pasta; enough for 4 standard servings. In Tuscany, oil is added to the dough, making it softer and somewhat easier to work than Emilian egg pasta (sfoglia). Emilians argue that the absence of oil makes the dough more porous and so able to absorb sauces more readily. Ideally, fresh pasta should be made with 00 flour (a refined white flour) or, if this is not available, a good unbleached all-purpose flour. Do not use semolina flour, which is sometimes marketed as "pasta flour." If using a flavoring, add it to the egg in step 1.

INGREDIENTS
2½ cups (300g) 00 flour (a little less if using unbleached all-purpose flour), plus extra to dust
⅛ tsp salt (optional)
3 extra large eggs
2 tsp vegetable oil (optional)

1 Combine the flour and salt, if using, directly on a large pastry board or work surface. Make a well in the center of the flour. Lightly beat the eggs with the oil and pour the mixture into the well.

Work very carefully to avoid breaking the flour wall

2 Using a fork, gradually draw in the flour from the inside wall of the well. Beat gently in a constant direction to prevent air pockets forming. Use your free hand to protect the outer wall until the wet mixture is well integrated.

3 When the mixture becomes too stiff to work with a fork, scrape the dough from the fork into the well and continue forming the dough with your hands. Draw in the flour very gradually from the bottom of the wall, again being careful to keep air out of the dough and prevent air pockets forming.

4 Continue forming the dough into a very soft ball. It should be firm enough to handle, but soft and very pliable. If there is too much flour to be absorbed, do not use it all. Conversely, work in a little more flour if necessary. The perfect consistency is soft but not sticky, responsive to being touched and worked with.

6 Cover the dough with an inverted bowl or plastic wrap and let it rest for 15 minutes, or up to 3 hours.

5 Using the heels of your hands, flatten the dough ball and knead it from the middle outward, folding it in half after working it each time. Knead both sides, maintaining a round shape, for about 10 minutes, until the dough is even and elastic.

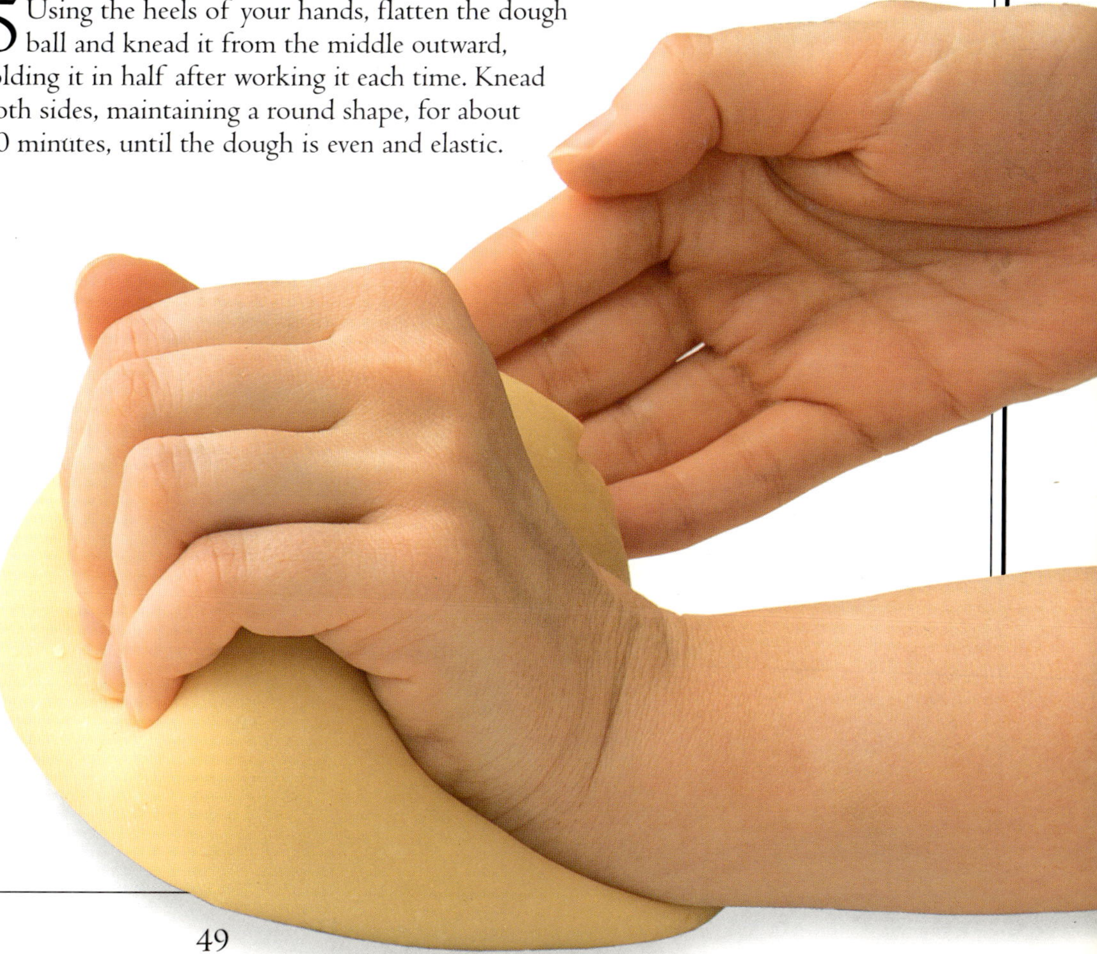

Mixing Dough in a Food Processor

Pasta dough can be mixed in a food processor. Place the dry ingredients in the bowl. Combine the eggs, oil, if using, salt, and any other flavoring such as tomato paste separately, then pour into the bowl. Turn the machine on and process until a ball is formed and the ingredients are well mixed. If the mixture is too dry to form a ball, add a little water and pulse once.

ROLLING FRESH PASTA

MACHINE-ROLLING FRESH PASTA not only allows you to achieve the desired thickness accurately, but helps to knead the dough. For all filled pasta, *lasagne* and *cannelloni,* and for all noodles, except the thicker *trenette, spaghetti,* and *spaghetti alla chitarra,* set the machine for the thinnest possible dough (if numbered, usually the highest number on the wheel). Use the next to last notch for the slightly thicker noodles mentioned. *Fettuccine,* which are meant to be a little thicker than *tagliatelle,* cannot be made thin enough when the pasta is rolled on the next to last setting, and it is best to use the last setting. Do not use extrusion-type pasta machines, which do not knead the dough and produce poor-quality pasta.

1 Attach the pasta machine to the work surface. Divide the dough into six portions. Use your hands to flatten one piece of dough; keep the others covered with an inverted bowl or with plastic wrap. Dust the piece of dough with flour. Put the rollers at their widest setting.

Flatten the dough portion and make it into a roughly rectangular shape

2 Pass the dough through the rollers without pulling or stretching it at the other end. Drape the rolled out dough strip over your hands, keeping your thumbs in the air to avoid puncturing it.

TIP

The coarser-textured pasta made with buckwheat, whole-wheat, and cornmeal flour is best rolled very thin. Once dry, noodles that are too thick remain hard, even when cooked. Since the numbers and notch widths on pasta machines vary from make to make, it is best to experiment on your own machine until you find the notch that works best for the type of noodles you are making.

3 Fold the dough strip into thirds as you would a letter, overlapping the top third then the bottom third over the middle portion to make a rectangular shape. Dust the strip very lightly with flour on one side (the other side remains unfloured so that it will adhere to itself when the pasta is folded again). Dough containing vegetable purée will require considerably more flour.

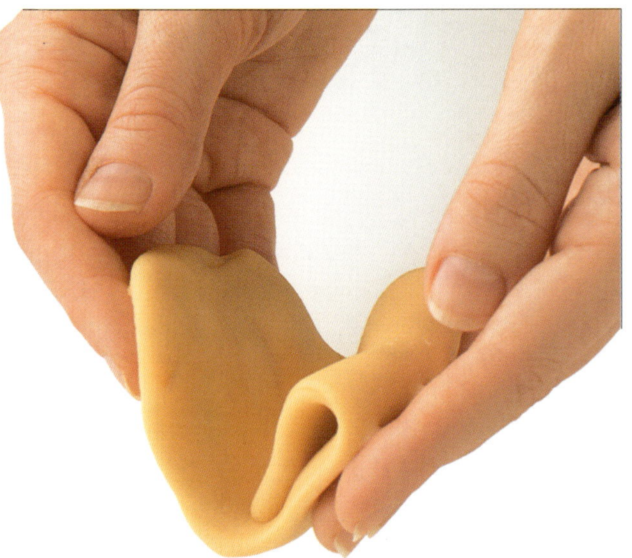

4 Feed the dough strip through the first setting at least six times, each time folding the dough into thirds, pressing out the air, passing it through the rollers, and dusting the strip with flour.

5 Set the rollers at the next notch. Flour the strip lightly on both sides to prevent the dough sticking to the rollers. Feed the dough through once, collecting it at the other end. A fairly well-shaped rectangular strip will form. Mend any breaks by pinching the pasta together.

6 Feed the flattened piece of dough through the rollers once at each remaining setting (unless preparing *trenette, spaghetti,* and *spaghetti alla chitarra,* which are rolled only up to the next to last notch). If the dough begins to stick, dust it lightly with flour.

7 When the sheet of pasta has passed through the rollers for the last time, collect it carefully in your hands and unfold it to its full length, keeping your thumbs in the air. Roll out the other five portions of dough in the same way. If you intend to make filled pasta, roll out only one strip of dough at a time as the dough must be very soft to seal properly.

8 Lay the strips on dry dish towels for 5–10 minutes, keeping them covered with more dry dish towels, until the dough has dried slightly. Do not leave the pasta to dry for too long or it will become brittle and impossible to cut.

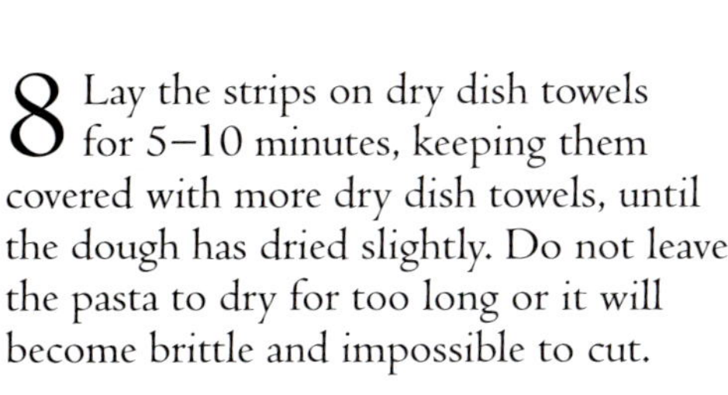

CUTTING FRESH PASTA

ONCE ROLLED, FRESH PASTA must be cut, whether by machine or by hand, when it is at exactly the correct stage of drying. If the dough sticks to the machine cutters, sprinkle it with more flour. Conversely, do not let the strips dry too much as the edges will become brittle, making it impossible to feed them through the cutting attachment. If this happens, trim the edges with a sharp knife and try cutting them again. Work quickly in order to prevent the dough drying out. If you think it is drying out too quickly, place a slightly damp dish towel over the strips waiting to be cut.

CUTTING NOODLES AND SHAPES

CUTTING MALTAGLIATI

These are irregular-shaped (literally "badly cut") handmade noodles. Using a knife or a fluted or straight pastry wheel, make diamond-shaped or triangular pieces of dough approximately 3in (7cm) in length.

CUTTING QUADRUCCI

Cut the pasta dough into *tagliatelle* noodles, as shown right. Then take a large chef's knife and cut the *tagliatelle* crosswise into tiny squares while the noodles are still soft. Place them on a dry cotton dish towel and leave to dry.

CUTTING PAPPARDELLE

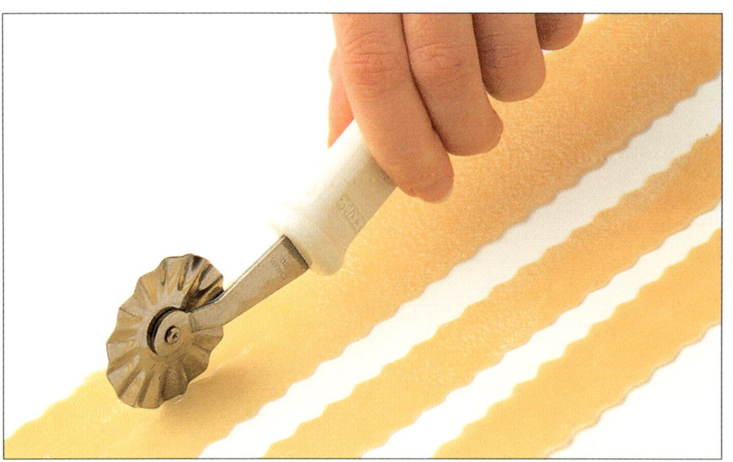

Cut the thinly rolled sheets of pasta in half to make *pappardelle* about 14in (35cm) long. Use a fluted pastry wheel to cut the *pappardelle* to a width of ¾–1in (1.5–2.5cm), taking care to cut them evenly.

CUTTING FARFALLE

Cut the pasta as for *pappardelle* (left). Use a fluted wheel to cut the noodles across into 2in (5cm) lengths. Pinch the middle of each piece to form little bows. Cook within 3–4 hours of making, or dry thoroughly and store.

CUTTING TAGLIATELLE

1 Fix the *tagliatelle* cutting attachment to the machine. Take a strip of pasta dough (it should now have a slight patina). Cut the strips of dough in half across to shorten the strands. Pass each strip through the cutter.

2 Collect the cut noodles at the base of the attachment. Line four baking sheets with dry dish towels. Lay the noodles out to dry flat for 10–15 minutes, or up to 3 hours.

3 To make *nidi* (pasta nests), wrap a few strands loosely around your fingers immediately after cutting. Lay them flat and leave to dry thoroughly. They can be stored for up to 3–4 weeks in a clean container.

CUTTING TAGLIERINI

To make fine noodles, such as *taglierini* or the slightly thicker *spaghetti alla chitarra,* feed the dough through the very narrow cutter. Leave to dry flat or curl into nests.

Making Colored Fresh Pasta

Subtly tinted and flavored doughs can make agreeable companions for many sauces. Tomato and spinach are two of the most popular additions, but in recent years a wide variety of ingredients has found its way into fresh pasta. It is unusual to find herbs in pasta, as aromatics are typically part of the sauce, not the pasta. However, there are some regional recipes for herb pasta, and some that have been invented since pasta's meteoric rise in popularity. Colored fresh pasta is softer than plain egg pasta and so takes less time to cook. Whole-wheat and buckwheat doughs take a few seconds longer.

Recipes

BEET PASTA

Of all the flavorings that are added to pasta dough, beet imparts the most dramatic color, but the intensity of the crimson tint fades to a soft, muted ivory pink when cooked. Makes approximately 1lb (500g).

INGREDIENTS

- 1 medium beet or 3 small ones (yields 1 tbsp cooked purée)
- 2½ cups (300g) 00 flour (a little less if using ordinary unbleached all-purpose flour), plus additional for dusting
- 3 extra large eggs
- 1 tsp vegetable oil

1 Scrub the beet and remove the outer leaves, but leave the stem intact at the base to prevent color leaching out as the beet boils. Place the beet in a pan, cover with cold water and bring to a boil. Cook over medium heat until tender, 30 minutes–1 hour, depending on size.

2 Drain the beet and, when cool enough to handle, slip off the skin. Grate or mash the beet finely by hand, or purée in a food processor. Leave the pulp to drain in a sieve for about 1 hour or overnight. Measure out exactly 1 level tablespoon of purée.

3 Proceed as for fresh egg pasta (see pages 48–49), thoroughly mixing the beet purée into the egg mixture. Because beet pasta is more likely to stick to the work surface and rollers, extra flour will be needed for kneading and rolling out. Leave the dough to dry for an additional 5–6 minutes before cooking.

SPINACH PASTA

Adding spinach to the dough gives a deep green color and definite flavor. The added moisture from the spinach makes the dough softer and a little more tricky to handle than basic egg pasta. This is easily rectified by having extra flour to hand. Makes approximately 1lb (500g).

INGREDIENTS

- 5oz (150g) fresh spinach, washed and stems removed
- 1 tsp salt, or to taste
- 2¼ cups (285g) 00 flour (a little less if using ordinary unbleached all-purpose flour), plus additional for dusting
- 3 extra large eggs
- 2 tsp vegetable oil

1 Place the spinach in a lidded pan with the salt and just enough boiling water to cover. Cook until tender, about 10 minutes. Drain thoroughly then transfer to a colander or sieve and leave to stand until cool. Squeeze the spinach as dry as possible. Wring in a dry, clean dish towel to absorb more of the moisture. You should have about ¼ cup (75g) of pulp.

2 Chop the spinach very finely by hand or, preferably, in a food processor or blender.

3 Proceed as for fresh egg pasta (see pages 48–49), beating the spinach into the egg mixture. Use extra flour to dust the pasta, the machine rollers, and work surface. Because the dough is softer than plain egg dough, it should be allowed to dry for an additional 5–6 minutes before cooking.

MUSHROOM PASTA

I came across this unusual pasta in a small village in the mountains of Abruzzo some years ago. It was served with a light tomato sauce, though sauces of meat or game would also be perfectly suitable. Unlike many ingredients commonly added to fresh pasta, porcini do add substantial flavor to this dough. Makes approximately 1lb (500g).

INGREDIENTS

- 1oz (30g) dried porcini
- 2½ cups (300g) 00 flour (a little less if using ordinary unbleached all-purpose flour)
- 2 extra large eggs
- 2 tsp vegetable oil

1 Soak the dried porcini in ¾ cup (175ml) of boiling water. Let stand for about 1 hour to rehydrate. Remove the porcini without disturbing the sediment. Squeeze out as much water as possible from the porcini, then chop them as finely as you can (large pieces of mushroom will make holes in the dough when it is rolled).

2 Strain the mushroom soaking liquid through paper towels to remove any impurities, and reserve (it can be used as a stock in other recipes).

3 Proceed as for fresh egg pasta (see pages 48–49), beating the chopped porcini into the egg mixture with a fork. If the porcini cause excessive tearing when the first strip of dough is passed through the rollers, fold it in half and pass through the rollers again, but roll no further than the penultimate notch on the machine.

CHILI PASTA

This recipe produces pasta with a real sting. Lovers of hot pepper can add more chili to taste. Choose sauces that will not be overshadowed by the fiery pasta. Makes approximately 1lb (500g).

INGREDIENTS

- *2½ cups (300g) 00 flour (a little less if using ordinary unbleached all-purpose flour)*
- *3 extra large eggs*
- *2 tsp vegetable oil*
- *1 tsp red pepper flakes, coarsely ground*

1 Proceed as for fresh egg pasta (see pages 48–49), beating the pepper flakes into the egg mixture until well incorporated.

2 If the flakes cause excessive tearing when the first strip of dough is passed through the rollers, fold it in half and pass it through the rollers again, but roll no further than the penultimate notch on the machine.

BUCKWHEAT PASTA

Buckwheat was brought to Italy by the Saracens or Crusaders. These noodles, called pizzoccheri, *are a specialty of Valtellina in Lombardy. Buckwheat is very nutritious with a lovely, nutty flavor. Because it has no gluten, it must be combined with wheat flour when making pasta. Makes approximately 1lb (500g).*

INGREDIENTS

- *2 cups (250g) buckwheat flour combined with 1 cup (125g) 00 flour or unbleached all-purpose flour*
- *2 extra large eggs*
- *½ cup (125ml) warm milk*
- *⅛ tsp salt*

1 Proceed as for fresh egg pasta (see pages 48–49), but use extra white flour if the dough appears to be too soft.

2 Cut as for *fettuccine* (see step 1, page 85), then cut the strands diagonally in half.

WHOLE-WHEAT PASTA

The flavor of whole-wheat noodles (bigoli) *is particularly suited to sauces that feature anchovies. The nutty taste of the wheat is obscured by tomato and olive-oil based sauces. Instead, dress* bigoli *with more delicate unsalted butter-based sauces. Makes approximately 2lb (1kg).*

INGREDIENTS

- *3 cups (375g) whole-wheat flour combined with 1 cup (125g) 00 flour or unbleached all-purpose flour*
- *5 extra large eggs*
- *2 tbsp olive oil*

1 Proceed as for fresh egg pasta (see pages 48–49), but knead the dough for an additional 3–4 minutes.

2 Cut the dough using a *spaghetti*-cutting attachment or cut it into *tagliatelle* noodles (see page 53).

HERB PASTA

Any of the fresh herbs listed below make suitable additions to the dough. Sauces should be very simple with no competing flavors. Makes approximately 1lb (500g).

INGREDIENTS

- *2½ cups (300g) 00 flour (a little less if using ordinary unbleached all-purpose flour)*
- *¼ cup (15g) fresh parsley, chives, or basil, or 1 tbsp (5g) fresh sage or rosemary*
- *3 extra large eggs*
- *2 tsp vegetable oil*

1 Remove any stems from the parsley, chives, basil, sage, or rosemary then chop the leaves very fine.

2 Proceed as for fresh egg pasta (see pages 48–49), beating the chopped herbs into the egg mixture with a fork.

3 If the herbs cause excessive tearing on the first strip of dough passed through the rollers, fold it in half and pass it through the rollers again, but roll no further than the penultimate notch on the machine.

SAFFRON PASTA

Saffron casts a bright golden hue and gives a slight flavor to the dough that is perfect with seafood and tomato sauces. Saffron strands may be used, but saffron powder gives a more even tint. Vary the amount used according to taste. Makes approximately 1lb (500g).

INGREDIENTS

- *2½ cups (300g) 00 flour (a little less if using ordinary unbleached all-purpose flour)*
- *3 extra large eggs*
- *2 tsp vegetable oil*
- *2–4 envelopes saffron powder, or large pinch of saffron strands*

1 If using saffron strands, warm them in a dry skillet and crush finely using a mortar and pestle.

2 Proceed as for fresh egg pasta (see pages 48–49), beating the saffron into the egg mixture with a fork.

3 Knead the dough thoroughly so that its vibrant color is uniform, then roll it on the pasta machine.

TOMATO PASTA

Adding a little tomato paste gives pasta dough a lovely soft, warm pale red blush. It also makes the dough softer. Have flour on hand as you roll out the dough to prevent it from becoming sticky. Makes approximately 1lb (500g).

INGREDIENTS

- *2½ cups (300g) 00 flour (a little less if using ordinary unbleached all-purpose flour), plus additional for dusting*
- *3 extra large eggs*
- *1 tsp vegetable oil*
- *1½ tbsp tomato paste*

1 Proceed as for fresh egg pasta (see pages 48–49), beating the tomato paste into the egg mixture, and incorporating it thoroughly with a fork.

2 As with beet and spinach pasta, tomato pasta is more likely to stick to the work surface and machine rollers. You will probably find that you need more flour for dusting. Because the dough is slightly softer, leave it to dry for an additional 5–6 minutes before cooking.

MAKING STUFFED PASTA

THE MANY SHAPES OF STUFFED PASTA are made from the thinnest possible dough (see pages 50–51). Roll out only one sixth of the pasta at a time as the dough must be very soft to seal properly. Keep in mind that fillings should not be too wet or they will soak through the pasta envelopes, causing them to stick to the surface and break when lifted. Most filled pasta should not rest longer than 15 minutes at room temperature, or 1–2 hours if refrigerated, but if fillings are not too moist, they can be left for up to 4 hours before cooking. Ricotta or vegetable fillings are wetter than most meat fillings.

MAKING RAVIOLI

If not cooking stuffed pasta parcels within the times indicated above, refrigerate them, leaving adequate space around them to prevent sticking, and turning them frequently. Alternatively, freeze them after making, or even as you make them, placing them on trays lined with waxed paper. When they have frozen solid, transfer to freezer bags or containers.

The dough must be very soft and pliable

1 Cut one strip of dough in half across; keep the other half covered with a damp cloth. Working quickly, place a teaspoon of filling at 2in (5cm) intervals in rows along one half of the pasta strip.

2 Dip a pastry brush in egg white, milk, or water and paint a grid between the mounds of filling (and paint around the actual mounds, if desired), so that each one is surrounded by a square of egg white.

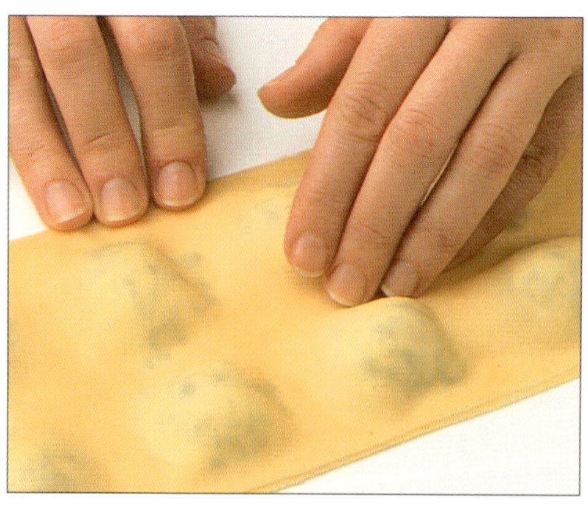

3 Place the second half of the pasta strip over the filled sheet. Press down firmly around each mound of filling to seal the bundle, forcing out any trapped pockets of air.

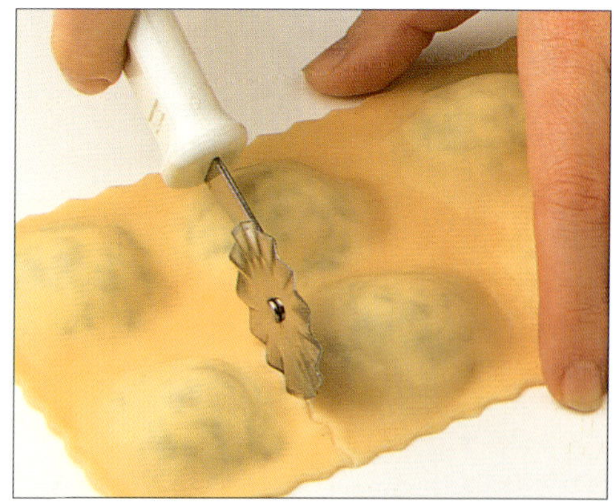

4 Use a fluted pastry wheel or a knife to cut 2in (5cm) square *ravioli* along the egg white lines. Press down around each bundle to secure the seal. Repeat with the remaining dough and filling.

MAKING PANSOTTI

Cut the pasta into 2½in (6cm) squares. Spoon ½ teaspoon of filling into the center of each square (test with the first one and use more filling if possible). Moisten the edges, fold diagonally in half, and seal.

MAKING CARAMELLE

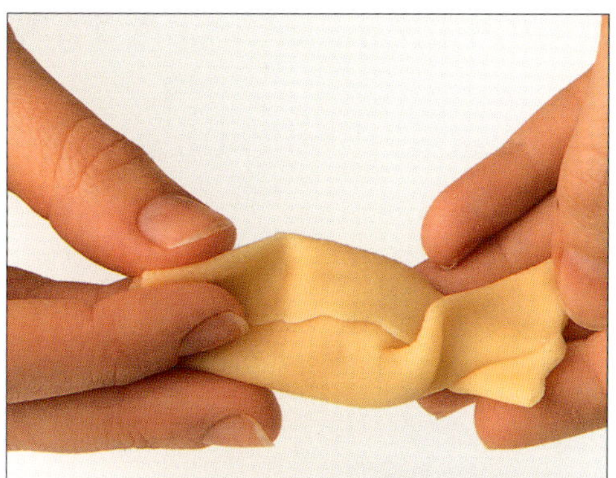

Cut the pasta into 1 x 3in (2.5 x 7cm) squares. Place ½ teaspoon of filling in the center of each piece. Fold the pasta over the center to make a narrow parcel. Twist the two ends to resemble a candy wrapper.

MAKING TORTELLI (ANOLINI)

Cut 2in (5cm) disks of pasta using a cookie cutter or glass. Place ½ teaspoon of filling in the center of each disk. Paint around the edges with egg white, milk, or water, fold in half, and press to seal.

MAKING TORTELLINI

Tortellini *and* **cappellacci** *are basically the same shape except that the former are made from 2in (5cm) disks of pasta and the latter from 3in (7cm) disks.* **Cappelletti** *("little hats") are made along the same lines, but they start out as 2in (5cm) squares rather than disks. The rest of the filling and folding procedure is the same.*

1 Work with one strip of pasta at a time. Use a 2in (5cm) cookie cutter or glass to cut the pasta into disks. Spoon approximately ¼ teaspoon of filling into the center of each disk.

2 Paint around the edges of the disk with egg white, milk, or water. Fold in half to form a crescent shape, bringing the edges of one side up slightly below the level of the other.

3 Press around the dumpling to make a secure seal, letting out any air that might inflate the filled section and cause the *tortellini* to burst during cooking. The dumpling will now look like a little stuffed half-moon.

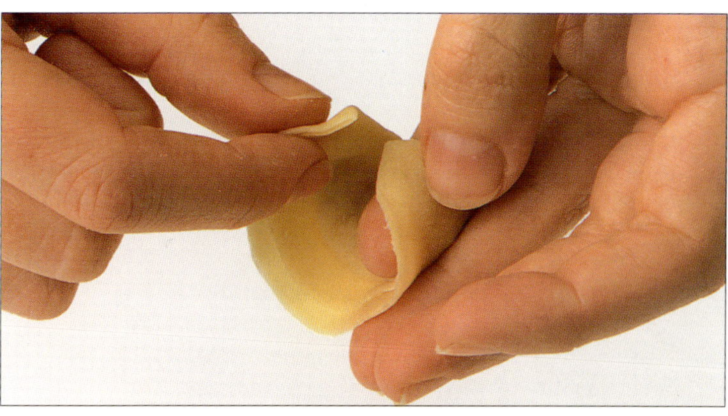

4 Take the dumpling and wrap it around your little finger, stuffed side facing away from you, keeping the arched end (or pointed end if making *cappelletti*) up. Slightly overlap the two corners and pinch them together.

Cooking and Draining Pasta

PROPER COOKING AND DRAINING is essential for fresh and dried pasta. Italians eat their dried pasta very firm and it is truly at its best when quite firm to the bite. The Italian term for this ideal texture is *al dente,* meaning "to the tooth," and it is the use of hard durum wheat semolina flour which allows dried pasta to retain its resilience during cooking.

The texture of cooked fresh pasta, on the other hand, can never be termed *al dente* as it is made from soft wheat flour and does not dry to such a hard texture. In both cases, the pasta should be cooked in an abundant quantity of water, salt must be added, and the pasta should be stirred frequently during cooking.

COOKING FRESH PASTA

It is important to cook fresh pasta in plenty of water to avoid the strands or parcels sticking together. The quantity of water suggested here is the minimum for 1lb (500g) of pasta.

Tips

✦ *Oil should not be added to the cooking water. It does not prevent the pieces of pasta from sticking together, but only coats the pasta, preventing it from fully absorbing the sauce after draining.*

✦ *When draining pasta, save at least half a cup of cooking water. The pasta will continue to absorb moisture after draining, and it is often necessary to add some of the water to the serving bowl so that sauce and pasta combine well. This is essential when using unctuous sauces, such as pesto, or thick cheese sauces.*

1 Bring 4 quarts (5 liters) of water to a boil. Add salt, according to recipe, and the pasta. Long pasta will stick out of the pan for a few moments until the submerged portion softens enough to allow the strands to slip into the water.

COOKING DRIED PASTA

Cooking dried pasta in too little water crowds the pan as the pasta swells, making the pasta gummy. Dried pasta cuts, such as *bucatini,* and thick-walled macaroni shapes, such as *penne* and *rigatoni,* require at least 4 quarts (5 liters) of cooking water per 1lb (500g). The amount of salt for this quantity of pasta would generally be 1½ tablespoons. This quantity should be increased proportionately.

✦

Undersalted or unsalted pasta is virtually tasteless.

✦

Accurate cooking times are printed on most pasta packaging, but it is best to lift out a piece of pasta and taste. If in doubt, drain. There is a startling difference between pasta that is truly *al dente* and pasta that is overcooked, even by half a minute. *Spaghetti* and other long pasta may be broken in half, but it is best to keep the strands whole so they will coil around the tines of the fork without falling off.

2 Stir the pasta then cover the pan. Bring back to a boil, uncover and cook for 5 seconds for fine noodles, 15 for thicker cuts. Total cooking time should not exceed 1½ minutes, or 3–5 minutes for stuffed pasta. Cook dried or frozen fresh pasta for 1 minute after the water has reboiled, then test.

3 Drain the pasta without delay in a capacious, handled colander. Scoop stuffed pasta out gently with a slotted spoon as a colander will damage the parcels. Reserve at least half a cup of the cooking water. The pasta should retain some moisture, though not be dripping wet, unless the recipe indicates otherwise. Combine the pasta with the sauce, adding some of the reserved cooking water if necessary.

Recipes

THE RECIPES IN THIS BOOK might be most accurately described as eclectically Italian, for while many are classic in their composition, they are by and large a product of Italian thinking, rather than historical tradition. Many of them were spontaneous in their composition. Some were arrived at out of necessity when particular ingredients were on hand; others were born in an inspired moment. There are some recipes that were gathered from friends and colleagues whose cooking I admire or who invited me to their table for a plate of pasta that was so good as to require memorializing.

MINESTRE

SOUPS

ORIGINALLY, PASTA WAS MEANT to be eaten as an ingredient in soup. It was only later that the custom evolved of serving it "dry," that is, with a sauce, hence the term "*pastasciutta*" (see page 162). There are numerous categories of pasta soups, and different types of pasta for which they are designed. *Pasta in brodo* refers to a clear meat broth, perhaps infused with the flavors of saffron or herbs, in which a small amount of tiny soup pasta (*pastina*), or fine angel hair is cooked. A *minestrina*, "little soup," is a fairly light soup to which small soup pasta, such as *farfalline*, is added. Also included here is *minestrone*, a lavish, deeply savory "big soup" incorporating larger pasta, perhaps *ditalini*.

MINESTRA DI LENTICCHIE CON SALSICCIE E TUBETTINI
Lentil Soup with Swiss Chard, Sausage, and Tubettini

MINESTRA DI LENTICCHIE CON SALSICCIE E TUBETTINI

Lentil Soup with Swiss Chard, Sausage, and Tubettini

There are many different Italian lentil soups, invariably including pasta. Some are thick and almost stew-like; others are true soups, such as this one. Spinach makes a good alternative to Swiss chard, and water can replace meat broth, if preferred.

KCal 695 P 29g C 74g S 3092mg SFA 11g UFA 21g (4)

INGREDIENTS
½lb (250g) brown lentils, rinsed
10 cups (2.5 liters) light meat broth (see page 68)
1 celery rib with leaves
1 bay leaf
1 tbsp salt
2 tbsp extra-virgin olive oil
2 large garlic cloves, finely chopped
1 onion, finely chopped
10oz (300g) sweet Italian sausages with fennel seeds, casings removed, crumbled
2 tbsp tomato paste
2 tsp fresh marjoram, or 1 tsp dried marjoram
1¼ cups (300g) chopped fresh or canned drained plum tomatoes, peeled, seeded, and chopped
½ cup (125g) tubettini
½lb (250g) Swiss chard leaves, chopped

1 Place the lentils in a large pan with the broth or water, celery, bay leaf, and salt. Bring to a boil, then reduce to a simmer and cook until the lentils are nearly tender, about 20 minutes.

2 Meanwhile, in a skillet, combine the olive oil, garlic, and onion. Sauté over medium-low heat until softened, about 5 minutes. Add the sausage meat and sauté for 10 minutes, until golden.

3 Add the tomato paste dissolved in a little of the lentil broth and stir well. Stir in the marjoram and tomatoes.

4 Stir the sausage and onion mixture, the *tubettini*, and Swiss chard into the lentils. Simmer until the chard is tender and the pasta is *al dente*, about 7 minutes. Discard the celery and bay leaf, and serve.

MINESTRA DI POLLO CON TAGLIATELLE ALL'ALESSANDRO

Chicken Soup with Tagliatelle, Alessandro Style

In a typical Italian chicken-based soup, the cooked bird is separated from the broth and served as a second course with one or more sauces, such as the classic* salsa verde*. In this original hearty soup, the meat of the chicken is served in the soup with the vegetables. Steps 1–3 contain the basic recipe for chicken broth.

KCal 387 P 40g C 31g S 948mg SFA 3g UFA 8g (4)

INGREDIENTS
3½lb (1.75kg) chicken, fat removed, cut into quarters
8 cups (2 liters) water
salt, to taste
3 sprigs fresh flat-leaf parsley
1 large celery rib
2 carrots, cut in half lengthwise then thinly sliced
2 medium potatoes, peeled and cut into small dice
1 tbsp olive oil
1 onion, chopped
2oz (60g) fresh or dried tagliatelle, broken into 2in (5cm) lengths
freshly ground white pepper, to taste

1 Combine the chicken pieces, water, 2 teaspoons of salt, the parsley, and celery in a large pan. Bring to a boil and then immediately reduce to a simmer. Simmer gently but steadily until the chicken is nearly cooked, about 40 minutes. Frequently skim off the foam that forms on the surface.

2 Take the pan off the heat, transfer the chicken to a cutting board, and remove the skin and bones. Cut the meat into bite-sized pieces.

3 Strain the broth, skim off the fat, and return it to the stove. Add the carrots and partially cover the pan. Simmer over medium heat until they are half-cooked. Add the potato and continue to simmer, partially covered, until the vegetables are cooked through, about 15 minutes.

4 Meanwhile, warm the oil in a small skillet and add the onion. Sauté over medium-low heat until the onion is soft and lightly golden, about 5 minutes. Remove from the heat.

5 If using dried pasta, bring 10 cups (2.5 liters) of water to a boil. Add the *tagliatelle* and 1½ tablespoons of salt. Cook until half-done, then drain.

6 Add the half-cooked pasta, if using, or the fresh pasta to the broth with the chicken pieces and cooked onion; stir well. Simmer over low heat for 5 minutes, then check the seasoning, and serve.

Minestrone Estivo con Prosciutto e Parmigiano

Summer Minestrone with Ham and Parmesan

Minestrone *is crowded with many seasonal vegetables and beans, with pasta being an optional ingredient. My family has always added a meaty ham bone (smoked ham hocks or pork neck bones, or ham steak can be substituted), but it can be made without meat. Use unblemished fresh vegetables, good quality, flavorful extra-virgin olive oil, and authentic parmigiano-reggiano cheese. The rinds of the cheese are cooked in the soup, and grated Parmesan is sprinkled over the soup at the table. The ingredients list is lengthy, as the soup is rich with many fresh summer vegetables, but the cooking method is simple. Serves 10–12.* *(See page 13 for illustration.)*

KCal 360 P 26g C 32g S 1422mg SFA 4g UFA 10g (10)

INGREDIENTS

½lb (250g) fresh or canned borlotti or pinto beans, rinsed, or ⅔ cup (125g) dried beans, preferably soaked overnight (see step 1)

1 large meaty ham bone, excess fat removed, or 2 smoked ham hocks, or 2lb (1kg) smoked pork neck bones, or 1½lb (750g) ham steak

12 cups (3 liters) water

approximately 6oz (175g) Parmesan cheese rinds, cut into small pieces, if available

3 tbsp extra-virgin olive oil

2 tsp fresh rosemary, or 1 tsp dried rosemary, or 2 bay leaves

2 vine-ripened fresh plum tomatoes, or 2 canned drained tomatoes, seeded and finely chopped, or 2 tbsp tomato paste

1 large onion, coarsely chopped

1 medium potato, peeled and diced

1 large celery rib, finely sliced, with the leaves, chopped

¾lb (375g) butternut or hubbard squash, diced

1 large carrot, chopped

½lb (250g) finely shredded cabbage

1 tbsp salt, or to taste

2 small zucchini 6–8oz (175–250g) each, cut into small dice

2 small yellow summer squash, 6–8oz (175–250g) each, diced

½lb (250g) cauliflower florets

½lb (250g) Swiss chard leaves, finely shredded and roughly chopped, if available

½lb (250g) green beans, tips trimmed and cut into 1in (2.5cm) lengths

1 cup (125g) conchigliette ("little shells") or ditalini ("little thimbles")

3 tbsp chopped fresh flat-leaf parsley

plenty of freshly ground black pepper, to serve

freshly grated Parmesan, to serve

1 If using presoaked dried beans, place them in a pan with cold water to cover by 3in (7cm). Bring to a boil, then reduce the heat and simmer until tender, about 1 hour. Drain well. Alternatively, place dried beans in a pan with cold water to cover by 3in (7cm), bring to a boil, cover and let stand, off the heat, for 1 hour, then cook as described above. Fresh or canned beans need no advance preparation.

2 Place the ham bone(s) or ham steak in a large pan with the water. Bring to a boil and cook over medium-low heat, partially covered, for 1 hour for the ham bone(s), 30 minutes for ham steak. Skim the surface to remove any scum that forms. Let the stock cool.

3 Remove the ham bone(s) or steak from the stock. Separate the meat from the bone and cut it into bite-sized pieces; set aside. Skim the fat off the stock and add enough cold water to make 12 cups (3 liters). Transfer the stock to a large clean saucepan.

4 Add all the ingredients listed up to and including the salt to the ham stock. Cover the pan and bring to a boil. Immediately reduce to a simmer and cook over medium-low heat, partially covered, for approximately 30 minutes.

5 Add the zucchini, summer squash, cauliflower, Swiss chard, cooked or fresh or canned beans, green beans, pasta, and parsley to the pan. Cook until the vegetables are tender and the pasta is not quite *al dente*, about 10 minutes (it will continue to cook in the hot soup). Check the seasoning and return the cooked ham pieces to the soup.

6 Serve the *minestrone* with pepper to taste, accompanied by plenty of freshly grated Parmesan.

Stracciatella con Polpettine e Pastina

Stracciatella with Meatballs and Pastina

Another marvelous broth-based soup, this one with the addition of beaten egg. It is not unlike the renowned stracciatella *of the Roman kitchen, but this original version contains a larger variety of vegetables. Small, light soup pasta such as* semi di melone *("melon seeds"),* acini di pepe *("peppercorns"), or* orzi *("barley") should be used. (See page 12 for illustration.)*

KCal 455 P 24g C 31g S 1301mg SFA 7g UFA 18g (4)

INGREDIENTS

- 1 quantity chicken broth (see page 63) or light meat broth (see page 68)
- 1 carrot, very finely chopped
- 1 onion, grated
- ½lb (250g) shredded young zucchini or fresh peas
- ½ cup (90g) pastina
- 1 quantity meatballs (see recipes on page 69)
- salt, to taste
- 2 eggs
- 2 tbsp extra-virgin olive oil
- 2 tbsp freshly grated Parmesan, plus extra to serve
- ⅛ tsp freshly grated nutmeg
- freshly ground black pepper, to taste
- 1 tbsp chopped fresh flat-leaf parsley

1 Combine the broth, carrot, onion, and zucchini or peas in a large pan. Bring the broth to a boil, then reduce to a steady simmer and cook over medium heat until the vegetables are almost tender, about 10 minutes.

2 Add the *pastina*, meatballs, and salt to taste. Continue to simmer over medium heat until the *pastina* and meatballs are cooked, about 5 minutes.

3 Meanwhile, beat the eggs with the olive oil, Parmesan, and nutmeg in a bowl. Stir the mixture into the simmering soup to solidify and distribute the beaten egg. Season with pepper, add the parsley, and serve immediately.

Minestra di Fagioli con Prosciutto e Cicoria

Bean Soup with Ham and Curly Endive

Southern Italy has many permutations of this type of soup in which beans and greens are combined with pasta. In some variations, thinly sliced diced salame is added in the last stage of cooking instead of ham. Escarole, cime di rapa *(broccoli rape) or other greens are often substituted for curly endive, and tomatoes may or may not be included. If a large meaty ham bone is available, it can make a very tasty stock for the soup. If not, use ham steak.*

KCal 810 P 60g C 49g S 3020mg SFA 11g UFA 31g (4)

INGREDIENTS

- 1¼ cups (250g) dried cannellini beans, preferably soaked overnight (see step 1)
- 1 bay leaf
- 1 large meaty ham bone, excess fat removed, or 1½lb (750g) ham steak
- 1½lb (750g) head curly endive, outer leaves trimmed
- ⅓ cup (75ml) extra-virgin olive oil
- 3 garlic cloves, finely chopped
- 1 small onion, finely chopped
- pinch of crushed red pepper flakes
- ½ cup (60g) medium soup pasta, such as ditali
- 2 tsp salt
- freshly ground black pepper, to taste

1 If using presoaked dried beans, place them in a pan with cold water to cover by 3in (7cm). Bring to a boil, reduce the heat, and simmer with the bay leaf and ham bone, if using, until tender, about 1 hour. If using ham steak, add a third of it to the beans after 30 minutes. Alternatively, place dried beans in a pan with cold water to cover by 3in (7cm), bring to a boil, cover and let stand, off the heat, for 1 hour, then cook as above.

2 When the beans are tender, remove the ham bone, if using, cut off the meat, dice it, set it aside and discard the bone. If using ham steak, dice the piece that has cooked with the beans, and reserve.

3 Trim the bottom off the curly endive. Wash it, pat dry and cut into ¼in (5mm) wide ribbons then chop roughly.

4 Warm the olive oil in a skillet large enough to hold the curly endive. Add the garlic and onion. Sauté over medium-low heat just until softened, about 5 minutes. Add the pepper flakes. If using ham steak, cut the remainder into dice and sauté it in the skillet for 1–2 minutes to marry the flavors.

5 Add the curly endive to the skillet, and toss well. Cover the pan and cook over medium-low heat for 5 minutes. Transfer the mixture to the bean pot. Turn the heat to medium-high and add the pasta and salt. Cook until the curly endive and pasta are tender, about 10 minutes. Stir in the pepper and the reserved cooked ham, and check the seasoning before serving.

Minestra di Piselli con Ditalini alla Romana

Pea Soup with Ditalini, Roman Style

This thick, satisfying pea soup is a variation of a soup I grew up with. No doubt my mother learned to make it during the pre-war years when she lived in Rome, as it is a very typical Roman dish. It is hearty enough to serve as a full meal for lunch or a light supper. When available, a little chopped mint can be added to the soup with the parsley.

KCal 776 P 60g C 89g S 2370mg SFA 6g UFA 15g (4)

INGREDIENTS
1lb (500g) dried split peas
8 cups (2 liters) water
1 large celery rib with leaves
3 sprigs flat-leaf parsley
1 beef or chicken bouillon cube, crushed
1 large bay leaf
1 carrot, coarsely chopped
1lb (500g) thick slice of ham, rinsed and finely diced
3 tbsp extra-virgin olive oil
1 small onion, very finely chopped
1 tsp salt
½ cup (60g) ditalini
1 tbsp chopped fresh flat-leaf parsley
freshly ground black pepper, to taste

1 Wash the peas, place them in a large pan, and cover with the water. Using kitchen string, tie together the celery and parsley and add to the pan with the bouillon cube, bay leaf, carrot, and one third of the ham. Bring to a boil, then lower the heat and simmer until the peas disintegrate, about 1 hour.

2 Meanwhile, warm the olive oil in a small pan. Add the onion and sauté gently until soft, about 5 minutes. Stir the onion, remaining ham, salt, and *ditalini* into the soup pan and cook over medium heat until done, about 9 minutes. Stir in the parsley and pepper and check for salt before serving.

Minestra di Patate e Porri con Farfalline

Leek and Potato Soup with "Little Butterflies"

My mother invented this delicious soup one day in order to use up some leeks that were languishing in my refrigerator. Based on butter, not olive oil, it is typical of my mother's delicate hand. If fresh marjoram can't be found, substitute chives or finely chopped scallion tops.

KCal 327 P 7g C 39g S 366mg SFA 10g UFA 5g (4)

INGREDIENTS
3 large leeks, trimmed
5 tbsp (75g) unsalted butter
1lb (500g) potatoes, peeled and cut into small dice
1 small onion, very finely chopped
2 large garlic cloves, unpeeled and bruised
1 celery rib with leaves, cut into very fine dice
1 medium yellow summer squash, about ½lb (250g), cut into small dice
8 cups (2 liters) chicken broth (see page 63)
½ tsp very finely chopped fresh marjoram or chives or scallion tops
salt, to taste
¼ cup (30g) pastina such as farfalline ("little butterflies") or tripoline ("little bowties"), tubettini, orzi ("barley"), or semi di melone ("melon seeds")
freshly ground white pepper, to taste
freshly grated Parmesan, to serve

1 Slice the leeks in half lengthwise and spread open the sheaths under cold running water to wash out any soil or grit lodged between them. Cut the leeks across into very thin slices, then chop them into small dice.

2 Warm the butter in a large pot. Add the leeks, potatoes, onion, garlic, celery, and squash. Sauté over medium heat until the vegetables sweat, about 10 minutes. Add the chicken broth and marjoram, chives, or scallion tops. Simmer until the vegetables are tender, about 20 minutes.

3 Bring 10 cups (2.5 liters) of water to a boil and add 1 teaspoon of salt and the *pastina*. Cook the *pastina* until half-done, about 5 minutes. Drain and add to the soup.

4 Remove the whole garlic cloves from the pot and discard. Taste the soup for salt and adjust if necessary. Season with white pepper, and serve, passing freshly grated Parmesan at the table.

MINESTRA DI FAVE CON LINGUINE

Linguine and Fava Bean Soup in the Style of Sicily

Fresh fava beans have a pleasant tang with rich yet delicate creamy flesh that is entirely unique in the bean family. They are a particular favorite of the Italians. Bear in mind that they are worth eating fresh only if young and tender; older beans are hard and bitter. The beans that nestle in the woolly interior of the pod should be a clear green. To prepare them, first shell the beans from the long pods, then remove the outer shell of the bean itself before using.

KCal 300 P 15g C 35g S 1191mg SFA 3g UFA 6g (4)

INGREDIENTS
1½ tbsp extra-virgin olive oil
1 onion, very finely chopped
2oz (60g) prosciutto or ham, coarsely chopped
7 cups (1.8 liters) water
1lb (500g) fresh fava beans, shelled and pale green inner skins removed
¼lb (125g) linguine, broken into 2in (5cm) lengths
2 tsp salt
1 tbsp very finely chopped fresh basil
1 tbsp very finely chopped fresh mint
¼ tsp freshly ground black pepper, or to taste

1 Warm the oil in a large pan. Add the onion and sauté until tender, about 3 minutes. Add the prosciutto and sauté until lightly browned, about 2 minutes.

2 Pour in the water and bring to a boil. Add the fresh beans and simmer, partially covered, over medium-low heat until tender, about 30 minutes. Stir in the *linguine* and salt. Cook over medium heat until just tender, about 10 minutes.

3 Stir the basil and mint into the hot soup just before serving, then season with pepper. Serve immediately.

Brodo Magro di Carne

Light Meat Broth

Meat broth is the basis of many soups. For maximum flavor, the meat and accompanying vegetables should begin cooking in cold water, which allows the meat juices to be released into the broth rather than being sealed in by immediate intense heat. The best broth is made with a combination of red meats and poultry. For a richer broth, beef can be substituted for veal, and turkey wings or legs can replace chicken pieces.

KCal 20 P 3g C tr S 786mg SFA tr UFA 1g (4)

Advance Preparation

This broth can be made up to four days in advance. Strain out the meat and vegetables, cover, and refrigerate for up to four days, or freeze for up to six months.

INGREDIENTS

3lb (1.5kg) chicken backs or wings, washed

2lb (1kg) veal neck bones, or other economy cut

1 fresh or canned plum tomato

1 onion, unpeeled and washed, quartered

1 large carrot, peeled and cut into quarters

1 large celery rib with leaves

handful of flat-leaf parsley leaves and stems

⅛ tsp whole peppercorns

approximately 8 cups (2 liters) water

2–3 tsp salt, depending on quantity of water used

1 Trim any excess fat from the chicken pieces and veal.

2 Select a deep soup pan in which all the meat will fit comfortably. Put in all the ingredients up to and including the peppercorns. Add the cold water to cover the ingredients by 2in (5cm), up to a maximum of 8 cups (2 liters).

3 Cover the pan and bring to a boil. Immediately reduce the heat to low and simmer steadily and gently, partially covered, for 2½ hours, until the liquid is full-bodied and tasty. Check the broth occasionally, keeping it at a gentle simmer. Skim the surface to keep the broth clear. Do not allow it to return to a boil.

4 When the broth is finished, skim off any fat that has risen to the surface. Using tongs, remove the meat and bones (the meat can be eaten separately). Strain the broth through cheesecloth or a very fine sieve into a bowl. Add salt to taste if you are using the broth immediately.

Pastina in Brodo per Bambini

Pastina in Broth for Children

While** pastina **cooked in broth is by no means a dish confined to the nursery, it is associated with my childhood and that of most Italians. It is still a favorite of mine and of my own children. The freshly made broth is clear and flavorful – perfect when the stomach requires gentle food.

KCal 130 P 7g C 24g S 791mg SFA tr UFA 1g (4)

INGREDIENTS

1 quantity light meat broth (see above)

1 cup (125g) pastina, such as semi di melone ("melon seeds"), acini di pepe ("peppercorns"), or orzi ("barley")

1 tbsp chopped fresh flat-leaf parsley

freshly grated Parmesan, to serve (optional)

1 Bring the broth to a boil in a saucepan. Add the *pastina* and simmer at a lively pace (medium or medium-high heat) until the *pastina* is cooked, according to package directions. It should be tender but not overcooked.

2 Remove the pan from the heat, add the parsley, and serve, passing Parmesan at the table.

Brodo con Zafferano e Quadrucci

Saffron Broth with Quadrucci

This is a** minestrina, **a light soup, which typically includes a little light pasta. I like to use** quadrucci **(tiny squares), either homemade or dried. Angel hair, broken up, would also be suitable. (See page 12 for illustration.)

KCal 149 P 8g C 25g S 808mg SFA 1g UFA 2g (4)

INGREDIENTS

1 quantity light meat broth (see above) or other broth

⅓ quantity (5½oz/165g) fresh egg fresh pasta (see page 48), cut into quadrucci (see page 54), or ⅔ cup (90g) dried quadrucci

⅛ tsp saffron threads, or 1 envelope (130mg) pure saffron powder

salt, to taste

2 tbsp chopped fresh flat-leaf parsley

freshly ground black pepper, to taste

freshly grated Parmesan, to serve

1 Bring the meat broth to a boil in a large pan. Add the *quadrucci* and saffron threads or powder. Simmer, partially covered, until the pasta is cooked, about 1 minute for fresh *quadrucci*. If using dried *quadrucci*, follow the package cooking directions.

2 Take the soup from the heat. Taste and adjust for salt then sprinkle in the chopped parsley. Season to taste with pepper. Serve hot, accompanied by plenty of fresh Parmesan.

BRODO CON POLPETTINE DI SALSICCIA E TACCHINO E PASTINA

Sausage and Turkey Meatballs in Broth with Escarole and Pastina

There is so much that can be done with broth for a really first-rate soup, assuming the broth is good, flavorful, and homemade. It is a common practice in the Italian kitchen to add mild greens, such as escarole, spinach, or Swiss chard, to a pot of home-cooked broth for color, flavor, and body. The tiny meatballs are a wonderfully savory addition. Be sure to use high-quality, lean sausage meat to avoid adding fat to the broth. As for the pasta, almost any type of soup pasta can be used, or even broken up angel hair.

KCal 260 P 20g C 25g S 1152mg SFA 3g UFA 6g (4)

INGREDIENTS

- 1 quantity light meat broth (see opposite)
- ⅔ cup (90g) pastina, such as orzi ("barley"), acini di pepe ("peppercorns"), or semi di melone ("melon seeds")
- ¼lb (125g) escarole, washed well, cut across and shredded
- freshly ground salt and black pepper, to taste

For the meatballs

- 6oz (175g) raw ground turkey
- 3oz (90g) lean sweet Italian sausage meat, ground twice if possible
- ¼ cup (20g) fresh bread crumbs
- ¼ tsp ground fennel seeds
- 1 tbsp chopped fresh flat-leaf parsley
- ⅛ tsp salt
- 1 egg white
- ½ small onion, grated

1 In a bowl, combine the ingredients for the meatballs, using your hands to mix everything together well. Form the mixture into small meatballs about the size of a large grape. Set aside.

2 Bring the broth to a boil. Stir in the *pastina* and cook over medium heat for 3 minutes. Add the meatballs and the escarole. Cook until the meatballs and escarole are tender, 3–4 minutes. Remove from the heat, check for salt and add pepper. Serve immediately.

BRODO CON POLPETTINE DI POLLO E PROSCIUTTO E CAPELLI D'ANGELO

Tiny Chicken and Prosciutto Meatballs in Broth with Angel Hair

One usually thinks of frying or sautéing meatballs, but they are marvelous cooked in broth: they remain succulent and also impart their aromatic flavor to the broth. These meatballs are more delicate than those above, which contain sausage, so be sure to cook them very briefly as they will harden quickly.
(See page 12 for illustration.)

KCal 442 P 49g C 25g S 1744mg SFA 7g UFA 7g (4)

INGREDIENTS

- 1 quantity light meat broth (see opposite)
- 3oz (90g) capelli d'angelo ("angel hair" pasta)
- freshly grated Parmesan, to serve

For the meatballs

- 1¼lb (625g) raw ground chicken
- 1 egg white
- 4 slices (60g) stale white bread, soaked in milk or broth and squeezed dry
- 2oz (60g) chopped prosciutto or ham
- 1 large garlic clove, finely chopped
- 2 tbsp chopped fresh flat-leaf parsley
- 1 tsp chopped fresh marjoram, or ½ tsp dried marjoram
- 3 tbsp freshly grated Parmesan or pecorino
- ½ tsp salt
- ¼ tsp freshly ground black pepper

1 Thoroughly combine the ingredients for the meatballs, using your hands to mix everything together thoroughly. Form the mixture into small balls, each approximately the size of a cherry.

2 Bring the broth to a boil in a large saucepan. Drop the meatballs into the broth. Bring to a boil once more and add the angel hair pasta. Reduce the heat to medium and simmer gently until the meatballs and pasta are cooked, about 5 minutes. Do not overcook the meatballs. Serve immediately, passing fresh Parmesan at the table.

SALSE, SUGHI, E RAGÙ

SAUCES

IN ITALY, SAUCES are not as critical to the cuisine as they are in France. The Italians like to experience the natural flavor of food, not mask it with sauces. But when it comes to pasta, sauces are crucial. In general, the Italians do not sauce pasta as heavily as foreigners: the quality of the pasta is so good that they want to taste it. The word *salsa,* "sauce," derives from *sale,* "salt" – probably because the first sauce was one of meat drippings mixed with salt. There are many sauces offered throughout this book, but in this chapter are gathered some of the essential sauces of the pasta kitchen: *salse* made of any number of ingredients; *sughi,* which are simple sauce essences with few ingredients; and *ragù,* meat-based sauces.

RAGÙ CON PORCINI E PINOLI ALLA LIGURE
Ragù with Porcini and Pine Nuts in the Style of Liguria

RAGÙ CON PORCINI E PINOLI ALLA LIGURE

Ragù with Porcini and Pine Nuts in the Style of Liguria

There are many ways to make ragù, *and numerous regional variations that reflect historical and geographical influences. The tomato and meat sauce of Liguria is lent extra body and flavor by pine nuts, a popular ingredient in many of the local dishes, most notably* pesto alla genovese. *Makes approximately 3¼ cups (800ml).*

KCal 342 P 16g C 14g S 290mg SFA 4g UFA 19g (4)

INGREDIENTS

- *½ cup (30g) dried porcini*
- *4 tbsp extra-virgin olive oil*
- *1 small onion, very finely chopped*
- *2 large garlic cloves, very finely chopped*
- *½lb (250g) lean ground beef*
- *½ tsp salt*
- *½ cup (125ml) dry red wine*
- *¼ cup (30g) pine nuts*
- *1 tsp chopped fresh rosemary, or ½ tsp dried rosemary*
- *1 bay leaf*
- *4 tbsp tomato paste*
- *1¼lb (625g) fresh or canned drained plum tomatoes, peeled, seeded, and chopped*
- *freshly ground pepper, to taste*

1 Soak the dried porcini in ¾ cup (175ml) of warm water for 30 minutes. Drain, reserving the soaking liquid. Squeeze out the excess water and then chop the porcini. Strain the liquid through paper towels and reserve.

2 Warm the oil in a wide pan over medium-low heat. Add the onion and garlic and sauté until soft, 3–4 minutes.

3 Add the ground beef and salt, using a wooden spoon to break up the meat and turn it so that it browns evenly. Sauté until light brown on the surface but still pinkish inside, about 5 minutes.

4 Pour in the wine and allow it to evaporate, about 2 minutes. Add the porcini, pine nuts, rosemary, bay leaf, and tomato paste. Stir, then add the porcini soaking liquor. Simmer until most of the liquid has evaporated, 5 minutes.

5 Stir in the tomatoes and simmer, partially covered, stirring frequently, until the sauce is thick and aromatic, about 45 minutes. Remove the pan from the heat. Check for salt and add pepper.

VARIATION

Substitute ¼lb (125g) fresh porcini, chanterelles, cremini, or shiitake mushrooms for the dried porcini. Brush them well with a soft cloth to remove any dirt. Cut off woody tips and thinly slice them. Add the mushrooms to the pan with the meat and stir in ¼ cup (125ml) of water with the tomato paste.

RAGÙ DI MANZO E FUNGHI

Beef and Mushroom Ragù

Unlike many ragù, *this one cooks quickly, though it still exhibits the characteristic deep, rich flavor of a meat-based tomato sauce. It is a good choice for most macaroni cuts, including* rigatoni, penne, creste di gallo, *and* fusilli, *and also suits shorter pasta cuts such as* pennette *and* anelli. *This* ragù *is also perfect for* lasagne *and other baked dishes. Makes approximately 2½ cups (600ml).*

KCal 332 P 32g C 13g S 714mg SFA 4g UFA 10g (4)

INGREDIENTS

- *2oz (60g) wild or cultivated mushrooms*
- *2 tbsp extra-virgin olive oil*
- *2oz (60g) pancetta, finely chopped, or lean bacon, blanched for 1 minute then finely chopped*
- *1 onion, chopped*
- *1 large garlic clove, very finely chopped*
- *1 small carrot, chopped*
- *1 tbsp chopped fresh flat-leaf parsley*
- *1 tbsp chopped fresh basil, or 1 tsp chopped fresh thyme, or ½ tsp dried thyme*
- *1lb (500g) lean ground beef*
- *½ cup (125ml) dry red wine*
- *½lb (250g) tomato paste*
- *2 cups (500ml) water*
- *½ tsp salt*

1 Use a soft brush or cloth to clean the mushrooms. Trim off any woody tips, then chop the caps and stalks. Set aside.

2 Warm the oil in a pan and add the pancetta or bacon. Sauté for 2 minutes until golden. Add the onion, garlic, carrot, parsley, basil or thyme, and mushrooms. Sauté until soft, about 5 minutes. Add the beef and sauté over medium-low heat until lightly colored but not hard, about 1 minute, using a spoon to break it up.

3 Stir in the wine and let it evaporate. Add the tomato paste, water, and salt. Bring the mixture to a boil, then reduce to a gentle simmer. Cook, partially covered, until the sauce is thick and aromatic, about 30 minutes.

Ragù alla Toscana

Tuscan Ragù

I learned to make this style of ragù *from a Tuscan chef many years ago. It is simpler than the Bolognese variation (see page 73), but is still exceptionally tasty. It is made with olive oil rather than butter, and its style is correspondingly lighter. For a variation, fresh chicken livers can be added. The sauce can be made, omitting the pepper, three or four days in advance and stored tightly covered in the refrigerator, or it may be frozen for up to three months. Add 2 tablespoons of meat broth or water when reheating, keeping the heat low to prevent the meat from hardening. Stir in the pepper just before serving. Makes approximately 3¼ cups (800ml).*

KCal 317 P 21g C 9g S 290mg SFA 4g UFA 15g (4)

INGREDIENTS

- *4 tbsp extra-virgin olive oil*
- *1 small onion, very finely chopped*
- *2 large garlic cloves, very finely chopped*
- *1 carrot, very finely chopped*
- *¾lb (375g) lean ground beef*
- *½ cup (125ml) dry white wine*
- *2 tbsp tomato paste*
- *2 cups (500g) fresh or canned drained plum tomatoes, peeled, seeded, and chopped*
- *½ tsp salt, or to taste*
- *1 tbsp very finely chopped fresh flat-leaf parsley*
- *freshly ground pepper, to taste*

1 Warm the oil in a large pan over medium-low heat. Add the onion, garlic, and carrot, and sauté until soft, 8–10 minutes.

2 Stir in the beef, using a wooden spoon to break it up. Continue to sauté over medium-low heat, turning the meat constantly, until it becomes light pink. Do not allow it to harden.

3 Pour in the wine and let it evaporate, about 2 minutes, continuing to turn the meat. Dissolve the tomato paste in a tablespoon of water and stir it in. Simmer for 8–10 minutes over medium-low heat, until thickened.

4 Add the tomatoes and salt. Continue to simmer until the sauce is thick and aromatic, about 40 minutes. Stir in the parsley and pepper to taste, and remove from the heat.

VARIATION

Take 3 plump, impeccably fresh chicken livers and trim of any fat, membranes, or discolored areas. Cut into dice. Warm 1 tablespoon of extra-virgin olive oil in a skillet. Add the livers and sauté until lightly browned, but still pink inside. Stir them into the sauce 5 minutes before the end of cooking.

Ragù con Manzo e Maiale

Beef and Pork Ragù

This classic Italian meat sauce is made without tomato. It cooks for a very long time, simmering ever-so-gently over the lowest possible flame so that the meat disintegrates into the sauce, which is made delicate and aromatic by the inclusion of cloves, lemon zest, and wine. Pork, which lends its characteristic sweetness, can be combined with beef, as this recipe suggests, or beef can be used alone. Serve the sauce with fresh pasta or medium-weight macaroni cuts such as rigatoni, lumache, fusilli, eliche *("helixes"),* ziti, orecchiette, *or* penne. *Makes approximately 2½ cups (600ml).*

KCal 319 P 27g C 9g S 203mg SFA 9g UFA 7g (4)

INGREDIENTS

- *¼ cup (15g) dried porcini*
- *½lb (250g) boneless beef chuck, trimmed of all fat*
- *½lb (250g) lean boneless pork, trimmed of all fat*
- *3 tbsp unsalted butter*
- *3 shallots, chopped*
- *1 celery rib with leaves, very finely chopped*
- *1 small carrot, very finely chopped*
- *2 tbsp very finely chopped fresh flat-leaf parsley*
- *⅛ tsp ground cloves*
- *1 tbsp flour*
- *¾ cup (175ml) meat broth*
- *⅔ cup (150ml) dry white wine*
- *salt and freshly ground pepper, to taste*
- *1in (2.5cm) strip lemon zest, without any white pith*

1 Soak the porcini in 1 cup (250ml) of warm water for 30 minutes. Meanwhile, cut the meat into ½in (1cm) dice. Drain the porcini, reserving the liquid. Squeeze the water out of the porcini and then chop them. Strain the liquid through paper towels.

2 Melt the butter in a large pan over medium-low heat. Add the shallots, celery, carrot, and porcini. Increase the heat to medium and sauté until lightly colored, about 5 minutes. Stir in the parsley.

3 Reduce the heat and add the meat. Brown it lightly, about 5 minutes. Stir in the cloves and flour. Pour in the porcini liquid, broth, and wine, and season.

4 Twist the lemon zest to release its oil and add to the sauce. Stir, cover, and simmer at the lowest heat until the meat begins to disintegrate and thickens the sauce, 2½–3 hours, stirring occasionally. If the sauce is not thick enough, remove the cover and let it evaporate gently.

SALSA ALLA BOLOGNESE

Bolognese Sauce

The authentic salsa bolognese *of Emilia-Romagna is delicate, richly complex, and aromatic – vastly different from the popular, rather ordinary hybrid. A variety of meats, typically beef, veal, pork, and chicken, and sometimes* salumi *(cured meats such as prosciutto and mortadella), is used. These are combined with a generous* battuto (see page 162) *of carrots, celery, and onion, and cooked gently with a touch of milk, white wine, and tomato to form an extraordinarily tasty and fragrant sauce. Homemade egg pasta in the form of* tagliatelle or fettuccine, *or layers of delicate* lasagne *noodles are the other half of the legend. The crowning touch is Emilia's great cheese, parmigiano reggiano.*

There are innumerable variations of this sauce throughout the region. I always add ground pork because it adds so much flavor and sweetness. Mortadella, the delicious, subtly spiced sausage, is also included. It is essential to cook this sauce over extremely low heat so that it never boils. Preventing the meat from hardening allows it to absorb the flavors of the other ingredients and to become delicate and creamy.

Makes approximately 3 cups (750ml).

KCal 461 P 28g C 8g S 307mg SFA 17g UFA 14g (4)

INGREDIENTS

2 tbsp unsalted butter

1 tbsp extra-virgin olive oil

1 small yellow onion, finely chopped

1 small celery rib with leaves, finely chopped

1 small carrot, finely chopped

1 tbsp chopped fresh flat-leaf parsley

½lb (250g) good-quality lean ground beef

½lb (250g) lean ground pork

2oz (60g) mortadella or prosciutto crudo, thinly sliced and finely chopped (optional)

¼ tsp salt, or to taste

½ cup (125ml) dry white wine

⅓ cup (75ml) milk

⅛ tsp freshly grated nutmeg

4 tbsp tomato paste

1½ cups (350ml) light meat broth (see page 68), plus extra as needed

½ cup (125ml) heavy cream

freshly ground white or black pepper, to taste

1 Melt the butter with the olive oil in a large, wide, heavy-bottomed pan or a large, deep skillet over low heat. Add the onion, celery, carrot, and chopped parsley, and sauté until the vegetables are fairly soft but not at all browned, stirring occasionally, about 12 minutes.

2 Keeping the heat very low, add the ground meats, the mortadella or prosciutto, if using, and the salt. The meat must heat very gently, only enough to color it lightly on the outside, for about 2 minutes. Use a wooden spoon to break up the meat and stir it as it colors.

3 Stir in the wine and simmer over low heat until the alcohol evaporates and the liquid begins to be absorbed by the meat and vegetables, about 3 minutes.

4 Add the milk and nutmeg. Simmer gently for 5 minutes, then stir in the tomato paste dissolved in ⅓ cup (90ml) of the meat broth. As soon as the sauce begins to simmer, turn the heat down as low as possible (use a heat-diffusing mat, if necessary). Add the remaining broth.

5 Cover the pan partially and continue to simmer, always over the lowest possible heat and stirring occasionally, until the sauce is thick, creamy, and fragrant, about 2 hours. Add additional meat broth as necessary, several tablespoons at a time, to prevent the sauce from becoming too dry.

6 Remove the sauce from the heat and stir in the cream and pepper. Taste and adjust for salt.

ADVANCE PREPARATION

The sauce can be made three or four days in advance and stored tightly covered in the refrigerator, or it can be frozen for up to three months. Whether storing it in the refrigerator or freezer, leave out the cream and the pepper. Add 2 tablespoons of meat broth or water when reheating the sauce, being sure to keep the heat low. Stir in the cream and pepper.

Ragù meridionale

Sugo di pomodoro semplice

Sugo di pomodoro fresco

Salsa di pomodoro con verdure

Ragù Meridionale

Southern-Style Ragù with Pork

Southern Italy does not produce or use very much beef compared to regions of the north; thus, the ragù sauces of the south are frequently based on pork. I am particularly fond of this recipe because the sweetness of both the pork and the fennel seeds lends an appealing, mildly sweet savoriness, which foils and complements the natural acidity of the tomatoes.

Makes approximately 3 cups (750ml).

KCal 232 P 15g C 9g S 316mg SFA 3g UFA 11g (4)

INGREDIENTS

3 tbsp extra-virgin olive oil

1 small onion, very finely chopped

2 large garlic cloves, very finely chopped

1 small carrot, chopped

1 small celery rib with leaves, chopped

1 tbsp chopped fresh flat-leaf parsley

½lb (250g) ground pork

1 tsp fennel seeds, ground

¼ cup (60ml) dry red wine

2 tbsp tomato paste dissolved in ¼ cup (60ml) water

2 cups (500g) canned drained tomatoes, seeded and finely chopped, or fresh crushed tomatoes

salt and freshly ground white pepper, to taste

1 Warm the olive oil in a saucepan over medium heat. Sauté the onion and garlic until softened, about 4 minutes. Add the carrot, celery, and parsley, and continue to cook, tossing occasionally, until the vegetables are soft, about 10 minutes.

2 Add the pork and fennel seeds. Use a wooden spoon to break up the meat. Reduce the heat to low and sauté until the meat colors lightly, about 2 minutes.

3 Pour in the wine and let it evaporate, 3 minutes. Stir in the thinned tomato paste, tomatoes, and ½ teaspoon of salt. Partially cover and simmer over low heat for 1 hour, stirring occasionally. Take off the heat, check for salt and add pepper.

Sugo di Pomodoro Semplice

Simple Tomato Sauce

This basic, simple tomato has many uses, including as a base for other sauces, or for spreading between layers of lasagne. When used to sauce pasta, Parmesan, pecorino, or even shredded ricotta salata are typically scattered on top.

Makes approximately 2½ cups (750ml).

KCal 163 P 2g C 5g S 207mg SFA 2g UFA 13g (4)

INGREDIENTS

¼ cup (60ml) extra-virgin olive oil

2 large garlic cloves, bruised

2½ cups (625g) canned chopped tomatoes

⅓ tsp salt, or to taste

1½ tbsp chopped fresh basil or parsley

freshly ground black pepper, to taste

1 Warm the olive oil and garlic in a pan over medium-low heat, until the garlic is golden. Add the tomatoes, salt, and herbs. Simmer gently for 15 minutes. Remove the garlic, if desired. Let cool.

2 Pass the sauce through a food mill (see page 127), or purée in a blender or food processor. Reheat just before serving, adjusting for salt and adding pepper.

Sugo di Pomodoro Fresco

Fresh Tomato Sauce

No one with access to luscious sun-ripened tomatoes should miss the opportunity to make this sauce. Plum tomatoes are the best variety to use because of their thick fleshy skins and low water content. The less cooking time needed to evaporate excess liquid, the fresher and clearer the taste of the sauce. Other tomato varieties may be used – squeeze out as much of their liquid as possible, then skim off the water that accumulates around the edges of the pan. Almost any type of pasta is a good match. Makes approximately 2½ cups (750ml).

KCal 204 P 2g C 6g S 211mg SFA 3g UFA 16g (4)

INGREDIENTS

- *⅓ cup (75ml) extra-virgin olive oil*
- *6 large garlic cloves, bruised*
- *½ small onion, very finely chopped*
- *2 tbsp very finely chopped fresh flat-leaf parsley, or 8 large basil leaves*
- *5 cups (1.25kg) fresh, mature vine-ripened plum tomatoes, peeled, seeded, coarsely chopped, and drained*
- *½ tsp salt*
- *freshly ground black or white pepper, to taste*

1 Warm the olive oil in a saucepan over medium-low heat. Add the bruised garlic cloves, onion, and parsley, if using. Sauté until the onion softens and the garlic turns pale golden. Remove and discard the garlic.

2 Add the tomatoes and salt. Use a potato masher or fork to break the tomatoes into fairly small pieces. Raise the heat to high and bring the tomatoes to a simmer. Reduce the heat to medium-low and simmer, stirring occasionally, until the tomatoes acquire a thick, saucelike consistency, about 20 minutes.

3 Add pepper to taste and then remove the sauce from the heat. If using basil instead of parsley, shred it with your fingers and stir it gently into the sauce just before serving.

Salsa di Pomodoro con Verdure

Tomato Sauce with Vegetables

This elegant, butter-based, fragrant sauce is suitable for fresh, dried, or stuffed pasta. If you do not have a food mill, the sauce can be puréed in a food processor, although the result will be less velvety. Makes approximately 2½ cups (750ml).

KCal 197 P 2g C 10g S 244mg SFA 9g UFA 7g (4)

INGREDIENTS

- *4 tbsp unsalted butter*
- *1 tbsp extra-virgin olive oil*
- *1 small–medium onion, very finely chopped*
- *1 carrot, very finely chopped*
- *1 celery rib with leaves, very finely chopped*
- *1 tbsp chopped fresh flat-leaf parsley*
- *2 tbsp tomato paste*
- *2½ cups (625g) fresh or canned drained plum tomatoes, peeled, seeded, and chopped*
- *½ tsp salt*
- *freshly ground black or white pepper, to taste*

1 Warm 3 tablespoons of butter with the oil in a wide pan over medium-low heat. Add the onion, carrot, celery, and parsley. Sauté until the vegetables are softened but not browned, 10 minutes.

2 Stir in the tomato paste, the tomatoes, and salt. Simmer, partially covered, stirring frequently, until the mixture has thickened, about 40 minutes. Remove from the heat and let cool.

3 Pass the sauce through a food mill (see page 127), or purée in a food processor or blender. Return the sauce to the pan and reheat gently. Stir in the remaining butter and the pepper. Check the seasoning before serving.

Variations

To make a creamy tomato sauce (Salsa Aurora) add ¼ cup (60ml) heavy cream to the finished sauce.

To make a wine-enriched version, add ¼ cup (60ml) of dry white or red wine with the tomatoes and tomato paste. Simmer the sauce for an additional 5 minutes or so, if necessary.

Salsa di Pomodoro con Funghi Selvatici e Vino Rosso

Tomato Sauce with Wild Mushrooms and Red Wine

No mushroom's flavor can compare with that of the porcino (cèpe in France), and while fresh porcini are rarely found in our markets, dried porcini are excellent substitutes. This tomato-based sauce is lent depth and complexity by the intense flavor and aroma of these mushrooms, and so there is no need for meat. Fresh mushrooms are also added for texture and body. This sauce has many uses; it is suitable for both fresh and dried pasta, and as a filling for baked pasta dishes. Makes approximately 2¾ cups (650ml).

KCal 205 P 3g C 15g S 281mg SFA 7g UFA 6g (4)

INGREDIENTS
½ cup (30g) dried porcini
¼lb (125g) fresh wild mushrooms, such as chanterelles, morels, oyster or cremini mushrooms, or cultivated mushrooms
3 tbsp unsalted butter
1 tbsp extra-virgin olive oil
1 small white or red onion, very finely chopped
1 celery rib, very finely chopped
1 small carrot, very finely chopped
2 tbsp very finely chopped fresh flat-leaf parsley
1 tsp chopped fresh rosemary, or ½ tsp dried rosemary
3 tbsp tomato paste
¼ cup (60ml) dry red wine
2½ cups (625g) fresh or canned drained plum tomatoes, peeled, seeded, and chopped
½ tsp salt
freshly ground pepper, to taste

1 Soak the porcini in 1 cup (250ml) of warm water for 30 minutes. Drain, reserving the soaking liquid. Squeeze the water out of the porcini, then cut into thumbnail-size pieces. Set aside. Strain the soaking liquid through paper towels and reserve.

2 Meanwhile, use a soft cloth or brush to clean the fresh mushrooms. Separate the stems from the caps, discarding the stems if they are tough. Cut the mushrooms into halves, or quarters if large, then slice thinly.

3 Warm the butter and oil in a large pan over medium-low heat. Add the onion, celery, carrot, and parsley, and sauté until soft, about 12 minutes.

4 Stir in the rehydrated porcini and rosemary and sauté gently for 5 minutes. Add the fresh mushrooms and cook until soft, about 7–8 minutes.

5 Stir in the tomato paste and the reserved porcini liquor and combine thoroughly. Simmer gently to evaporate the liquid for about 5 minutes. Pour in the wine and simmer until the alcohol has evaporated, about 3 minutes.

6 Add the tomatoes and salt. Allow the sauce to simmer over very low heat, partially covered, until it is thickened and fragrant, about 40 minutes, stirring occasionally. Remove the sauce from the heat and check the seasoning.

Salsa ai Quattro Formaggi

Four Cheese Sauce

This is a very popular Italian sauce, used with macaroni cuts and between layers of lasagne. The foundation of this sauce is béchamel (see opposite), into which the cheeses are blended. Each cheese contributes its own unique flavor and blending characteristics: the fontina is nutty, sweet, delicate, and buttery; the Gruyère has depth and body; the mozzarella is bland but has great melting properties; and the Parmesan adds its incomparable complexity of flavor. Makes approximately 3 cups (750ml).

KCal 367 P 18g C 13g S 492mg SFA 18g UFA 8g (4)

INGREDIENTS
2¼ cups (550ml) milk
3 tbsp unsalted butter
2 tbsp all-purpose flour
¼ tsp salt
freshly ground white pepper, to taste
1½oz (45g) each, Gruyère, fontina, and high-quality mozzarella, shredded
⅓ cup (45g) freshly grated Parmesan

1 Heat the milk to just below boiling point, then keep warm.

2 Melt the butter in a saucepan over low heat. Using a whisk, blend in the flour. Let the flour and butter paste heat through for about 2 minutes, stirring constantly so that it does not stick and become brown.

3 Add the hot milk very gradually and slowly, stirring continually with a whisk or wooden spoon to prevent lumps from forming (see steps 3 and 4 for Besciamella, opposite).

4 When the sauce is thick and creamy, about 5 minutes, add the salt and pepper. Keeping the sauce over low heat, scatter in the Gruyère, fontina, and mozzarella, stirring until all the cheeses are thoroughly melted, about 2 minutes. Stir in the Parmesan and take the sauce off the heat immediately.

BESCIAMELLA
Béchamel Sauce

Besciamella is as fundamental to Italian cooking as tomato sauce, which did not become established in Italy until the late 19th century. It is indispensable in baked dishes, it anoints casseroles of chicory and cauliflower, and is a base for many sauces. It is a simple sauce, the success of which depends on using plenty of butter and heating the milk, then adding it slowly. Makes approximately 2 cups (500ml).

KCal 241 P 6g C 16g S 176mg SFA 12g UFA 5g (4)

INGREDIENTS

2¼ cups (550ml) milk

4 tbsp unsalted butter

3 tbsp all-purpose flour

¼ tsp salt

⅛ tsp freshly grated nutmeg

1 Heat the milk to just below boiling point, then keep warm.

2 Melt the butter in a heavy-based saucepan. Working over low heat, add the flour and stir with a wooden spoon or whisk to get rid of lumps. Let the flour and butter paste heat through for about 2 minutes, stirring constantly. Do not let the paste brown.

3 Add the hot milk, a tablespoon at a time, stirring constantly to incorporate it thoroughly. Continue to add the milk very slowly, just a few tablespoons at a time, until ½ cup (125ml) is used up.

4 If you are not an old hand at this, turn off the heat as you add the rest of the milk in a very slow and gradual trickle, stirring all the time. If the sauce is to be used as a binding, rather than as a pouring sauce, hold back a little of the milk. If lumps appear, you are probably adding the milk in too great a quantity, too quickly, or the heat is too high. Should this happen, turn off the heat and press the lumps against the side of the pan with a wooden spoon.

5 When all the milk has been added, simmer the sauce very gently for another 15 minutes or so, stirring constantly. Add the salt and nutmeg during the last 10 minutes of cooking.

SALSA AL MASCARPONE
Mascarpone Sauce

Here is a very simple, classic, and versatile pasta sauce made with Italy's sweet, delicate cream cheese. It is so simple that my young children make it themselves. They call it "baci" *sauce – sauce of kisses! Makes approximately 2½ cups (600ml).*

KCal 448 P 7g C 4g S 159mg SFA 32g UFA 12g (4)

INGREDIENTS

4 tbsp unsalted butter

10oz (300g) mascarpone

¼ cup (30g) freshly grated Parmesan

1 Warm the butter in a saucepan over low heat until it is melted. Add the mascarpone. Stir with a wooden spoon to make a consistent, creamy-smooth mixture. Do not let it heat longer than 4–5 minutes, or it will become too thin.

2 Remove the saucepan from the heat and quickly stir in the Parmesan just before serving.

SALSA DI GORGONZOLA
Gorgonzola Sauce

This superb sauce is typically served with fresh fettuccine, penne, *or* gnocchi *(see page 144). It is essential that the Gorgonzola be young and "sweet" (often called* dolcelatte*), not aged, which is too strong for pasta sauce. However, made with the right cheese, this sauce is exceptional. There are many versions, but I think this one, the simplest, is the best. Makes approximately 2 cups (500ml).*

KCal 481 P 14g C 1g S 687mg SFA 29g UFA 15g (4)

INGREDIENTS

5oz (150g) sweet (young) Gorgonzola

3 tbsp unsalted butter

¾ cup (175ml) heavy cream

pinch of salt

½ cup (60g) freshly grated Parmesan

freshly ground white pepper, to taste

1 Remove the rind from the Gorgonzola and discard. Cut the cheese into small, evenly sized pieces.

2 Warm the butter in the top of a double boiler over boiling water or in a saucepan over low heat. When it is melted, add the Gorgonzola. Using a wooden spoon, stir until the cheese is totally dissolved in the butter.

3 Add the cream. Heat until it begins to simmer, stirring constantly. When it is thick enough to coat the spoon, about 5 minutes, add the salt and Parmesan. Stir in the white pepper at the very last minute.

PASTA FRESCA

FRESH PASTA

TO EXPERIENCE THE DELIGHTS of true *pasta fresca,* it must be made at home (see page 48). So-called fresh pasta sold in the refrigerated sections of supermarkets is not fresh pasta at all; this product is made from hard-wheat flour, and not necessarily fresh eggs. The resulting pasta is thick, tough, and somewhat gummy when cooked. It lacks the flavor and delicacy of the true product and is to be avoided. In general, homemade pasta should be matched with butter-based sauces, cream sauces, or delicate vegetable or tomato creations. You should no more think of dressing *pasta fresca* with the robust sauces suited to dried pasta than you would drink a heavy red wine with a plate of delicate seafood.

PAPPARDELLE CON GRANCHI E ASPARAGI
Pappardelle with Crab and Asparagus

Special Ingredients

Crab *Asparagus* *Tarragon* *Cream* *Pappardelle*

Preparation

The Tuscans are particularly fond of pappardelle *and have developed a number of sauces that have been designed to accompany them, most notably* pappardelle *with hare sauce. Here is quite a different sauce, which is well suited to these very broad but delicate noodles. Other suitable pasta cuts include fresh or dried* fettuccine *or* tagliatelle.

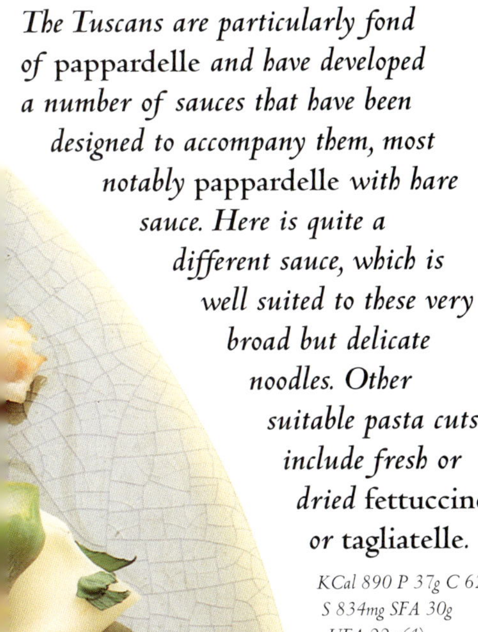

KCal 890 P 37g C 62g S 834mg SFA 30g UFA 22g (4)

INGREDIENTS
¾lb (375g) fresh cooked crabmeat, or ¾lb (375g) small or medium raw shrimp in their shells
½lb (250g) fresh asparagus, ends trimmed
salt, to taste
4 tbsp unsalted butter, plus ½ tbsp for sautéing crab, if necessary
1 onion, grated
1 tsp chopped fresh tarragon, or ½ tsp dried tarragon
1 cup (250ml) heavy cream
freshly ground white pepper, to taste
1 quantity (1lb/500g) fresh egg pasta (see page 48) cut into pappardelle (see page 52) or dried pappardelle

1 Check the crabmeat, if using, to make sure it is free of all shell and cartilage. If using shrimp, use a small knife to peel off the shells and remove the tails. Make a cut down the back of each shrimp and remove the dark intestinal vein. Wash well, making sure all traces of the intestinal vein are removed. Dry well with a dish towel and set aside.

2 Using a paring knife, peel off the thicker skin at the base end of each asparagus stalk to reveal the tender flesh inside. Cut the asparagus across on the diagonal into slices about ¼in (5mm) long, keeping the delicate tips intact.

3 Bring a large pan of salted water to a boil and immerse the asparagus. Cook until just tender, about 5 minutes; be careful not to damage the flowerlike buds at the top. Drain immediately and plunge into cold water to arrest cooking. Set the asparagus aside.

4 Melt the butter in a large skillet. Sauté the onion until soft, about 5 minutes. Add the reserved asparagus and sauté gently for 5 minutes longer.

5 If using crab, sauté it briefly in ½ tablespoon of butter, just until heated through, before adding it to the skillet. Alternatively, add the shrimp to the skillet, raise the heat to medium-high and cook until pink, 5 minutes.

6 Add salt to taste, tarragon, cream, and plenty of pepper, and stir thoroughly. Bring the sauce to a simmer, then remove from the heat.

7 Meanwhile, bring 4 quarts (5 liters) of water to a boil. Add the fresh pasta and 1½ tablespoons of salt. Let the water return to a boil and then cook for 15 seconds. Alternatively, cook the dried pasta until *al dente*. Drain the pasta and toss with the sauce in the skillet, then serve immediately.

Taglierini con Salsa di Pesce

Taglierini with Seafood Sauce

I fashioned this sauce in imitation of a dish I was served in Parma, where fresh pasta is preferred over dried pasta. The butter in the sauce gives it a delicacy and sweetness that is most suitable with fresh pasta, though it certainly can be served over dried pasta such as spaghetti or spaghettini. If making the sauce for dried pasta, extra-virgin olive oil may be used instead of butter.

KCal 682 P 45g C 61g S 526mg SFA 12g UFA 14g (4)

INGREDIENTS

- *½lb (250g) large shrimp in their shells*
- *1 tbsp extra-virgin olive oil*
- *4 tbsp unsalted butter*
- *2 garlic cloves, very finely chopped*
- *2 cups (500g) fresh or canned drained plum tomatoes, peeled, seeded, and chopped*
- *½ cup (125ml) dry white wine*
- *1lb (500g) whole fish, such as sea bass, mullet, or porgy, scaled and gutted but with head intact*
- *½lb (250g) firm white-fleshed fish fillet, such as cod or swordfish*
- *1 envelope (130mg) pure saffron powder, or ⅛ tsp saffron threads*
- *salt and freshly ground white pepper, to taste*
- *1 quantity (1lb/500g) fresh egg pasta (see page 48), cut into taglierini (see page 53)*

1 Use a small knife to peel the shells off the shrimp and remove the tails. Make a cut down the back of each shrimp and remove the dark intestinal vein. Wash thoroughly, making sure all traces of the intestinal vein are removed. Dry well with a dish towel, then chop them into small pieces and set aside.

2 Warm the oil and 3 tablespoons of butter in a deep, broad skillet. Add the garlic and sauté until softened, 3–4 minutes. Add the tomatoes and simmer for 5 minutes over medium heat.

3 Stir in the wine. Allow it to evaporate for 2 minutes. Place the whole fish and the fillet in the pan. Cook for 10 minutes over medium heat, turning once. Remove the pan from the heat.

4 Take the whole fish out of the pan and remove its bones and skin. Flake the meat and return it to the pan.

5 Warm the remaining butter in a small skillet and add the shrimp. Sauté until they turn pink, about 3 minutes. Add the shrimp, saffron, and salt to the sauce and heat it through. Season with pepper and remove from the heat.

6 Meanwhile, bring 4 quarts (5 liters) of water to a boil. Add the *taglierini* and 1½ tablespoons of salt. Let the water return to a boil and then cook for 15 seconds. Drain and toss with the sauce in the skillet, then serve immediately.

Taglierini con Sugo di Arrosto di Maiale alla Veneta

Taglierini with Pork Roast Pan Juices in the Style of the Veneto

It is a typical Sunday or holiday ritual in Italian families to dress freshly made noodles with the juices of a roast, which is then served as the second course. In this recipe, the pan juices, richly flavored with garlic, rosemary, and fruity olive oil, are fortified with wine and butter. Pork is far leaner today than it once was, so it is important to keep the fat on the loin intact to ensure that there will be plenty of meat drippings in the bottom of the roasting pan, not just burnt juices. After cooking, the fat can be separated from the meat juices and discarded. The juices are then used to make the sauce.

KCal 378 P 11g C 40g S 2471mg SFA 7g UFA 11g (6)

Tip

If there is not enough fat round the roast, lard it with fat before cooking. If the joint has been boned by the butcher, ask for the bones and place them in the roasting pan with the meat; they will help to keep the pork moist and contribute to the pan juices.

Advance Preparation

The meat can be prepared for roasting as directed, and refrigerated a day in advance. Bring back to room temperature before cooking.

INGREDIENTS

1 boneless center-cut pork loin, about 4lb (2kg), plus bones, or 1 unboned center-cut pork loin, about 6lb (3kg), fat intact

6 large garlic cloves, cut into slivers

bunch (6 or so) long rosemary sprigs, if available

⅔ cup (150ml) dry white wine

sea salt, to taste

For the rub

2 tbsp extra-virgin olive oil

coarsely ground black pepper, to taste

2 tbsp finely chopped fresh rosemary leaves, or 3 tsp crushed dried rosemary

For the sauce

4 tbsp unsalted butter

4 large garlic cloves, bruised

reserved pan juices

¼ cup (60ml) dry white wine

1 quantity (1lb/500g) fresh egg pasta (see page 48), cut into taglierini (see page 53)

TO ROAST THE PORK

1 Bring the meat to room temperature. Combine the ingredients for the rub and massage it into the surface of the meat. Using the point of a knife, make ½in (1cm) deep incisions on all sides of the roast, and in between the meat and bones if using an unboned center-cut. Slip the garlic slivers into the incisions. At this point, the pork can be covered and refrigerated overnight if desired.

2 Preheat the oven to a temperature of 350°F (180°C).

3 If using a boneless loin, score the fat on top of the roast. Place the detached bones in a large roasting pan, slipping the rosemary sprigs between them, and set the meat fat side up on top of the bones. If using a center-cut, fold the bones under the meat.

4 Add several tablespoons of water to the bottom of the pan to prevent the meat juices from burning on contact. Slide the pan onto the middle or upper-middle rack for 30 minutes. Pour ⅔ cup (150ml) of wine into the pan; this will keep the pork moist during roasting.

5 Cook the meat for a total of about 1 hour and 35 minutes, basting every 20 minutes or so with the juices in the bottom of the pan. If the bottom of the roasting pan appears too dry, pour a little more water into the pan. Insert a meat thermometer into the thickest part of the meat during the last 30 minutes of cooking. The pork should be removed from the oven when the thermometer reads 150°F (65°C).

6 Sprinkle the roast with sea salt to taste and cover completely with foil. Allow it to rest for 15 minutes. The meat will continue to cook as it rests. Carve the meat and transfer to a serving dish; cover well and set in a warm place.

7 Defat the pan juices by skimming of the excess oil. Combine them with the juices that have accumulated from carving; you should have about 1 cup (250ml). If less, increase the amount of butter in the sauce.

TO MAKE THE SAUCE

1 Warm the butter in a saucepan and add the garlic. Sauté over medium-low heat until the garlic is golden, about 5 minutes, pressing down on the cloves with a wooden spoon to release their juices. Add the pan juices and the wine and allow to evaporate, about 3 minutes. Remove and discard the garlic.

2 Bring 4 quarts (5 liters) of water to a boil. Add the fresh *taglierini* and 1½ tablespoons of salt. Let the water return to a boil and then cook for 15 seconds. Drain the *taglierini* and toss them thoroughly with the sauce. Serve as a first course, following with the roast pork as a second course.

Tagliatelle con Asparagi e Zafferano

Saffron Tagliatelle with Asparagus

This culinary "fantasia" brings together not only the harmonious flavors of asparagus, sherry, prosciutto, and onion, but also shows off the beautiful colors of the sauce and the golden saffron noodles. Fresh egg tagliatelle may be substituted. (See illustration opposite.)

KCal 1007 P 32g C 65g S 1380mg SFA 37g UFA 28g (4)

INGREDIENTS

1½lb (750g) asparagus, ends trimmed

salt, to taste

5 tbsp (75g) unsalted butter

1 onion, grated

½ cup (125ml) dry sherry

1 cup (250ml) heavy cream

3 tbsp fresh chives, snipped

¼ cup (30g) freshly grated Parmesan, plus extra for serving

¼lb (125g) prosciutto, thinly sliced and cut into matchstick strips

freshly ground white or black pepper, to taste

1 quantity (1lb/500g) saffron pasta (see page 54), cut into tagliatelle (see page 53)

1 Using a paring knife, peel off the thicker skin at the base end of each asparagus stalk to reveal the tender stalk. In a skillet large enough to accommodate the length of the asparagus, bring enough water to cover the asparagus to a boil.

2 Add 1 teaspoon salt per 5 cups (1.25 liters) of water and the asparagus to the pan. Boil until tender but not mushy, 5–6 minutes, depending on the freshness and maturity of the asparagus. Drain the asparagus immediately and plunge it into chilled water to arrest cooking. Cut the stalks across into diagonal slices about ¼in (5mm) thick, keeping the tips whole.

3 Melt the butter in a large skillet over medium-low heat. Add half the asparagus pieces and the grated onion. Stir and sauté until the onion wilts, about 1 minute. Cover and sauté gently for 1–2 minutes until soft. Stir in the sherry and allow the alcohol to evaporate, approximately 3 minutes.

4 Add the cream and allow it to come to a simmer. Remove the pan from the heat, stir in the remaining asparagus, the chives, Parmesan, prosciutto, ¼ teaspoon of salt, and pepper.

5 Bring 4 quarts (5 liters) of water to a boil. Add the fresh *tagliatelle* and 1½ tablespoons of salt. Let the water return to a boil and then cook for 15 seconds. Drain the pasta and add to the sauce. Toss together and serve immediately, topping each serving with 2 teaspoons or so of extra Parmesan.

Tagliatelle al Limone

Tagliatelle with Lemon Sauce

It may seem strange to put cream, butter, and lemon together in the saucepan, but the combination is a winning one. The richness of the cream sauce is cut by the tartness of the lemon zest, and brandy adds complexity. Don't exclude the Parmesan cheese – it is a necessity for the delicate balance of flavors, but don't add too much (1 tablespoon per serving should be adequate), or the subtle fragrance of the lemon will be lost.

KCal 889 P 16g C 59g S 495mg SFA 36g UFA 23g (4)

INGREDIENTS

4 tbsp unsalted butter

1½ cups (350ml) heavy cream

freshly grated zest of 4 large lemons (about 6 tsp)

¼ cup (60ml) brandy or Cognac

salt and freshly ground white pepper, to taste

1 quantity (1lb/500g) fresh egg pasta (see page 48), or spinach or herb pasta (see page 54), cut into tagliatelle (see page 53)

freshly grated Parmesan, to serve

1 Melt the butter in a wide skillet over medium-low heat. Add the cream, half the lemon zest, and the brandy. Increase the heat to medium and allow the cream to come to a simmer and the alcohol to evaporate, 3–5 minutes. Sprinkle in the remaining zest and season with salt and pepper to taste. Remove the pan from the heat.

2 Bring 4 quarts (5 liters) of water to a boil. Add the fresh *tagliatelle* and 1½ tablespoons of salt. Let the water return to a boil and then cook for 15 seconds. Drain the pasta and add to the pan with the sauce. Toss everything together and serve, sprinkling each serving with Parmesan.

TAGLIATELLE CON MELANZANE ARROSTO, POMODORO, E MOZZARELLA

Tagliatelle with Roasted Eggplant, Fresh Tomato, and Mozzarella

Most recipes for eggplant sauces prescribe cooking the eggplant at the same time as the other ingredients, which usually include tomatoes. This results in the eggplant marrying in texture and flavor with the other components. In this sauce, the eggplant is first roasted or grilled, then tossed with the light, fresh tomato sauce and chunks of mozzarella at the last minute. The eggplant acquires a nutty, pleasantly bitter flavor and a smoky quality when cooked in this style. *(See page 15 for illustration.)*

KCal 826 P 30g C 69g S 610mg SFA 12g UFA 34g (4)

INGREDIENTS

- *2 small eggplants, about 1½lb (750g) total weight*
- *salt, to taste*
- *⅓ cup (90ml) extra-virgin olive oil, plus extra for brushing eggplants*
- *6 large garlic cloves, very finely chopped*
- *2lb (1kg) vine-ripened plum tomatoes, peeled, seeded, and chopped*
- *1 handful of fresh basil, torn into small pieces*
- *6oz (175g) fresh mozzarella, diced*
- *freshly ground black pepper, to taste*
- *1 quantity (1lb/500g) fresh egg pasta (see page 48) or chili pasta (see page 55), cut into tagliatelle (see page 53)*

1 Cut the stems and navels off the eggplants and cut them across into ¼in (5mm) thick slices. Sprinkle the slices with salt and stand them upright in a colander to drain off the bitter juices, about 40 minutes. Blot the salt and sweat from the slices with paper towels.

2 Preheat the oven to 450°F (230°C) if roasting the eggplant.

3 Brush both sides of the eggplant slices with oil. Place them on baking sheets, well spaced, and roast for 30–35 minutes. Alternatively, preheat the broiler, or prepare a charcoal grill, and cook until lightly colored on both sides. When cooled, dice and set aside.

4 Meanwhile, warm the olive oil in a large skillet over medium-low heat. Add the garlic and sauté until just softened, 3–4 minutes. Add the tomatoes, basil, and ½ teaspoon of salt, or to taste, and stir well. Simmer gently until the excess water evaporates, about 15 minutes.

5 Add the diced eggplant, mozzarella, and pepper to taste and toss well. Check the seasoning. Turn off the heat and cover the pan for several minutes, until the mozzarella is soft and almost melted.

6 Bring 4 quarts (5 liters) of water to a boil. Add the fresh *tagliatelle* and 1½ tablespoons of salt. Let the water return to a boil and then cook for 15 seconds. Drain well, toss with the sauce, and serve.

TAGLIATELLE DI POMODORO CON PORRI E GAMBERI

Tomato Tagliatelle with Leeks, Shrimp, and Tarragon

Outside Italy and France, leeks are often overlooked as being useful for anything but soups, but with their mild oniony flavor and firm structure, they are ideal vegetables around which to center a sauce. Do not substitute onions or scallions, which are much more assertive in flavor. Fresh egg pasta, saffron pasta, or beet pasta can replace tomato pasta. Dried tagliatelle, pappardelle, *or* nidi *can also be used.* *(See page 14 for illustration.)*

KCal 693 P 27g C 64g S 537mg SFA 20g UFA 13g (4)

INGREDIENTS

- *¾lb (375g) fresh raw shrimp in their shells*
- *3 leeks, roots and tops trimmed*
- *4 tbsp unsalted butter*
- *6 scallions, including 2in (5cm) of green tops, trimmed and thinly sliced*
- *1½ tbsp fresh tarragon, or 2 tsp dried tarragon*
- *salt, to taste*
- *zest of 1 lemon*
- *⅓ cup (75ml) dry vermouth*
- *½ cup (125ml) heavy cream*
- *freshly ground white pepper, to taste*
- *1 quantity (1lb/500g) tomato pasta (see page 54), cut into tagliatelle (see page 53)*

1 Peel the shrimp. Make a cut down the back of each and remove the dark intestinal vein. Wash well and cut into dice.

2 Halve the leeks lengthwise, spread open the sheaths, and rinse carefully. Cut across into very thin slices.

3 Warm the butter in a large skillet. Add the leeks and scallions. Sauté until soft, about 4 minutes. Add the shrimp, tarragon, ⅓ teaspoon of salt, or to taste, and the lemon zest. Sauté until the shrimp begin to color, tossing to cook them evenly, about 2 minutes.

4 Add the vermouth and allow to evaporate, 2 minutes. Stir in the cream and pepper to taste. Remove from the heat.

5 Bring 4 quarts (5 liters) of water to a boil. Add the *tagliatelle* and 1½ tablespoons of salt. Let the water return to a boil and then cook for 15 seconds. Drain, toss with the sauce, and serve.

FETTUCCINE DI BARBABIETOLE CON SALSA DI ZUCCHINE

Beet Fettuccine with Creamy Zucchini Sauce

Only very fresh, small zucchini should be used in this sauce because the larger vegetables have thicker, bitter skins that impart an unpleasant taste to the sauce, as well as large seeds. Other suitable pasta cuts for this dish include fresh or dried* tagliatelle *or* trenette*, dried* nidi*, or dried* fettuccine*.

KCal 663 P 24g C 65g S 585mg SFA 20g UFA13g (4)

INGREDIENTS

1 quantity (1lb/500g) beet pasta (see page 54) or fresh egg pasta (see page 48), rolled (see pages 50–51)

4 tbsp unsalted butter

1lb (500g) zucchini, trimmed and shredded

1 small onion, grated

1 cup (250ml) cream

3 tbsp freshly grated Parmesan

pinch of freshly grated nutmeg

salt and freshly ground pepper, to taste

1 Using a sharp chef's knife, cut the pasta strips into *fettuccine* noodles ⅛–¼in (2.5–5mm) wide.

2 Melt the butter in a deep, large skillet. Add the shredded zucchini and onion. Stir and sauté until the onion is wilted, about 4 minutes. Cover the pan and sauté for 3 minutes longer, until soft. Stir in the cream and allow it to come to a gentle simmer.

3 Remove the pan from the heat and stir in the Parmesan, nutmeg, salt, and pepper to taste.

4 Meanwhile, bring 4 quarts (5 liters) of water to a boil. Add the fresh *tagliatelle* and 1½ tablespoons of salt. Let the water return to a boil and then cook for 15 seconds. Drain the pasta and add to the skillet with the sauce, toss all together, and serve immediately.

Fettuccine con Salmone Affumicato e Uova di Salmone

Fettuccine with Smoked Salmon and Salmon Roe

No caviar lover will want to pass over this luxurious recipe. While the sauce deserves delicate fresh pasta, dried tagliatelle or nidi ("nests") would be suitable. A herb-flavored fresh pasta (see page 55), either a parsley, chive, or basil version, would also work well. As for the sauce, although genuine salmon roe is costly, very little is needed and it is really worth procuring. Many inferior substitutes are simply not palatable, and contain red food coloring which runs when the fish eggs are exposed to heat – resulting in an unsightly mess!

KCal 983 P 34g C 59g S 1988mg SFA 37g UFA 25g (4)

INGREDIENTS
1 quantity (1lb/500g) fresh egg pasta (see page 48), rolled (see pages 50–51)
4 tbsp unsalted butter
½lb (250g) smoked salmon, thinly sliced and cut into julienne strips
3 tbsp brandy
freshly grated zest of 2 small lemons (about 2 tsp)
1½ cups (350ml) heavy cream
freshly ground white pepper, to taste
salt, to taste
4 tbsp salmon roe (caviar)

1 Using a sharp chef's knife, cut the pasta strips into *fettuccine* noodles ⅛–¼in (2.5–5mm) wide.

2 Warm the butter in a skillet over medium-low heat. Add the salmon, stirring well to coat it with the butter. Add the brandy, half the lemon zest, and the cream. Allow the alcohol to evaporate, about 3 minutes. Season with pepper and remove the sauce from the heat.

3 Bring 4 quarts (5 liters) of water to a boil. Add the fresh *fettuccine* and 1½ tablespoons of salt. Let the water return to a boil and then cook for 15 seconds. Drain, and transfer the pasta to the skillet with the sauce. Add the remaining lemon zest and toss the pasta and sauce together. Transfer the sauced pasta to individual serving plates. Top each one with a tablespoon of salmon caviar, then serve immediately.

Fettuccine ai Funghi con Pomodoro, Fegatini di Pollo, e Vermouth

Mushroom Fettuccine with Tomato, Chicken Livers, and Vermouth

Mushrooms and liver have a great affinity for each other. Likewise, mushroom-flavored fettuccine *are well suited to this tomato-based chicken liver sauce. I like to use tomatoes with chicken livers because their sweetness foils the natural bitterness of the liver. Vermouth, green peppercorns, and rosemary provide a harmonious depth of flavors. Fresh egg* fettuccine *or fresh or dried* tagliatelle, spaghetti, *or* linguine *may be used.*

KCal 713 P 35g C 68g S 589mg SFA 11g UFA 17g (4)

INGREDIENTS

- *1 quantity (1lb/500g) mushroom pasta (see page 54), cut into fettuccine (see below) or tagliatelle (see page 53)*
- *¾lb (375g) very fresh chicken livers, washed*
- *3 tbsp unsalted butter*
- *2 tbsp extra-virgin olive oil*
- *1 onion, very finely chopped*
- *2 garlic cloves, very finely chopped*
- *3 tbsp tomato paste*
- *½ cup (125ml) dry vermouth*
- *1 tsp fresh rosemary leaves, chopped, or ½ tsp dried rosemary*
- *½ tsp crushed green peppercorns, or freshly ground white pepper, to taste*
- *salt, to taste*
- *2½ cups (625g) fresh vine-ripened or canned drained tomatoes, peeled, seeded, and chopped*
- *freshly grated Parmesan, to serve*

1 Using a sharp chef's knife, cut the pasta strips into *fettuccine* noodles ⅛–¼in (2.5–5mm) wide.

2 Trim any connective tissue, discolored areas, or fat from the livers. Separate the pairs of livers, but leave them whole. Place in a pan, add water to cover, and bring to a boil. Blanch the livers until their shape is firm and they are lightly cooked, about 30 seconds. Remove and plunge into cold water. Drain, let cool, then thinly slice and set aside.

3 Warm the butter and oil together in a skillet over medium-low heat. Add the onion and garlic and sauté until soft, about 4 minutes. Add the livers and sauté over medium heat, turning them, until they brown nicely on the outside but remain pinkish inside, about 3 minutes. Transfer the livers to a dish and set aside.

4 Add the tomato paste, vermouth, rosemary, pepper, and ½ teaspoon of salt, or to taste, to the pan. Let evaporate for 3 minutes. Add the tomatoes and cook until a thick sauce forms, about 30 minutes. Stir in the chicken livers and simmer until heated through, 2–3 minutes. Check the seasoning of the sauce and remove the pan from the heat.

5 Bring 4 quarts (5 liters) of water to a boil. Add the fresh *fettuccine* and 1½ tablespoons of salt. Let the water return to a boil, then cook for 15 seconds. Drain the pasta and toss with the sauce. Serve immediately, passing Parmesan.

Bigoli al Burro con Acciughe e Cipolle

Whole-Wheat Pasta with Butter, Anchovies, and Onions

The flavor of whole-wheat pasta is particularly suited to sauces that feature anchovies. These sauces are always made without tomatoes, because the nutty taste of the wheat is obscured by the strong presence of tomato. Dried whole-wheat pasta is typically combined with an anchovy sauce founded on extra-virgin olive oil, while fresh bigoli *noodles are better suited to the more delicate flavor of butter.*

KCal 834 P 30g C 96g S 951mg SFA 16g UFA 18g (4)

INGREDIENTS

- *6 tbsp (90g) unsalted butter*
- *4 onions, quartered and thinly sliced*
- *1 can (2oz/60g) anchovy fillets, drained*
- *3 tbsp chopped fresh flat-leaf parsley*
- *1 quantity (1lb/500g) whole-wheat pasta (see page 55), cut into tagliatelle (see page 53)*
- *salt and freshly ground black pepper, to taste*

1 Warm the butter in a large skillet and add the onions. Sauté gently until lightly colored, about 12 minutes. Transfer the onions to a dish. Add the anchovies to the pan and heat just until they begin to dissolve into the butter; do not let them harden. Return the onions to the pan, then stir in the parsley.

2 Bring 4 quarts (5 liters) of water to a boil. Add the fresh pasta and 1½ tablespoons of salt. Let the water return to a boil and then cook for 15 seconds. Drain, reserving a little of the cooking water. Toss the pasta in the skillet with the onion sauce. Add some of the pasta water, if necessary, to moisten. Sprinkle with plenty of pepper, and serve.

FARFALLE CON CARNE DI VITELLO E PINOLI

Farfalle with Veal, Lemon, and Pine Nut Sauce

This superb sauce, one of my mother's inventions, is designed for an economy cut of veal, such as the shoulder, that responds well to lengthy cooking. The addition of pine nuts provides an interesting texture and a wonderful nutty flavor. Slow braising produces enough gravy to sauce 1lb (500g) of short-cut pasta. Delicate, homemade **farfalle** ***("butterflies") are ideal for this sauce, but fresh or dried*** **tagliatelle** ***or*** **fettuccine** ***and short*** **macaroni** ***cuts are also suitable. The sauce can be made 2–3 days in advance and refrigerated. When reheating, stir in about 4 tablespoons of chicken stock. (See page 14 for illustration.)***

KCal 877 P 80g C 63g S 988mg SFA 10g UFA 22g (4)

INGREDIENTS

1 quantity (1lb/500g) fresh egg pasta (see page 48), cut into farfalle (see page 52, and step 1, below)

4 x 1in (2.5cm) thick boneless veal shoulder steaks, each about 10–12oz (300–375g)

¼ cup (30g) all-purpose flour for dredging

2 tbsp unsalted butter

2 tbsp safflower or corn oil

½ cup (125ml) dry white wine

1 tbsp chopped fresh rosemary leaves, or ½ tsp dried rosemary

2 cups (500ml) chicken or veal broth

2 x 1in (2.5cm) strips lemon zest

salt, to taste

1 tbsp pine nuts, coarsely chopped

freshly ground white or black pepper, to taste

1 Let the *farfalle* dry on dish towels while you make the sauce. (*Farfalle* are best eaten within several hours of being made, or the pinched center of the "bow" will remain hard after cooking, while the rest of the pasta is tender.)

2 Trim excess fat from the veal and cut each steak in half. If there is bone, include it in the dish, as it will add flavor to the sauce and the marrow can be eaten like a miniature *osso buco*. Spread the flour for dredging on a piece of waxed paper or on a wide plate.

3 Heat half the butter and half the oil in a large, heavy, deep, lidded skillet until sizzling hot. Dredge the veal in the flour and add half the meat to the pan. Cook the steaks over moderately high heat, turning once, until brown on both sides, about 15 minutes. Transfer the veal to a platter and warm the remaining butter and oil in the skillet. Brown the second batch of veal steaks, then transfer to the platter.

4 Add the wine and rosemary to the pan and cook, stirring with a wooden spoon, until the wine evaporates, about 1 minute. Stir in about ⅓ cup (90ml) of the broth. Return the veal to the pan in a single layer, cover, and simmer over moderately low heat until the broth is absorbed, about 10 minutes. Stir in about ¼ cup (60ml) of broth and keep adding this quantity at 10-minute intervals, or as needed to keep the meat moist, for 1 hour.

5 Add the lemon zest to the pan. Continue to cook the veal gently, keeping the pan covered, until tender, for 45–60 minutes longer. Keep adding the remaining broth at 10-minute intervals, as necessary, and add ½ teaspoon of salt and the pine nuts 15 minutes before the meat has finished cooking.

6 Transfer the veal to a work surface, cut it into slices about ¼in (5mm) thick or ½in (1cm) dice, and return to the sauce. Stir in the pepper.

7 Bring 4 quarts (5 liters) of water to a rolling boil. Pick up the towels holding the *farfalle* and drop the pasta into the water so that it all begins cooking at the same time. Stir at once and add 1½ tablespoons of salt. Stir again and cover. The pasta is cooked when it rises to the surface, about 15 seconds from the time the water returns to a boil. Be careful not to overcook it; the cooking process should take no longer than 3–4 minutes.

8 Drain the *farfalle* thoroughly, toss with the veal sauce in the pan, and serve immediately.

Maltagliati con Piselli, Cipolla, e Pancetta

Maltagliati with Baby Peas, Onion, and Pancetta

Here is a delicious sauce to make when fresh shelled peas are available, although frozen baby peas can be substituted. If bacon is used instead of pancetta, blanch it in boiling water for 1 minute before using. A little butter is added to the pasta when it is tossed with the hot sauce, which contributes to the delicate flavor of the dish. Dried pasta cuts that are good matches for this sauce include orrecchiette, gnocchi, *and* maruzzelle *(medium-sized shells).*

KCal 660 P 28g C 70g S 986mg SFA 9g UFA 19g (4)

INGREDIENTS
3oz (90g) pancetta or lean bacon
3 tbsp extra-virgin olive oil
3 shallots, very finely chopped (about 4 tbsp)
14oz (425g) fresh or frozen shelled baby peas
2 tbsp chopped fresh flat-leaf parsley
1½ tbsp chopped fresh mint
½ cup (125ml) dry white wine
1¼ cups (300ml) tasty chicken broth (see page 63)
salt, to taste
1 tsp green peppercorns, or freshly ground white or black pepper, to taste
1 quantity (1lb/500g) fresh egg pasta (see page 48), cut into maltagliati (see page 52)
2 tbsp unsalted butter at room temperature
freshly grated Parmesan, to serve

1 If using bacon, blanch it in boiling water for 1 minute. Chop the pancetta or bacon and set aside.

2 Warm the oil in a large, deep skillet over medium-low heat. Increase the heat to medium and add the pancetta or bacon. Sauté until the meat begins to color, 3 minutes. Add the shallots and sauté until wilted, about 3 minutes.

3 Stir in the peas, parsley, and mint, and continue to sauté for 3 minutes. Add the wine and let evaporate for 3 minutes. Stir in the broth and ½ teaspoon of salt, or to taste. If using peppercorns, add them now. Simmer gently, partially covered, until the peas are cooked, about 15 minutes. Check for salt and sprinkle with ground pepper, if using.

4 Bring 4 quarts (5 liters) of water to a boil and add the *maltagliati* and 1½ tablespoons of salt. Let the water return to a boil and cook for 15 seconds. Drain the pasta and toss with the sauce and butter. Serve at once with Parmesan.

PASTA SECCA

DRIED PASTA DISHES

THE TASTE AND TEXTURE of dried pasta suit it to robust, often rustic, sauces that use some of the most characteristic ingredients of the Italian peasant kitchen – cold-pressed olive oil, plum tomatoes and combinations of seasonal vegetables, spicy or sweet sausages, piquant olives, and pungent aromatics. However, dried pasta should by no means be confined purely to tomato-and-oil-based sauces; it also lends itself perfectly to subtle, delicately balanced sauces based on butter and cream. The most important consideration is to match the myriad pasta shapes with compatible sauces.

PAPPARDELLE CON SALSA VELLUTATA ROSA DI FUNGHI SELVATICI
Pappardelle with Creamy Pink Wild Mushroom Sauce

Special Ingredients

Porcini

Basil

Brandy

Tomato paste

Oyster mushrooms

Chanterelles

Pappardelle

Preparation

Wild mushrooms, with their deep, woodsy flavor, are ideal for sauces such as this. Because their taste is so intense, there is little need for elaboration or a profusion of other ingredients. Dried or fresh pappardelle, fettuccine, *or* tagliatelle *may be used.*

KCal 850 P 18g C 100g S 439mg SFA 24g UFA 16g (4)

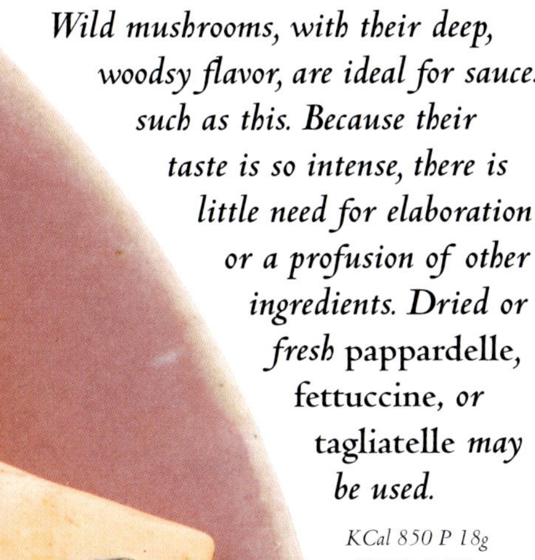

INGREDIENTS

6oz (175g) fresh wild mushrooms such as porcini, chanterelles, morels, hedgehog, oyster or cremini mushrooms, or a mixture of any of these

2 tbsp unsalted butter

1 tbsp extra-virgin olive oil

1 small onion, finely chopped

5 large basil leaves, torn into very small pieces, or 1 tsp chopped fresh thyme, or ½ tsp dried thyme

3 tbsp brandy

3 tbsp tomato paste

salt, to taste

1 cup (250ml) heavy cream

freshly ground white or black pepper, to taste

1lb (500g) dried pappardelle or tagliatelle, or 1 quantity (1lb/500g) fresh egg pasta (see page 48), cut into pappardelle (see page 52)

freshly grated Parmesan, to serve

1 Remove any dirt from the wild mushrooms with a soft brush or cloth. Trim the stems, removing any woody parts. Cut the mushrooms in half or quarter them, depending on size, then thinly slice and set aside.

2 Warm the butter and oil in a broad skillet over medium heat. Add the onion and sauté until softened but not browned, about 4 minutes. Add the sliced mushrooms and basil or thyme, and continue to sauté until the mushrooms are very tender, 5–6 minutes.

3 Pour in the brandy and stir. Dissolve the tomato paste and ⅓ teaspoon of salt in ¼ cup (60ml) of water and add to the pan. Allow the mixture to come to a simmer, then stir in the heavy cream. When the sauce begins to simmer, remove the skillet from the heat and stir in pepper, according to taste.

4 Bring 4 quarts (5 liters) of water to a boil. Add the pasta and 1½ tablespoons of salt. Cook the pasta until *al dente,* stirring frequently to prevent the strands from sticking together. Drain the cooked pasta and transfer it to the skillet. If using fresh pasta, follow the cooking directions on page 58. Toss the pasta and sauce together thoroughly and serve immediately, passing fresh Parmesan at the table.

Pasta e Fagioli alla Napoletana

Pasta and Beans with Tomato in the Style of Naples

There are endless permutations on the theme of* pasta e fagioli*, pasta and beans. This one is* "di magro," *meatless, and derives most of its flavor from high-quality, fruity extra-virgin olive oil, a large quantity of garlic, and plenty of flavorful fresh basil. When making* pasta e fagioli*, select a size of tubular pasta that is comparable to the size of the bean. If desired, a little extra-virgin olive oil can be drizzled over each serving.

KCal 565 P 19g C 80g S 492mg SFA 3g UFA 18g (4)

INGREDIENTS

2½lb (1.25kg) fresh, mature vine-ripened plum tomatoes, peeled, seeded, and coarsely chopped, or 2½ cups (625g) canned drained tomatoes, seeded and chopped

⅓ cup (75ml) extra-virgin olive oil, plus additional if desired

5 large garlic cloves, chopped

salt, to taste

1 bay leaf

1lb (500g) cooked borlotti or pinto beans

1½ cups (250g) ditali

generous handful of fresh basil leaves, chopped

freshly ground white or black pepper, to taste

freshly grated Parmesan or pecorino, to serve

1 If using fresh tomatoes, let the chopped pulp drain in a colander for 5 minutes. You should have about 2½ cups (625g) of tomato pulp. Set aside.

2 Meanwhile, warm the olive oil and garlic together in a pan. Sauté until the garlic is softened but not browned, about 4 minutes.

3 Immediately, add the tomatoes, ½ teaspoon of salt and the bay leaf to the pan. Use a potato masher to crush the tomatoes into fairly fine pieces. Turn the heat to high, bring the sauce to a rapid simmer, then reduce the heat to medium-low and simmer gently, stirring occasionally, until the tomatoes acquire a thick, saucelike consistency, about 20 minutes.

4 Add the beans and continue to simmer until all the flavors marry, about 15 minutes.

5 Meanwhile, bring 4 pints (2.5 liters) of water to a boil. Add the *ditali* and 1 tablespoon of salt. Cook until tender. Drain and add to the pan with the tomatoes and beans.

6 Remove the pan from the heat, stir in the basil and pepper, and check the seasoning. If desired, drizzle each serving with a little extra-virgin olive oil before scattering with Parmesan.

Farfalle con Peperoni Arrostiti

Farfalle with Roasted Red and Yellow Peppers

Sweet peppers are typically cut into strips and sautéed over the stove for many pasta sauces, but I like to roast them over charcoal first, which produces a delightful smoky flavor. The peppers can be cooked up to several days in advance, and the sauce assembled quickly just before serving. ***(See page 16 for illustration.)***

KCal 586 P 15g C 85g S 786mg SFA 3g UFA 19g (4)

INGREDIENTS

3 mixed large red and yellow peppers

⅓ cup (75ml) extra-virgin olive oil

5 large garlic cloves, bruised

pinch of crushed red pepper flakes

⅓ cup (75g) sharp green olives, pitted and chopped

salt, to taste

12oz (375g) farfalle

4 tbsp chopped fresh flat-leaf parsley

1 Place the whole peppers on a rack above a charcoal fire, or on wire racks on the stove top, or under a hot broiler, or in an oven preheated to 400°F (200°C). Roast them until charred all over and tender, turning them so they blacken evenly.

2 When the peppers are cool enough to handle, peel, then cut in half and remove the stems, ribs, and seeds. (Do not do this under running water.) Cut the peppers into ½in (1cm) square pieces.

3 Warm the olive oil in a deep skillet. Add the garlic and sauté gently until golden, pressing with a wooden spoon to release its flavor. Add the pepper flakes and olives. Raise the heat to medium-high and sauté quickly, stirring constantly, for 1 minute. Remove from the heat and discard the garlic, if desired.

4 Bring 4 quarts (5 liters) of water to a rapid boil and add 1½ tablespoons of salt. Cook the *farfalle* until *al dente*, stirring occasionally. Drain, reserving about 5 tablespoons of water. Transfer the pasta to the skillet. Add the parsley and toss everything together, adding the pasta water if necessary to moisten the sauce.

Rigatoni con Broccoli e Cavolfiore

Rigatoni with Broccoli and Cauliflower Sauce

Broccoli and broccoli rape (cime di rapa) *are typically cooked with pasta in Apulia in the south of Italy. My mother learned the original version of this peasant dish from my paternal grandmother, and it is one of many pasta dishes I grew up on. I have since made it with a combination of broccoli and cauliflower, and found it to be very good this way, too. The anchovies do not remain whole, but rather melt and disintegrate in the simmering olive oil, forming a tasty sauce base.* Orecchiette, cavatelli, pennette, fusilli, *or* maruzzelle *("shells") may be substituted for* rigatoni.

KCal 621 P 25g C 76g S 1105mg SFA 3g UFA 22g (4)

INGREDIENTS
1 bunch of broccoli, about 1¼lb (625g)
salt, to taste
½lb (250g) cauliflower florets
¾lb (375g) mixed rigatoni
⅓ cup (75ml) extra-virgin olive oil
2 large garlic cloves, finely chopped
1½ cans (3oz/90g) anchovy fillets in olive oil
pinch of crushed red pepper flakes

1 Trim the broccoli, cutting off any tough or discolored parts. Divide the top part into small florets and slice the top half of the stalk into thin pieces, about 2in (5cm).

2 Bring 5 quarts (6 liters) of water to a rapid boil and add 2 tablespoons of salt, the broccoli, cauliflower florets, and *rigatoni*. Stir occasionally to prevent the pasta from sticking together.

3 Meanwhile, gently heat the olive oil, garlic, anchovy fillets, including their packing oil, and pepper flakes in a large, wide skillet or in a saucepan large enough to accommodate the pasta, broccoli, and cauliflower later. The anchovies will dissolve completely in the olive oil, forming the sauce.

4 When the pasta is *al dente*, drain it, reserving some of the cooking water. (The pasta should still be moist and dripping slightly when mixed with the sauce.) Transfer the pasta and vegetables to the anchovy sauce and toss everything together well. If necessary, add a little of the cooking water to moisten the sauce. Serve immediately.

Cavatelli con Biete

Cavatelli with Swiss Chard

This is another simple Apulian dish that is typically made with broccoli and broccoli rape (cime di rapa, *or "broccoli raab," as it is also known) but also works well with Swiss chard.* Ziti, rigatoni, *or* orecchiette *may be substituted for* cavatelli.

KCal 697 P 21g C 99g S 1108mg SFA 4g UFA 20g (4)

INGREDIENTS
⅓ cup (90ml) extra-virgin olive oil
1 can (2oz/60g) anchovy fillets in olive oil
3 large garlic cloves, finely chopped
pinch of crushed red pepper flakes
1lb (500g) Swiss chard, green leafy parts only, washed, finely shredded, then coarsely chopped
salt, to taste
1lb (500g) cavatelli

1 Combine the olive oil, anchovies and their oil, garlic, and pepper flakes in a large, broad skillet. Cook over medium-low heat until the anchovies disintegrate and the garlic is soft, 3–4 minutes. Set aside.

2 Bring 5 quarts (6 liters) of water to a rolling boil. Add the Swiss chard, 1½ tablespoons of salt, and the *cavatelli*. Cook, stirring occasionally, to prevent the pasta from sticking together. When the pasta is *al dente*, drain everything, reserving about ⅓ cup (75ml) of the cooking water.

3 Transfer the pasta and Swiss chard to the skillet with the anchovy, oil, and garlic mixture. Toss everything together with a wooden spoon, making sure the sauce ingredients are evenly distributed throughout the pasta. If the pasta sauce needs additional moisture, stir in a little of the reserved cooking water before serving.

Ziti con Salsiccia e Peperoni

Ziti with Sausage and Peppers

There is no reason why sausages and peppers can't be put together in a sauce for pasta as felicitously as they are in the famous Italian-American sausage and pepper hero sandwich. In Italian cooking, however, red and yellow peppers are preferred to green peppers because they are sweeter and easier to digest (green peppers are the same species, but they are not yet mature). Other appropriate pasta cuts include **penne** ***and*** **rigatoni.** ***Serves 3–4.***

KCal 1105 P 30g C 77g S 1780mg SFA 25g UFA 47g (4)

INGREDIENTS

- *4 tbsp extra-virgin olive oil*
- *1 onion, halved and thinly sliced*
- *1 large garlic clove, finely chopped*
- *1½lb (750g) sweet Italian sausage, casings removed and crumbled*
- *¼ cup (60ml) dry white wine*
- *½ tsp crushed fennel seeds*
- *½ cup (125ml) water*
- *salt, to taste*
- *pinch of freshly ground black pepper*
- *1 red and 1 yellow pepper, seeded and cut into julienne strips*
- *½lb (250g) ziti, broken into pieces*

1 Heat half the olive oil in a deep skillet. Add the onion and garlic. Sauté until the onion is wilted, about 4 minutes.

2 Add the crumbled sausage and sauté over medium heat, stirring occasionally, until it is nicely colored but has not hardened, about 5 minutes. Pour in the wine and sauté until the alcohol has evaporated, 1 minute.

3 Add the fennel seeds and water. Cover and simmer for 10–12 minutes, stirring occasionally and adding a tablespoon or two of water, as needed, to prevent the sausage meat from drying out. Season with salt and pepper to taste.

4 Heat the remaining oil in another skillet. Add the pepper strips and cook over medium-low heat, partially covered, until completely tender, about 15 minutes. Add the peppers to the skillet with the sausage mixture and toss together thoroughly.

5 Bring 4 quarts (5 liters) of water to a boil. Add the *ziti* and 1½ tablespoons of salt. Cook until *al dente*, stirring frequently to prevent sticking. Drain the pasta and toss it with the sauce in the pan. Serve immediately.

Pennette con Cavolfiore

Pennette with Cauliflower

There are numerous Italian sauces for pasta that feature cauliflower, most of which include tomato. However, the combination of cauliflower and tomato does not appeal to me. Here is one of the recipes I have developed to bring pasta and cauliflower together. Serves 3–4.

KCal 524 P 17g C 57g S 737mg SFA 4g UFA 20g (4)

INGREDIENTS

- *1 medium head cauliflower, trimmed and cut into florets*
- *salt, to taste*
- *⅓ cup (90ml) extra-virgin olive oil*
- *4 large garlic cloves, finely chopped*
- *6 anchovy fillets in olive oil, drained*
- *pinch of crushed red pepper flakes*
- *2 tbsp chopped fresh flat-leaf parsley*
- *1 cup (250ml) chicken broth (see page 63) or stock*
- *½lb (250g) pennette*
- *¼ cup (30g) bread crumbs, lightly toasted*

1 Bring 4 quarts (5 liters) of water to a rapid boil. Add the cauliflower and 1½ tablespoons of salt. Boil until tender, about 7 minutes. Use a slotted spoon to retrieve the florets, then cut them into dice, and set aside. Reserve the cooking water.

2 Warm all but a tablespoon of the oil in a large skillet. Add the garlic and anchovies, and sauté until the garlic is soft and the anchovies dissolve into the oil, 2–3 minutes. Add the pepper flakes and cauliflower, and continue to sauté for 3 minutes. Add the parsley and broth and continue to cook, stirring constantly, until the cauliflower disintegrates in the liquid, about 5 minutes.

3 Bring the cauliflower cooking water to a boil, adding enough fresh water to make 4 quarts (5 liters). Add the *pennette* and 1½ tablespoons of salt, stirring frequently to prevent sticking. When the pasta is *al dente*, drain and add to the skillet with the cauliflower sauce.

4 Quickly, in a separate small skillet over medium or medium-low heat, warm the remaining oil and add the bread crumbs. Cook, stirring constantly, until the crumbs are just golden, about 1 minute. Sprinkle the bread crumbs over the pasta, and serve immediately.

Penne con Broccoli, Salame, e Fagioli

Penne with Broccoli, Salami, and Beans

I first sampled a variation of this dish many years ago in a Westchester County restaurant run by the Saparito family. I was reviewing restaurants for a local newspaper, and in those days it wasn't commonplace to find good, authentic Italian cooking on the peripheries of New York City. This robust and highly flavorful pasta dish was memorable. Many years later, I am still making it in my own kitchen.
(See page 17 for illustration.)

KCal 965 P 44g C 122g S 1026mg SFA 8g UFA 25g (4)

INGREDIENTS

- *1 large bunch of broccoli, about 1½lb (750g)*
- *salt, to taste*
- *⅓ cup (75ml) extra-virgin olive oil*
- *5 garlic cloves, finely chopped*
- *1 small onion, thinly sliced*
- *6oz (175g) Italian salami or peperoni sausage, thinly sliced and cut into julienne strips*
- *1 tsp chopped fresh marjoram, or ½ tsp dried marjoram*
- *pinch of crushed red pepper flakes*
- *1 cup (250ml) chicken broth (see page 63)*
- *6oz (175g) dried cannellini beans, soaked and cooked, or 1lb (500g) canned cannellini beans*
- *1lb (500g) penne*

1 Cut the tough stalks off the broccoli and discard, leaving the florets and approximately 2in (5cm) of stalk. Bring 5 quarts (6 liters) of water to a rolling boil. Add the broccoli and 1½ tablespoons of salt, and boil for 4 minutes. Use a slotted spoon to transfer the broccoli florets to a dish; reserve the cooking water.

2 Warm the oil in a deep skillet. Add the garlic and onion and sauté over low heat until the onion softens, 3–4 minutes. Add the salami or peperoni and cook until the fat is melted, 3 minutes.

3 Stir in the parboiled broccoli, marjoram, and pepper flakes. Sauté over medium heat to marry the flavors, about 3 minutes. Pour in the broth, cover, and simmer for 5 minutes. Add the beans and ⅓ teaspoon of salt, or to taste. Cover and cook for another 5 minutes.

4 Meanwhile, bring the broccoli cooking water back to a boil. Add the *penne* and cook until *al dente*. Drain the pasta and toss with the sauce in the skillet, then serve.

Spaghetti alla Puttanesca

Spaghetti with Harlot's Sauce (Cooked Version)

This dish has become immensely popular and I am often asked for the recipe, but as with other Italian classics, there are many different variations. In one interpretation, the sauce is cooked, while in another, it is uncooked (see page 106). Both sauces, however, are robust and zesty, in the spirit of their name. Use good canned tomatoes for the cooked version.

(See illustration opposite.)

KCal 621 P 18g C 98g S 987mg SFA 3g UFA 15g (4)

INGREDIENTS

- *2½ cups (625g) canned plum tomatoes in juice*
- *3 tbsp extra-virgin olive oil*
- *3 large garlic cloves, cut into small pieces*
- *3 tbsp chopped fresh flat-leaf parsley*
- *1 tsp chopped fresh marjoram, or ½ tsp dried marjoram*
- *3 anchovy fillets in olive oil, cut up, plus 1 tbsp of their oil*
- *4 tbsp sharply flavored black olives, pitted and sliced*
- *½ tsp crushed red pepper flakes*
- *4 tbsp small capers, drained*
- *salt, to taste*
- *1 lb (500g) spaghetti*

1 Drain the tomatoes, reserving the juice. Strain the juices through a sieve to hold back the seeds. Using your fingers, push out the excess seeds. Chop the tomatoes and set aside with the juice.

2 Combine the olive oil and garlic in a large skillet. Place over medium-low heat and sauté gently until the garlic softens, 3–4 minutes. Do not allow the garlic to brown.

3 Add the parsley and marjoram and sauté gently, just until the herbs release their aroma, about 30 seconds. Add the anchovies, using a wooden spoon to mash them, and let dissolve slightly, about 1 minute.

4 Add the tomatoes and juice, the olives, pepper flakes, and capers. Simmer, stirring frequently, until the sauce thickens, about 20 minutes. Check for salt, though the anchovies and capers may provide enough.

5 Bring 4 quarts (5 liters) of water to a boil and add the *spaghetti* and 1½ tablespoons of salt. Cook until *al dente*, stirring frequently to prevent the strands from sticking together. Drain the pasta and toss with the sauce in the skillet, then serve immediately.

Spaghetti con Aglio, Olive, ed Erbette

Spaghetti with Garlic, Olives, and Herbs

Many Italian sauces contain no meat or fish at all, and yet are wonderfully flavorful. The trick is to use fruity, extra-virgin olive oil and other ingredients that provide intense flavors, such as herbs, aromatics, olives, and capers. This recipe is an example of such a simple meatless and tasty sauce. The only pasta cuts appropriate for this sauce are spaghetti, spaghettini, *or* mezze linguine.

(See page 16 for illustration.)

KCal 754 P 17g C 99g S 675mg SFA 5g UFA 28g (4)

INGREDIENTS

- *⅓ cup (60g) sharply flavored black olives, such as Gaeta or Niçoise*
- *½ cup (125ml) extra-virgin olive oil*
- *6 large garlic cloves, very finely chopped*
- *3 tbsp chopped fresh flat-leaf parsley*
- *1 tsp chopped fresh marjoram, or ½ tsp dried marjoram*
- *pinch of crushed red pepper flakes*
- *salt, to taste*
- *1 lb (500g) spaghetti*
- *¼ cup (30g) fresh bread crumbs, lightly toasted*

1 Pit and slice the olives. Combine all but 2 tablespoons of the olive oil and the garlic in a deep, broad skillet. Turn the heat to medium-low and sauté until the garlic softens and begins to color lightly, about 5 minutes. Stir in the parsley, marjoram, olives, and pepper flakes and warm through, about 20 seconds. Remove from the heat.

2 Meanwhile, bring 4 quarts (5 liters) of water to a boil. Add 1½ tablespoons of salt and the *spaghetti*. Cook until *al dente*, stirring frequently to prevent the strands from sticking together. Drain the pasta, reserving some of the cooking water to moisten the pasta after saucing.

3 While the pasta is still dripping and moist, transfer to the skillet with the sauce and toss together. If it needs more moisture, add a little of the reserved cooking water.

4 In a separate small skillet, heat the remaining olive oil and add the bread crumbs. Sauté over medium-low heat, stirring, until crunchy. Sprinkle the crumbs over the pasta, and serve.

SPAGHETTI CON ACCIUGHE E TONNO

Spaghetti with Anchovies and Tuna

Canned Italian tuna packed in olive oil (see page 162) is a marvelous product that has myriad uses in the Italian kitchen. If it is not available, high-quality canned "light" tuna packed in olive oil is a second choice. Avoid tuna packed in water, which is dry and relatively bland.

KCal 761 P 38g C 70g S 903mg SFA 10g UFA 22g (4)

INGREDIENTS

- ¼ cup (60ml) extra-virgin olive oil
- 3 tbsp unsalted butter
- 2 garlic cloves, finely chopped
- 6 anchovy fillets in olive oil
- 2 x 7oz (200g) cans tuna packed in olive oil, or good-quality "light" tuna packed in oil, drained and finely chopped
- ¾ cup (175ml) dry white wine
- plenty of freshly ground black pepper, to taste
- 6 tbsp (20g) finely chopped fresh flat-leaf parsley
- salt, to taste
- 12oz (375g) spaghetti, linguine, or mezze linguine

1 Warm the oil and butter in a large skillet over medium-low heat. Add the garlic and allow it to soften, about 3 minutes. Do not let it brown.

2 Add the anchovies and 1 tablespoon of their oil to the pan. Let the anchovies dissolve completely, 2–3 minutes. Add the tuna and stir, then pour in the wine. Allow it to evaporate, about 3 minutes, until a thick, fairly smooth sauce is formed. Season liberally with pepper and stir in the parsley.

3 While the sauce is cooking, bring 4 quarts (5 liters) of water to a rolling boil. Add 1½ tablespoons of salt and the pasta, and cook until *al dente*, stirring frequently. While the pasta is still dripping wet, toss it in the skillet with the tuna sauce, and serve.

BUCATINI CON POMODORI ARROSTO ALL'AMENDOLARA

Bucatini with Roasted Tomato Sauce the Amendolara Way

My friend, cooking teacher Anna Amendolara Nurse, has always generously shared her Pugliese recipes with me, and I always feel compelled to print them because they are simply so good. Here is one that was passed down from her mother, Rosa Amendolara. It is served as a first course, followed by roast lamb or pork and a green salad – simple and delicious food! Use only the sweetest summer plum tomatoes (other types of tomato will throw off too much water and reduce to nothing) and high-quality Italian bucatini.

KCal 762 P 17g C 103g S 670mg SFA 5g UFA 27g (4)

INGREDIENTS

- 2lb (1kg) sweet, vine-ripened plum tomatoes
- 4 large garlic cloves, finely chopped
- ½ cup (30g) chopped fresh flat-leaf parsley
- ½ cup (125ml) extra-virgin olive oil
- salt and freshly ground black pepper, to taste
- 1lb (500g) bucatini
- freshly grated pecorino, to serve (optional)

1 Preheat the oven to a temperature of 375°F (190°C).

2 Wash the tomatoes and cut in half lengthwise. Push out the seeds and excess tomato liquid, and discard.

3 Place the tomato halves in a 9 x 13in (23 x 32.5cm) roasting pan, arranging them cut-side up in a single layer, as close together as possible. Scatter the garlic and parsley on top, then sprinkle with the olive oil, 1 teaspoon of salt, and pepper to taste.

4 Bake the tomatoes in the middle of the oven until they are very soft, nicely colored, and reduced in volume by about half, approximately 1 hour.

5 Bring 4 quarts (5 liters) of water to a boil and add the *bucatini* and 1½ tablespoons of salt. Cook until *al dente*, stirring frequently to prevent the strands from sticking to one another. Drain the pasta and toss it in the roasting pan with the sauce. Transfer to individual serving plates and serve, passing grated pecorino at the table, if desired.

Mezze Linguine con Salsa di Pomodoro e Tonno

Mezze Linguine with Tomato and Tuna Sauce

Either of the two tomato sauces listed right is suitable as a base for this excellent tuna sauce. If using Tomato Sauce with Vegetables, extra-virgin olive oil can be substituted for butter. I prefer to serve it with thin "half" linguine, mezze linguine, *but* linguine *or* spaghetti *are also good matches.*

KCal 711 P 30g C 103g S 719mg SFA 10g UFA 11g (4)

INGREDIENTS
1 quantity tomato sauce with vegetables (see page 75) or simple tomato sauce (see page 74)
1 x 7oz (200g) can imported Italian tuna in olive oil, drained and flaked
1lb (500g) mezze linguine, linguine, or spaghetti
salt, to taste
1 large clove garlic, finely chopped
1 tbsp chopped fresh flat-leaf parsley

1 Warm the tomato sauce through. Add the tuna and heat it through again.

2 Bring 4 quarts (5 liters) of water to a rolling boil and add the pasta and 1½ tablespoons of salt. Cook until *al dente*, stirring frequently to prevent the strands from sticking to one another. Drain the pasta and transfer it to a serving bowl with the sauce. Add the garlic and parsley, and toss together. Serve immediately.

Linguine con Calamari e Aglio

Linguine with Squid and Garlic

In Italy squid almost always appears in mixed seafood sauces for pasta, but it also makes a delightful sauce by itself. You can clean the squid yourself or ask your fishmonger to do it, but it is most important to procure small, tender squid. Larger squid make tough eating. Spaghetti *and* mezze linguine *are also suitable pasta cuts for this sauce. (See page 16 for illustration.)*

KCal 906 P 45g C 98g S 561mg SFA 6g UFA 29g (4)

INGREDIENTS
½ cup (125ml) extra-virgin olive oil
7 large garlic cloves, finely chopped
1½lb (750g) squid (cleaned weight), cut into rings and tentacle sections (see below)
¾ cup (175ml) dry white wine
3 large fresh vine-ripened plum tomatoes, or 1¼lb (625g) canned drained tomatoes, seeded and chopped
½ cup (30g) chopped fresh flat-leaf parsley
pinch of crushed red pepper flakes
salt and freshly ground black pepper, to taste
1lb (500g) linguine

1 Warm the oil and garlic together in a broad skillet over medium-low heat. Sauté gently until the garlic is softened, but do not allow it to color, about 4–5 minutes.

2 Add the squid and increase the heat to high. Sauté for 5 minutes, stirring frequently. Pour in the wine and reduce the heat to medium. Allow the alcohol to evaporate, about 3 minutes.

3 Stir in the chopped tomato, parsley, and pepper flakes. Cook for 5 minutes, then season with ¾ teaspoon of salt and black pepper to taste.

4 Meanwhile, bring 4 quarts (5 liters) of water to a rolling boil. Add the *linguine* and 1½ tablespoons of salt, and stir. Cook until *al dente*. Drain the pasta, toss with the sauce, and serve.

Preparing Squid

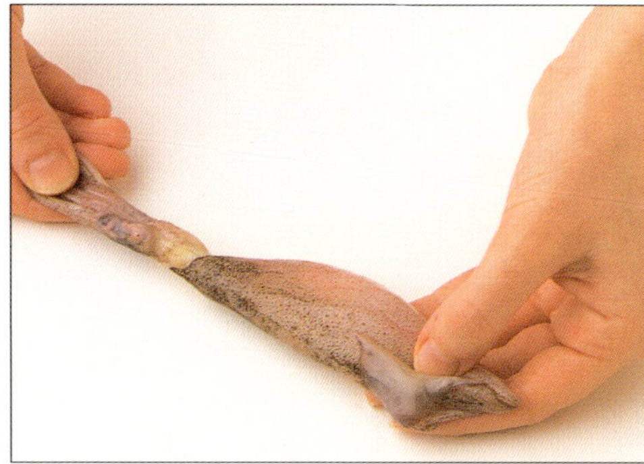

1 Separate the head and tentacles from the body by grasping the head below the eyes and pulling these parts away from the body cavity. Remove and discard the ink sac from the head.

2 Cut the head from the tentacles at the "waist" above the eyes. Cut the hard "beak" from the base of the tentacles. Peel off the speckled skin under cold running water.

3 Pull the transparent plasticlike "spine" from the body and clean out any insides remaining in the cavity. Rinse well. Cut the body and tentacles as directed in the recipe.

Fusilli Lunghi con Salsa di Pomodoro, Funghi, e Salsiccia

Long Fusilli with Tomato, Mushroom, and Sausage Sauce

Here is a richly flavored sauce that is ideal for long fusilli *and other shapes that cradle the bits of sausage and vegetables in their grooves.* Rigatoni, penne, *short* fusilli, creste di gallo *("cockscombs"),* lumache *("snails"),* maruzzelle *("shells"), and* gnocchi sardi *("Sardinian dumplings") are also perfectly suitable.*

KCal 875 P 33g C 104g S 1230mg SFA 9g UFA 25g (4)

INGREDIENTS

- ¼lb (125g) fresh cultivated or wild mushrooms
- ¼ cup extra-virgin olive oil
- 1 onion, chopped
- 2 large garlic cloves, finely chopped
- 1 large carrot, chopped
- 1 small celery rib with leaves, chopped
- 2 tbsp chopped fresh flat-leaf parsley
- 1 tsp fennel seeds, ground
- ½lb (250g) sweet Italian sausage meat, crumbled
- 2 tbsp tomato paste
- ½ cup (125ml) water
- ½ cup (125ml) dry red wine
- 2 cups (500g) fresh or canned plum tomatoes, peeled, seeded, and finely chopped
- salt, to taste
- good pinch of freshly ground black pepper, to taste
- 1lb (500g) fusilli lunghi
- freshly grated Parmesan, to serve

1 Remove any dirt from the mushrooms with a soft brush or cloth. Trim the stems. If the mushrooms are large, cut them into halves or quarters, then thinly slice. Set aside.

2 Warm the olive oil in a large pan. Add the onion, garlic, carrot, celery and parsley, and stir well. Sauté the mixture over medium-low heat until the vegetables soften, about 10 minutes.

3 Add the mushrooms, fennel seeds, and sausage meat to the pan, using a wooden spoon to break up the sausage. Sauté gently until the sausage loses most of its pink color and the mushrooms sweat, about 5 minutes. Do not overcook the sausage or it will toughen.

4 Stir in the tomato paste and water. Let the mixture come to a simmer. Add the wine, tomatoes, ⅓ teaspoon salt, and the pepper. Simmer the sauce over low heat, partially covered, until thick and aromatic, about 45 minutes.

5 Bring 4 quarts (5 liters) of water to a boil and add the *fusilli lunghi* and 1½ tablespoons of salt. Cook the pasta until *al dente,* stirring frequently to prevent sticking. Drain the cooked pasta and transfer to a serving bowl. Add the sauce to the bowl, toss well, and serve, passing Parmesan at the table.

Stelline con Burro e Latte per Bambini

"Little Stars" with Butter and Milk for Children

This was the first solid food my mother fed my sisters and me. When we reminisce about our upbringing, she is fond of telling how, in my highchair, I was always covered with these little stars from head to foot, and so were the walls and floor. I still love pastina *and so do my children.*

INGREDIENTS

- ½lb (250g) stelline ("little stars")
- 3 tsp salt
- about 3 tbsp unsalted butter (at room temperature)
- ⅓ cup (75ml) warm milk, or to taste

1 Bring 2 quarts (3.75 liters) of water to a boil. Stir in the *stelline* and salt. Cook the pasta according to package directions, stirring occasionally. Drain when it is tender but still firm.

2 Place the butter in a serving bowl. Transfer the drained *stelline* to the bowl. Stir well to mix the butter in thoroughly, add the warm milk, stir once more, and serve.

NIDI CON CARCIOFI E FINNOCHIO FRESCO

Pasta Nests with Artichokes and Fresh Fennel

This unusual, tasty sauce is excellent with dried or fresh pasta. Dried cuts that work well include* nidi *("nests"),* fresine, fettuccelle, lasagnette, mafalde, trenette, *and dried egg* tagliatelle. *Suitable fresh pasta varieties include fresh* trenette, tagliatelle, fettuccine, *and* pappardelle. *Serves 2–3.* *(See page 16 for illustration.)

KCal 493 P 16g C 51g S 658mg SFA 11g UFA 12g (4)

INGREDIENTS

2 fresh artichokes, each about 7oz (200g)

salt, to taste

1 large fennel bulb, about 1lb (500g)

2 tbsp extra-virgin olive oil

2 tbsp unsalted butter

2 large scallions, including 2in (5cm) of green tops, thinly sliced

4 large garlic cloves, finely chopped

½ cup (125ml) dry white wine

1 cup (250ml) tasty chicken or veal stock

¼ cup heavy cream

freshly ground pepper, to taste

¼ cup (30g) freshly grated Parmesan, plus extra to serve

½lb (250g) dried nidi

1 Prepare the artichoke hearts (see below), placing each one in a bowl of water acidulated with lemon juice until ready to use. When both artichokes have been trimmed, drain them. Place each artichoke half cut-side down on a work surface and cut lengthwise into ¼in (5mm) thick slices.

2 Bring enough water to cover the artichokes to a boil in a saucepan. Add ¼ teaspoon of salt and the artichoke slices. Cook until tender, 4–8 minutes, depending on their freshness. Drain and set aside until ready to use.

3 Trim the tough bottom off the fennel bulb. Cut off the tough stalks and feathery leaves, reserving some of the fronds. Cut the fennel bulb lengthwise into quarters, then slice very thinly. Chop 2 tablespoons of the tender fronds.

4 Warm the oil and butter together in a deep, broad skillet. Add the scallions, garlic, fennel, and chopped fennel fronds. Cover and sauté over medium-high heat until the vegetables sweat, stirring occasionally.

5 Reduce the heat to medium-low and cook, covered, for 5 minutes longer. Add the wine and allow to evaporate, uncovered, for 3 minutes. Add the stock and ½ teaspoon of salt. Cover and cook for 10 minutes. Stir in the cream; bring to a simmer and remove from the heat. Stir in pepper to taste and the Parmesan.

6 Meanwhile, bring 4 quarts (5 liters) of water to a boil and add the *nidi* and 1½ tablespoons of salt. Cook until *al dente,* then drain and toss with the sauce in the skillet. Serve immediately, passing extra Parmesan at the table.

PREPARING ARTICHOKES

1 Have ready a bowl filled with cold water, made acidic with 2 tablespoons of lemon juice or vinegar. Trim the bottom of the stem of each artichoke. Pull off the tough outer leaves until you reach leaves with tender, white bases.

2 Using a sharp chef's knife, cut off and discard the upper part of the inner leaves that are dark green at the top and greenish-yellow at the base. The inner rows of leaves are soft and tender.

3 Cut the artichoke in half lengthwise and, with a small knife, cut out the inedible hairy choke and any tough inner purple leaves. Slice according to recipe instructions, then place in the acidulated water until ready to use.

PASTA SECCA CON SALSE CRUDE

DRIED PASTA WITH UNCOOKED SAUCES

THESE LIGHT, REFRESHING PASTA dishes are often served in the summer months on the Italian table. They are worlds apart from the all too familiar chilly "pasta salads" containing inferior ingredients and overcooked pasta, drenched with vinaigrette, that are found in restaurants outside Italy. A truly successful uncooked dish uses only the best ingredients and should be a harmony of fresh flavors. The pasta, which is almost invariably used hot, is tossed with the sauce just prior to serving. Certain sauces should be left to stand for a little while to allow their flavors to meld and intensify, but others are truly spontaneous creations and can be made to serve immediately.

PENNETTE ESTIVA
Pennette with Summer Salad Vegetables

Pennette Estiva

Pennette with Summer Salad Vegetables

Special Ingredients

Plum tomatoes

Romaine lettuce

Arugula

Black olives

Pennette

Preparation

As with other sauces made with fresh tomatoes, this sauce is worth making only when sweet, luscious vine-ripened plum tomatoes are in season. This is one of only two or three recipes in this book that call for rinsing the pasta before combining it with the sauce. Cooling the pasta down prevents the lettuce from wilting instantly.

KCal 765 P 17g C 102g S 585mg SFA 5g UFA 28g (4)

INGREDIENTS
12 sharply flavored black olives, such as niçoise
1¼lb (625g) sweet, vine-ripened plum tomatoes, seeded and chopped
½ cup (60g) romaine lettuce, julienned and roughly chopped
½ cup (30g) arugula, stems removed and roughly chopped
1 small garlic clove, finely chopped
1 small sweet red onion, about 1oz (30g), finely chopped
6 large fresh basil leaves, torn into very small pieces
freshly ground black or white pepper, to taste
½ cup (125ml) extra-virgin olive oil
1lb (500g) pennette or other short pasta
salt, to taste

1 Pit and slice the olives. In a serving bowl, thoroughly combine the olives and all the other ingredients for the sauce.

2 Bring 4 quarts (5 liters) of water to a boil and add the *pennette* and 1½ tablespoons of salt. Cook the pasta until *al dente,* then drain and rinse quickly under cool running water. Drain well and toss with the sauce in the bowl. Check for salt, and serve immediately.

Gnocchetti con Rucola, Pomodoro Crudo, e Olive

Gnocchetti with Arugula, Tomatoes, and Green Olives

INGREDIENTS
3oz (90g) sharply flavored green olives, such as cracked Sicilian olives or picholine olives
1 bunch (150g) arugula, well washed and trimmed
½ cup (125ml) extra-virgin olive oil
¾lb (375g) fresh, sweet vine-ripened tomatoes or cherry tomatoes, seeded and coarsely chopped
2 medium-large garlic cloves, finely chopped
pinch of crushed red pepper flakes
¾lb (375g) gnocchetti
salt, to taste

KCal 653 P 13g C 75g S 870mg SFA 5g UFA 28g (4)

1 Pit the olives and cut them into small pieces. Shake the arugula dry, then chop it. In a serving bowl, combine the arugula, olives, and other sauce ingredients. Let the mixture marinate for up to 30 minutes, or while you cook the pasta.

2 Bring 4 quarts (5 liters) of water to a boil and add the *gnocchetti* and 1½ tablespoons of salt. Cook the pasta until *al dente,* then drain. Add ½ teaspoon of salt to the arugula sauce, or season to taste. Toss the pasta in the bowl with the sauce, and serve immediately.

Conchiglie con Pomodoro Crudo, Avocado, e Gamberetti

Pasta Shells with Uncooked Tomato, Avocado, and Shrimp

I consider avocado to be something of a secret sauce ingredient because it is not typically associated with pasta. Although avocados are never used cooked in pasta sauces, their creamy texture is enhanced by the heat of the cooked pasta. They are paired with shrimp here, adding body and a delightful distinctive flavor. Other suitable cuts are* cinese rigata *(ridged medium shells),* spaghetti, orecchiette, *and* eliche. *(See page 19 for illustration.)

KCal 793 P 34g C 67g S 1835mg SFA 7g UFA 35g (4)

INGREDIENTS

2¼lb (1.25kg) fresh, sweet, mature vine-ripened tomatoes or sweet, ripe cherry tomatoes, blanched, peeled, and cored

¾lb (375g) cooked and peeled small shrimp, cut in half lengthwise, or larger cooked shrimp, diced

1 tbsp chopped fresh basil or flat-leaf parsley

1 large garlic clove, finely chopped or passed through a garlic press

½ cup (125ml) extra-virgin olive oil

salt and freshly ground black or white pepper, to taste

1 large or 2 small ripe Hass avocado(s)

1lb (500g) conchiglie, cinese rigata, spaghetti, or orecchiette

1 Cut the tomatoes into quarters lengthwise then push out and discard the seeds. Cut the tomatoes into rough dice or chop coarsely. Place them in a serving bowl. Add the shrimp, basil or parsley, garlic, olive oil, ½ teaspoon of salt, and freshly ground pepper, to taste, to the tomato pulp.

2 Insert a knife into the avocado at the top, where the navel is. Cut into the avocado until you reach the pit, then make a clean incision all the way around the length of the fruit. Twist the halves in opposite directions to open the avocado. The pit should fall out. Peel and thinly slice each half crosswise; then cut the slices again into small strips or dice.

3 Add the avocado to the bowl with the other sauce ingredients. Toss to mix well and let stand at room temperature while the pasta cooks. Taste for salt before combining with the pasta.

4 Bring 4 quarts (5 liters) of water to a boil and add the pasta and 1½ tablespoons of salt. Cook until *al dente*, stirring frequently to prevent sticking. Drain and toss with the sauce.

Fusilli con Pomodoro e Mozzarella

Fusilli with Fresh Tomatoes, Mozzarella, and Basil

The addition of sweet, fresh mozzarella gives a nice twist to this uncooked tomato sauce. The heat from the pasta melts the cheese slightly, just enough to bring out its appealing milky quality – a contrast to the other ingredients. Try to find a good, freshly made, delicatessen-bought mozzarella. Anchovies or capers can also be added. Other medium pasta cuts such as* fusilli, gnocchi, *and* lumache *can be used. (See page 18 for illustration.)

KCal 861 P 25g C 105g S 524mg SFA 9g UFA 29g (4)

INGREDIENTS

2¼lb (1.25kg) fresh, sweet, mature vine-ripened tomatoes, peeled, seeded, and coarsely chopped

¼lb (125g) mozzarella, cut into small dice

½ cup (125ml) extra-virgin olive oil

2 large garlic cloves, chopped

20 large fresh basil leaves, torn into small pieces

5 anchovy fillets, cut into small pieces, or 1 tbsp drained small capers (optional)

⅛ tsp dried oregano, or ¼ tsp chopped fresh oregano

salt and freshly ground black or white pepper, to taste

1lb (500g) fusilli, gnocchi, or lumache

1 Place the chopped tomatoes in a serving bowl. Add all the remaining sauce ingredients to the tomatoes, seasoning with ½ teaspoon of salt and pepper to taste. Mix the sauce thoroughly then leave it to marinate for at least 1 hour and up to 3 hours at room temperature to develop the flavors.

2 Bring 4 quarts (5 liters) of water to a boil and add the *fusilli* and 1½ tablespoons of salt. Cook until *al dente*, stirring frequently to prevent sticking. Drain and add to the bowl with the sauce, tossing everything together. Serve immediately.

Fusilli con Ricotta e Basilico alla Paolo

Fusilli with Ricotta and Basil Sauce, Paolo's Style

My friend Paolo Destefanis is an excellent photographer, but his creativity is not limited to his work behind the lens. He is also a good cook, and this is one of his superb quick pasta recipes. The sauce is also suitable for other short pasta cuts such as penne and rigatoni. Much of the ricotta made outside Italy is very loose and runny, which is ideal for this recipe. If using firm, genuine Italian ricotta, work more of the pasta cooking water into it to make the ricotta creamy before adding the other ingredients for the sauce.

KCal 789 P 26g C 98g S 513mg SFA 10g UFA 23g (4)

INGREDIENTS
1 bunch of basil
salt, to taste
1lb (500g) short fusilli
1¼ cups (300g) ricotta
1 garlic clove, finely chopped
⅓ cup (90ml) extra-virgin olive oil
¼ tsp freshly ground nutmeg (optional)
freshly ground white pepper, to taste
¼ cup (30g) freshly grated Parmesan

1 Wash the basil thoroughly and remove all stems. Pat the leaves dry with a clean dish towel or paper towels. Tear the basil into small pieces and set aside.

2 Bring 4 quarts (5 liters) of water to a boil and add 1½ tablespoons of salt. Cook the *fusilli* until *al dente*, stirring frequently to prevent sticking.

3 Meanwhile, combine the remaining ingredients for the sauce with the basil, blending well with a wooden spoon. Add up to several tablespoons of the pasta cooking water, if necessary, to form a smooth, creamy-textured sauce.

4 Drain the pasta and combine it thoroughly with the sauce. Serve immediately, offering extra freshly grated Parmesan, if desired.

SPAGHETTI ALLA PUTTANESCA

Spaghetti with Harlot's Sauce (Uncooked Version)

Here is the uncooked version of the famous Neapolitan dish. In the spirit of its name, the sauce is coarse and zesty. Consider making this sauce only when sweet, luscious vine-ripened summer tomatoes are available.
(See page 18 for illustration.)

KCal 777 P 18g C 103g S 666mg SFA 5g UFA 28g (4)

INGREDIENTS
¼ cup (60g) good black olives, such as Gaeta or niçoise
2¼lb (1.25kg) fresh, sweet, mature vine-ripened tomatoes, peeled, seeded, and coarsely chopped
½ cup (125ml) extra-virgin olive oil
2 large garlic cloves, chopped
8 large fresh basil leaves, torn into small pieces
1 tbsp chopped fresh flat-leaf parsley
1 tbsp drained small capers
pinch of crushed red pepper flakes, or to taste
salt, to taste
1lb (500g) spaghetti

1 Pit the olives and cut them into small slices. Place the tomatoes in the serving bowl. Add the olives and remaining sauce ingredients to the tomatoes with ½ teaspoon of salt, and mix well. Let the sauce marinate for at least 1 hour at room temperature to give the flavors time to develop, or cover and chill in the refrigerator for up to 3 days.

2 Bring 4 quarts (5 liters) of water to a boil and add 1½ tablespoons of salt and the *spaghetti.* Cook until *al dente,* stirring frequently to prevent sticking. Drain and add to the bowl with the sauce, tossing thoroughly. Serve at room temperature.

SPAGHETTINI CON LIMONE, CAPPERI, E OLIVE

Spaghettini with Lemon, Capers, and Olives

While this is one of the simplest of sauces, it is packed with flavor. The briny tang of olives and capers, combined with the tartness of lemon, provides an interesting foil to the mild nuttiness of pasta and the fruity olive oil. The sauce can be prepared up to a day in advance and left at room temperature to marinate (do not refrigerate it).
(See page 18 for illustration.)

KCal 739 P 15g C 94g S 941mg SFA 5g UFA 28g (4)

INGREDIENTS
¼lb (125g) sharply flavored green olives
grated zest of 1 lemon
½ cup (125ml) extra-virgin olive oil
⅓ cup (75ml) freshly squeezed lemon juice
1½ tbsp drained small capers
1 large garlic clove, finely chopped
2 tsp chopped fresh thyme, or 1 tsp dried thyme
pinch of crushed red pepper flakes
salt, to taste
1lb (500g) spaghettini

1 Pit and chop the olives. Combine them with all the remaining sauce ingredients in a serving bowl, adding ½ teaspoon of salt, or to taste.

2 Bring 4 quarts (5 liters) of water to a boil and add 1½ tablespoons of salt and the *spaghettini.* Cook until *al dente,* stirring frequently to prevent sticking. Drain the pasta, reserving some of the water, and toss with the sauce in a serving bowl. If necessary, add a little cooking water to moisten the sauce so that it is evenly distributed. Serve immediately.

SPAGHETTINI CON PASSATO DI POMODORO CRUDO

Spaghettini with Uncooked Tomato Purée

The difference between this sauce and the classic* passato *tomato sauce is that the traditional* passato *is cooked. Cooking tomatoes evaporates much of their unwanted natural liquid, thus concentrating flavor and thickening the sauce. In this recipe, excess water is squeezed out prior to chopping, and the clear, true sweet flavor of the best summer tomatoes is captured, unaltered by the process of cooking.

KCal 690 P 18g C 103g S 472mg SFA 4g UFA 21g (4)

INGREDIENTS
2¾lb (1kg 375g) vine-ripened plum tomatoes, peeled
⅓ cup (90ml) extra-virgin olive oil
8–10 large basil leaves, torn into tiny pieces
1 garlic clove, passed through a garlic press
½ tsp chopped fresh marjoram, or ¼ tsp dried marjoram
freshly ground black or white pepper, to taste
salt, to taste
1lb (500g) spaghettini

1 Halve the tomatoes and push out the seeds. With your hands, squeeze out as much of the liquid in the flesh as possible. Purée the flesh in a food processor or blender.

2 In a serving bowl, combine the puréed tomato with the other sauce ingredients. Add ½ teaspoon of salt.

3 Bring 4 quarts (5 liters) of water to a boil and add 1½ tablespoons of salt and the *spaghettini.* Cook until *al dente,* stirring frequently to prevent sticking. Drain the pasta and toss with the sauce in the bowl. Serve immediately.

TRENETTE CON BASILICO, POMODORI SECCHI, E PINOLI

Trenette with Basil, Sun-Dried Tomatoes, and Pine Nuts

***This uncooked sauce has the unctuous consistency of* pesto alla genovese *(see above), but a very different flavor due to the addition of sun-dried tomatoes. As with pesto, this sauce needs a robust cut of pasta to support it. The best choices are* trenette *(fresh or dried),* linguine, bucatini, *or* spaghetti.**

KCal 595 P 16g C 45g S 640mg SFA 10g UFA 29g (4)

INGREDIENTS

1 cup (30g) dry-packed sun-dried tomatoes, or ¾ cup (125g) sun-dried tomatoes in oil, drained

½ cup (60g) pine nuts

1 cup (30g) fresh basil leaves

3 tbsp extra-virgin olive oil

2 large garlic cloves, finely chopped

salt, to taste

¾lb (375g) dried trenette or fresh pasta (see page 48) rolled to the penultimate notch and cut by hand into ⅛in (2.5mm) thick trenette

2 tbsp unsalted butter

¼ cup (30g) freshly grated Parmesan

freshly ground black pepper, to taste

1 If using dry-packed sun-dried tomatoes, soak them in hot water for 30 minutes, or until tender. Drain and squeeze dry, then chop them or the tomatoes in oil by hand. Set aside.

2 Using a mortar and pestle, a food processor, or a blender, pound or roughly grind the pine nuts, taking care not to pulverize them. They should retain a grainy texture and stand out in the dish rather than be overprocessed into a paste. Set aside.

3 In a food processor or mortar, combine the basil, olive oil, garlic, and ⅓ teaspoon of salt, and pound to a rough paste. Transfer to a serving bowl large enough to hold the pasta later.

4 Bring 4 quarts (5 liters) of water to a boil and add the *trenette* and 1½ tablespoons of salt. Cook dried pasta until *al dente* or fresh *trenette* until tender (see page 58), stirring frequently to prevent sticking. Drain, reserving some of the water.

5 Toss the pasta in the bowl with the basil mixture and butter. Add the sun-dried tomatoes, pine nuts, Parmesan, and pepper. Toss well, adding a little cooking water, if necessary, to moisten the pasta so that the sauce is evenly distributed.

TRENETTE AL PESTO ALLA SILVANA

Trenette with Basil Pesto, Silvana Style

In the traditional way of making* pesto alla genovese, *all the ingredients are pounded or ground together, then tossed with the pasta. In this method, which I learned many years ago from Silvana Pistolesi at the Ristorante Casaletto in Ostia, only the basil, oil, garlic, and salt are included in the basic* pesto. *The pine nuts, cheese, and butter are tossed in later with the cooked pasta, which makes the nuts and cheese stand out. Despite the recipe's nontraditional Roman origins, I very much like this interpretation of pasta with* pesto. *(See page 18 for illustration.)

KCal 713 P 19g C 60g S 595mg SFA 12g UFA 31g (4)

INGREDIENTS

½ cup (60g) pine nuts

2 cups (60g) fresh basil leaves

¼ cup (60ml) extra-virgin olive oil

2 large garlic cloves, finely chopped

salt, to taste

1lb (500g) dried trenette, linguine, mezze linguine, or bucatini, or fresh pasta (see page 48) rolled to the penultimate notch and cut by hand into ⅛in (2.5mm) thick trenette

3 tbsp unsalted butter at room temperature

¼ cup (30g) freshly grated Parmesan

freshly ground black pepper, to taste

1 Using a mortar and pestle, pound or roughly grind the pine nuts, taking care not to pulverize them. Alternatively, use a food processor to pulse the nuts, but bear in mind that they should retain a distinct grainy texture and not be overprocessed into an oily paste. Set aside.

2 Combine the basil, olive oil, garlic, and ⅓ teaspoon of salt in a food processor or mortar. Pound or grind to a rough paste, then transfer to a serving bowl large enough to hold the pasta later.

3 Bring 4 quarts (5 liters) of water to a boil and add 1½ tablespoons of salt. Cook the dried pasta until *al dente* or the fresh *trenette* until tender (see page 58), stirring frequently to prevent sticking. Drain the pasta, but don't overdrain. Reserve some of the water. Toss the wet pasta with the basil mixture and the butter in the bowl.

4 Add the pine nuts, Parmesan, and pepper to the serving bowl and toss together thoroughly, adding a little of the reserved pasta cooking water, if necessary, to moisten the *trenette* so that the sauce is evenly distributed throughout the pasta. Check the seasoning, and serve.

Linguine con Tonno, Capperi, e Olive

Linguine with Tuna, Capers, and Olives

Though the pasta is rinsed lightly for this dish, it should still be warm when combined with the sauce. No salt is necessary in the sauce, as the olives, capers, and lemon juice provide enough salt and tartness. The best tuna to use is the Italian variety (see page 162), which has a rosy color and exceptional flavor. (See illustration opposite.)

KCal 840 P 28g C 96g S 1253mg SFA 6g UFA 32g (4)

INGREDIENTS

1 x 7oz (200g) can imported Italian tuna packed in olive oil, drained and flaked

½ cup (125ml) extra-virgin olive oil

3 tbsp freshly squeezed lemon juice

2 tbsp chopped fresh flat-leaf parsley

¼lb (125g) mixed green and black sharply flavored olives

3 tbsp drained small capers

1 large garlic clove, finely chopped

5 anchovy fillets in olive oil, drained and cut into small pieces

freshly ground black pepper, to taste

1lb (500g) linguine or mezze linguine

salt, to taste

1 In a serving bowl, combine the tuna and remaining ingredients for the sauce, tossing thoroughly to distribute them evenly, then set aside.

2 Bring 4 quarts (5 liters) of water to a boil and add 1½ tablespoons of salt and the *linguine*. Cook until *al dente*, stirring frequently to prevent sticking. Drain the pasta, rinse it rapidly and toss with the sauce in the bowl. Serve immediately.

Linguine con Gamberi e Pomodoro Crudo

Linguine with Shrimp and Uncooked Tomato Sauce

The shrimp in this uncooked sauce can be cooked in advance and chilled, and the sauce assembled in the time it takes to boil the water and cook the pasta. Other pasta cuts, including maruzzelle ***(shells) and dried pasta*** gnocchi, ***are appropriate, but I like to use*** linguine.

KCal 776 P 24g C 97g S 771mg SFA 5g UFA 28g (4)

INGREDIENTS

¼ cup (60g) sharply flavored black olives

6oz (175g) raw shrimp, shelled, deveined, and washed

salt, to taste

½lb (250g) sweet vine-ripened tomatoes

½ cup (125ml) extra-virgin olive oil

2 tbsp freshly squeezed lemon juice

2 tsp drained small capers

1 small garlic clove, finely chopped

handful of fresh basil leaves, torn into small pieces, or 2 tbsp chopped fresh flat-leaf parsley

freshly ground black pepper, to taste

1lb (500g) linguine or mezze linguine

1 Pit and coarsely chop the olives. Bring enough water to cover the shrimp to a boil and add ⅓ teaspoon of salt. Boil until they turn pink, about 2 minutes, then drain. Do not overcook or they will toughen. Alternatively, steam the shrimp for 2 minutes. Remove their tails, cut in half lengthwise, then dice.

2 In a serving bowl, combine the shrimp and the remaining sauce ingredients. Let marinate for up to 30 minutes.

3 Bring 4 quarts (5 liters) of water to a boil and add 1½ tablespoons of salt and the *linguine*. Cook until *al dente*, stirring frequently to prevent the strands sticking together. Drain and toss immediately with the sauce.

PASTE RIPIENE

STUFFED PASTA DISHES

THERE ARE INNUMERABLE TYPES of stuffed pasta in the Italian kitchen, made either with pasta dough or a type of very thin crepe, variously called *crespelle, fazzoletti* (handkerchiefs), or *manicotti* (little muffs). Any of the flavored pasta described on page 43 can be used for the dough envelope, though the most popular casings are of egg or spinach pasta. Home-cooked pasta is far superior to commercially made stuffed pasta, which is prepared with a thick envelope of heavy and chewy dough. Not only are homemade fillings of higher quality, but the pasta itself is thin and delicate, producing a very appealing taste sensation. The sauces served with stuffed pasta should be carefully matched so as not to distract from the extraordinarily subtle and varied fillings.

RAVIOLI RIPIENI DI PATATE E PESTO CON SUGO DI NOCI
Ravioli with Potato and Pes[to] Stuffing in Walnut and Sour C[ream] Sauce

Special Ingredients

Preparation

Potatoes and pesto have a great affinity for one another, not only in the form of potato gnocchi al pesto, but also in the simplest variation on the theme, puréed potatoes dressed with a dollop of fragrant basil sauce. This filling of potato and pesto capitalizes on that happy marriage. The accompanying walnut sauce is a Ligurian classic that is traditionally made with a creamy type of soured milk, though sour cream is equally delicious here. Fresh Tomato Sauce (see page 75) would also be compatible. For the basic ravioli-making technique, which can be adapted for these round ravioli, see page 56.

KCal 1059 P 30g C 72g S812mg SFA 25g UFA 45g (4)

INGREDIENTS

1 quantity (1lb/500g) fresh egg pasta (see page 48), unrolled
1 egg white, to seal
salt, to taste

For the filling

5oz (150g) boiling potatoes, scrubbed but unpeeled
2 tbsp unsalted butter, softened
5 tbsp ricotta
2½ tsp pesto alla Silvana (see page 107)
3 tbsp freshly grated Parmesan
¼ tsp salt

For the sauce

1 slice stale white bread, crusts removed
⅓ cup (90ml) milk
½ cup (90g) walnuts, lightly toasted
2 tbsp (30g) pine nuts, lightly toasted
½ cup (125ml) sour cream
3oz (90g) mascarpone
¼ cup (60ml) olive oil
¼ tsp salt
freshly ground white pepper, to taste
2 tbsp freshly grated Parmesan, plus extra to serve

1 For the filling, place the potatoes in a pan with cold water to cover. Bring to a boil and cook over medium heat until tender, about 25 minutes. Drain and leave until cool enough to handle.

2 Remove the potato skins with a paring knife. Pass them through a potato ricer or finely mash with a potato masher. Do not use a blender or food processor. Place the mashed potato in a bowl and, while still warm, blend in the softened butter. Blend in the other filling ingredients, cover and set aside.

3 To make the sauce, soak the bread in the milk until soft, then squeeze dry. Meanwhile, place the nuts in a food processor. Add the damp bread and grind for a few seconds. Alternatively, use a mortar and pestle to grind them.

4 Combine the sour cream and mascarpone in a bowl and beat with a whisk or wooden spoon. Stir in the nuts. Gradually add the olive oil, stirring to amalgamate thoroughly, then season and stir in the Parmesan. Cover and set aside.

5 Roll the dough (see pages 50–51) and cut it into fluted disks using a 2in (5cm) cookie cutter. Form the pasta as for *ravioli*, but make them one at a time, painting around each filled disk with egg white and covering with a second disk. Press around the edges to seal. Leave to dry as described in step 7 on page 112.

6 Bring a pan of water to a boil. Pick up the cloths holding the *ravioli* and slide the first batch into the water, followed by 2 tablespoons of salt. Cook for 3–5 minutes once the water has returned to a boil, stirring gently. Taste for doneness, then transfer with a slotted spoon to a buttered serving dish.

7 While the *ravioli* are cooking, gently warm the walnut sauce. Spoon the hot sauce over the *ravioli*, and sprinkle with freshly grated Parmesan, if desired.

Ravioli Classici con Ricotta e Spinaci in Salsa di Pomodoro Leggera

Classic Ravioli with Ricotta and Spinach Filling in a Light Tomato Sauce

This is the classic central Italian filling for ravioli *and* tortelloni *(large filled pasta squares), though Swiss chard sometimes replaces spinach. The proportions of spinach to ricotta vary from cook to cook, and parsley is sometimes included, though nutmeg and Parmesan are obligatory. It is important to drain the ricotta; if the filling is too wet, it will soak through the pasta envelope. Once cooked, the* ravioli *are moistened with tomato sauce and sprinkled with a little Parmesan.*

The dough can be of egg, tomato, or spinach pasta, or a combination of all three for ravioli alla bandiera *— in the colors of the Italian flag. The traditional sauce for topping is a simple tomato sauce, such as those on pages 74–75, or even Salsa Aurora, a classic tomato sauce enriched with heavy cream (see page 75). For* ravioli*-making technique, see page 56.*

KCal 1045 P 47g C 68g S 1386mg SFA 29g UFA 32g (4)

INGREDIENTS

1 quantity (1lb/500g) fresh egg pasta (see page 48), unrolled

1 egg white, to seal

salt, to taste

For the filling

1½lb (750g) fresh spinach, washed and stems removed

1½lb (750g) ricotta, drained (see Tip, page 143)

2 egg yolks, lightly beaten

¼ tsp freshly grated nutmeg

½ tsp salt

¼ tsp freshly ground white or black pepper

½ cup (60g) freshly grated Parmesan

1 tbsp chopped fresh flat-leaf parsley

To serve

melted unsalted butter

1 quantity simple tomato sauce (see page 74) or creamy tomato sauce (see page 75)

freshly grated Parmesan, to serve

1 To make the filling, place the spinach in a deep lidded pan with no water except for the drops still clinging to the leaves after washing. Steam the spinach for 5–10 minutes until tender, tossing now and then but replacing the lid. Drain and leave until cool enough to handle. Squeeze out as much water as you can. Chop the spinach and set aside.

2 Combine all the ingredients for the filling in a bowl, blending well with a wooden spoon. Cover and refrigerate.

3 Divide the pasta dough into six portions. Work with only one piece at a time; keep the remainder covered with a bowl to prevent it from drying out. Roll the dough as thin as possible (see pages 50–51) into 4in (10cm) wide strips. Work with two strips at a time; keep the others covered with a damp cloth. Work quickly to prevent the dough drying out.

4 If using a *ravioli* mold, cut the pasta strips to the length of the mold. Dust the mold with flour. Press down lightly on the dough so it fills the pockets of the mold. Put a teaspoon of filling inside each pocket. Paint egg white along the filling. Place a second sheet of pasta over the top and roll a rolling pin across the top. The teeth of the mold will cut through the pasta, forming the *ravioli.*

5 Alternatively, place a teaspoon of filling at 2in (5cm) intervals in rows along one of the pasta strips. Dip a pastry brush in the egg white and paint around each spoonful of filling, so that each mound is surrounded by a square of egg white.

6 Place the second rolled-out strip of pasta over the filled sheet. Press down firmly around each mound of filling to seal it, forcing out any trapped air. Use a fluted pastry wheel or a knife to cut the *ravioli* into 2in (5cm) squares along the lines of egg white. Press down around each parcel to secure the seal. Repeat with the remaining dough and filling.

7 Place the *ravioli* on trays lined with clean dish towels sprinkled with flour. Do not let the *ravioli* overlap. Turn them occasionally so they dry evenly. They should not be left to dry for longer than 3–4 hours before being cooked, refrigerated, or frozen (see page 56).

8 Bring a pan of water to a rolling boil. Pick up the cloths holding the *ravioli* and slide the first batch of *ravioli* into the water, followed by 2 tablespoons of salt. Cover the pan until the water returns to a boil. Cook for 3–5 minutes once the water has returned to a boil, stirring gently. Taste for doneness.

9 Transfer the *ravioli* with a slotted spoon to a buttered serving dish. If you are layering the *ravioli* in the dish, drizzle melted butter between the layers to prevent sticking. Heat the tomato sauce until simmering. Spoon the sauce over the *ravioli,* and serve hot, passing freshly grated Parmesan at the table.

Ravioli/Pansotti di Ricotta e Prosciutto all'Aurora

Ravioli Filled with Ricotta, Prosciutto, and Parmesan with Creamy Tomato Sauce

The simple filling in these ravioli *makes them compatible with a wide variety of sauces, tomato-based or otherwise. I have suggested a creamy tomato sauce called Salsa Aurora that is often served with* penne *in Tuscany, but* ravioli *can also be served simply with melted unsalted butter and grated Parmesan. If desired, the pasta can be shaped into little triangles called* pansotti *(see page 57). (See page 20 for illustration.)*
For ravioli*-making technique, see page 56.*

KCal 1132 P 41g C 76g S 1515mg SFA 42g UFA 35g (4)

INGREDIENTS

- 1 quantity (1lb/500g) fresh egg pasta (see page 48), unrolled
- salt, to taste
- 1 egg white, to seal

For the filling

- 1lb (500g) ricotta, drained (see Tip, page 143)
- 1 egg yolk
- ½ cup (60g) freshly grated Parmesan
- 2oz (60g) thinly sliced prosciutto, minced
- ¼ tsp salt
- ⅛ tsp freshly grated nutmeg
- ⅛ tsp freshly ground white pepper
- 1 tbsp very finely chopped fresh flat-leaf parsley

To serve

- melted unsalted butter
- 1 quantity creamy tomato sauce (see page 75)
- freshly grated Parmesan, to serve

1 Combine the filling ingredients in a bowl, mixing well with a wooden spoon. Cover and refrigerate until ready to use.

2 Roll the pasta dough and form the *ravioli* as described in steps 3–7 on page 112, using egg white to seal them.

3 Bring a pan of water to a rolling boil and cook the *ravioli* as described in step 8, opposite. Taste for doneness, then transfer them with a slotted spoon to a buttered dish.

4 If you are layering the *ravioli* in the dish, drizzle melted butter between the layers. Heat the sauce, then spoon it over the *ravioli*. Serve hot, passing grated Parmesan at the table.

Ravioli di Zafferano con Spinaci, Ricotta, e Salsiccia

Saffron Ravioli with Spinach, Ricotta, and Sausage Stuffing in Tomato Sauce

These are inspired by a type of ravioli *from the Veneto called* casonziei, *which are stuffed with spinach, puréed potato, and sausage. I rather like this variation, which replaces the puréed potato with ricotta. Saffron pasta is perfect for the pasta envelopes, which can be in the form of half-moons* (anolini *or* tortelli), *or* ravioli. *However, egg or tomato pasta will also do nicely. The filling is also suitable for* cannelloni.

As for the sauce, unsalted butter is all that is needed, but a light tomato sauce is most complementary. If available, smoked dried ricotta can be sprinkled on top, in the tradition of the Veneto.
(See page 20 for illustration.)
For ravioli*-making technique, see page 56.*

KCal 1165 P 40g C 81g S 1555mg SFA 43g UFA 30g (4)

INGREDIENTS

- 1 quantity (1lb/500g) saffron pasta (see page 55) or fresh egg pasta (see page 48), unrolled
- salt, to taste
- 1 egg white, to seal

For the filling

- 1lb (500g) spinach, washed and stems removed
- 1 tbsp unsalted butter
- 1 small onion, very finely chopped
- 2oz (60g) sweet Italian sausage meat
- ½ tsp ground fennel seeds
- 1lb (500g) ricotta, drained (see Tip, page 143)
- salt and freshly ground white or black pepper, to taste
- 2 tbsp freshly grated Parmesan
- 1 egg yolk

To serve

- melted unsalted butter
- 1 quantity creamy tomato sauce or light tomato sauce (see page 75), made with butter instead of olive oil
- freshly grated smoked dried ricotta or Parmesan, to serve

1 For the filling, cook the spinach as described in step 1, opposite. Squeeze out as much water as possible, then chop and set aside.

2 Warm the butter in a skillet, add the onion, and sauté until softened. Add the sausage meat, breaking it up fine, and the fennel seeds. Cook until the sausage meat is browned, about 5 minutes. Remove from the heat, allow to cool slightly, then combine with the ricotta and spinach. Add the seasoning, Parmesan, and egg yolk.

3 Roll the pasta dough and form the *ravioli* as described in steps 3–7 on page 112, using egg white to seal them.

4 Bring a pan of water to a rolling boil and cook the *ravioli* as described in step 8, opposite.

5 Transfer the *ravioli* to a buttered dish. Heat the sauce and spoon it over the *ravioli*. Serve hot with the grated cheese.

RAVIOLI DI MANZO IN SALSA DI POMODORO, FUNGHI SELVATICI, E VINO

Beef Ravioli in Tomato Sauce with Wild Mushrooms and Red Wine

I like to fill** ravioli **with lean or good-quality ground beef because it is compatible with so many sauces. I have suggested Tomato Sauce with Wild Mushrooms and Red Wine as an accompaniment (see page 76), but any of the meatless tomato sauces would be suitable. While the flavors of** ragù **sauces are also compatible, their use for meat** ravioli **would be gilding the lily. For** ravioli**-making technique, see page 56. (See illustration opposite.)

KCal 1056 P 47g C 68g S 1386mg SFA 30g UFA 33g (4)

INGREDIENTS

1 quantity (1lb/500g) spinach pasta (see page 54) or fresh egg pasta (see page 48), unrolled

salt, to taste

1 egg white, to seal

For the filling

3 tbsp extra-virgin olive oil

1 small onion, chopped

3oz (90g) sliced prosciutto, very finely chopped

½ small carrot, very finely chopped

1 small celery rib with leaves, very finely chopped

3 tbsp coarsely chopped fresh flat-leaf parsley

1½lb (750g) lean ground beef

¾ tsp salt, or to taste

freshly ground black pepper, to taste

1 bay leaf

⅛ tsp ground cloves

3 tbsp chicken or meat stock or broth (see page 68)

1 egg, beaten

¾ cup (150g) freshly grated Parmesan, plus extra to serve

To serve

melted unsalted butter

1 quantity tomato sauce with wild mushrooms and red wine (see page 76)

freshly grated Parmesan, to serve

1 For the filling, warm the olive oil in a heavy-bottomed skillet and add the onion. Sauté over medium heat until soft, about 4 minutes. Add the prosciutto, carrot, celery, and parsley to the pan, stirring to coat with the oil.

2 Add the beef, salt, pepper, bay leaf, and ground cloves. Use a fork to break up the meat, tossing it with the other ingredients, and then add the stock or broth. Sauté over low heat, stirring frequently with a wooden spoon, until the meat is tender and the flavors marry, 25 minutes. Remove from the heat and discard the bay leaf. Allow to cool.

3 Pass the mixture through a meat grinder or food processor to grind it very fine. Add the egg and the Parmesan to the mixture and work in thoroughly with a wooden spoon.

4 Roll the dough and form the *ravioli* as described in steps 3–7 on page 112, using egg white to seal them.

5 Bring a pan of water to a rolling boil and cook the *ravioli* as described in step 8 on page 112.

6 Transfer the *ravioli* with a slotted spoon to a buttered serving dish. If you are layering the *ravioli*, drizzle melted butter between the layers to prevent sticking. While the *ravioli* are cooking, warm the sauce. Spoon it over the cooked *ravioli* and serve. Pass the freshly grated Parmesan at the table.

TORTELLONI AL POMODORO RIPIENI CON PESCE E PATATE IN BURRO FUSO

Tomato Tortelloni Stuffed with Fish, Potato, Tarragon, and Parsley with Butter Sauce

Fish and potatoes go very well together and the combination is particularly suitable for a pasta filling. These tortelloni *are very light and delicate. As* tortelloni *are much larger than* ravioli, *fewer are needed for each portion. This recipe makes enough for four main course portions, but if there is a little filling left over, form it into grape-sized balls and boil them in the pasta water after the* tortelloni *are cooked, just until they float to the surface. Serve them with the* tortelloni.

While grated hard cheeses are not typically served with seafood, a small quantity of pecorino can be sprinkled on this stuffed pasta to complement the potato in the filling. If you choose, shrimp, lobster, or crab may be substituted for some of the white fish. In this case, Parmesan, rather than pecorino, would be a more suitable accompaniment. As with other stuffed pasta, these tortelloni *can be frozen.* *(See page 21 for illustration.)*
For ravioli*-making technique, which can be adapted to* tortelloni, *see page 56.*

KCal 791 P 40g C 84g S 951mg SFA 17g UFA 13g (4)

INGREDIENTS
1 quantity (1lb/500g) tomato pasta (see page 55), unrolled
1 egg white, to seal
salt, to taste
For the filling
1 tsp vinegar
1 carrot, cut into quarters
1 small onion, cut into quarters
small handful of parsley stems
¾lb (375g) white-fleshed fish fillets such as sole, haddock, turbot, or hake
1lb (500g) boiling potatoes, peeled and cubed
2 tbsp unsalted butter
12 scallions, including 2in (5cm) green tops, chopped
2 tsp chopped fresh tarragon, or 1 tsp dried tarragon
¾ tsp salt
1 tbsp chopped fresh flat-leaf parsley, plus 1 tbsp for garnish
¼ tsp coarsely ground pepper
⅛ tsp cayenne
2 egg yolks
To serve
4 tbsp unsalted butter, melted
⅓ cup (45g) freshly grated pecorino
plenty of coarsely ground white pepper

1 To make the filling, combine the vinegar, carrot, onion, and parsley stems in a large skillet, covering with water by 2in (5cm). Bring to a boil, then simmer over medium heat, partially covered, for 15 minutes.

2 Add the fish fillets to the pan and cover. When the water returns to a boil, cook until just done, about 3 minutes. Lift the fillets out with a slotted spoon and transfer to a bowl; reserve the stock. When it is cool enough to handle, finely flake the fish, removing any stray bones, return it to the bowl, and set aside.

3 Pour the fish cooking stock into a pan and add the potato piecees. Partially cover, bring to a boil, and cook until fork-tender, about 20 minutes. Drain, reserving the stock, then finely mash them, preferably with a potato ricer, or mash them by hand. Add the potatoes to the flaked fish.

4 Warm the butter in a small skillet and add the scallions. Sauté until softened, about 2 minutes. Add them to the fish and potatoes with the tarragon, salt, parsley, pepper, cayenne, and egg yolks. Mix well, check the seasoning, and set aside.

5 Divide the pasta dough into six portions. Work with only one piece at a time; keep the rest covered with a bowl. Roll the pasta dough as thin as possible (see pages 50–51) into 4in (10cm) wide strips. Work with two strips at a time; keep the rest covered with a damp cloth.

6 Place 2 teaspoons of filling at 3in (7cm) intervals along the center of one of the strips. Dip a pastry brush in egg white and paint around the mounds of filling, so that each is surrounded by a square of egg white.

7 Place the second rolled-out strip of pasta over the filled sheet. Press down firmly around each mound to seal it. Use a fluted pastry wheel or a knife to cut the *tortelloni* into 3in (7cm) squares along the egg white lines. Press down around each one to secure the seal. Work quickly to keep the filling from seeping out. Repeat with the remaining dough and filling.

8 Place the *tortelloni* on trays covered with dish towels sprinkled with flour. Do not let them overlap and turn occasionally. They should not be left unrefrigerated or unfrozen.

9 Bring a pan of water to a boil. Pick up one of the cloths holding the *tortelloni* and slide the first batch into the water, followed by 2 tablespoons of salt. Cook for 3–5 minutes once the water has returned to a boil, stirring gently. Taste for doneness, then transfer the *tortelloni* to a warm buttered serving bowl. Drizzle liberally with melted butter, sprinkle with pecorino and pepper, and serve warm.

TORTELLINI IN BRODO ALLA BOLOGNESE

Tortellini Stuffed with Chicken and Pork in Meat Broth

Tortellini *are perhaps the most famous of all of Bologna's marvelous dishes. They are most often cooked in broth* (tortellini in brodo), *which becomes enriched with the flavors of the filling.* For tortellini in brodo, *first make the broth, then make the filling, and last, the dough. Alternatively, cook the* tortellini *in lightly salted water and serve with butter and fresh Parmesan. Makes enough for 10–12 as a soup dish and 4–6 as a sauced pasta dish. For* tortellini-*making technique, see page 57.*

KCal 257 P 17g C 23g S 540mg SFA 4g UFA 6g (10)

INGREDIENTS
1 quantity (1lb/500g) fresh egg pasta, made without oil (see page 48), unrolled
a little water, milk, or beaten egg, to seal
salt, to taste
For the filling
1⅓ tbsp unsalted butter
1 small boneless chicken breast, cut into small dice
3oz (90g) boneless pork loin, cut into small dice
1½oz (45g) prosciutto crudo, thinly sliced
2oz (60g) mortadella or high-quality salami, thinly sliced
¼ cup (30g) freshly grated Parmesan
⅛ tsp freshly grated nutmeg
⅓ tsp salt, or to taste
freshly ground white pepper, to taste
1 small egg, lightly beaten
To serve
1 quantity light meat broth (see page 68)
freshly grated Parmesan, to serve

1 To make the filling, melt the butter in a skillet. Add the chicken to the pan and sauté over medium-low heat until it loses its pinkness outside, up to 2 minutes. Do not allow it to brown and harden. Transfer the chicken to a bowl, leaving the butter in the pan. Add the pork to the pan and sauté over low heat in the same manner. Add it to the chicken and chill until the meat is cooled throughout, about 10 minutes.

2 Combine the prosciutto and mortadella on a chopping board or work surface. Use a sharp chef's knife to chop them fine. Alternatively, dice them and then grind in a food processor for no more than a few seconds at a time, being careful not to grind or pulverize the meat to a paste.

3 Chop the cooled pork and chicken in the same manner as the cured meats. Combine the meats, Parmesan, nutmeg, salt, pepper, and egg. Use a wooden spoon to mix the filling thoroughly, but do not beat it. Cover, and set the mixture aside until ready to use.

4 Divide the pasta dough into six portions. Work with only one piece at a time; keep the rest covered with a bowl. Roll the pasta dough as thin as possible (see pages 50–51) into 4in (10cm) wide strips. Work with two strips at a time; keep the rest covered with a slightly damp cloth. Work quickly to prevent the dough drying out.

5 Use a 2in (5cm) round cookie cutter to cut disks from the strips (see page 57). Alternatively, cut the strips into 2in (5cm) squares, which will result in *cappelletti* rather than *tortellini.* Spoon a heaping ¼ teaspoon of filling onto the center of each disk. Dip your finger into water, milk, or beaten egg and lightly run it along the inside edges of the disks.

6 Fold the disk in half to form a crescent shape, bringing the edges of one side slightly below the other. Press to seal well, being sure to let out any air. The dumpling will now look like a little stuffed half-moon. Take it and wrap it around your little finger, holding the arched end up, with the stuffed side away from you. Pinch the two corners together.

7 Place the *tortellini* on trays covered with clean dish towels sprinkled with flour. Do not allow them to overlap. Turn them occasionally so they dry evenly and do not stick to the tray. They should not be left to dry for longer than 3–4 hours before being cooked, refrigerated, or frozen (see page 58).

8 Bring the broth to a boil in a large pan. Pick up one of the cloths on which the *tortellini* are resting and slide them directly into the rapidly boiling liquid. Stir, and cover the pan until the broth returns to a boil, then cook the *tortellini* gently until they float to the surface, about 3 minutes from the moment the water has returned to a boil. Ladle the *tortellini* and broth into soup bowls, and serve with freshly grated Parmesan.

Tortellini con Salsa di Funghi e Panna

Tortellini with Mushroom Cream Sauce

***Tortellini** are excellent served with certain simple sauces. The traditional ones are a classic cream sauce of butter, cream, and Parmesan, or simply butter and fresh Parmesan, neither of which distract from the flavor or delicacy of the **tortellini**. Strongly flavored sauces would overshadow these **tortellini**, but I have found a simple mushroom and cream sauce to be a successful elaboration. (See page 20 for illustration.)*

KCal 837 P 30g C 32g S 1340mg SFA 36g UFA 23g (4)

INGREDIENTS

1 quantity tortellini alla bolognese (see page 117)

For the sauce

¾lb (375g) fresh wild mushrooms such as porcini, chanterelles, morels, oyster mushrooms, or cremini, or a mixture

4 tbsp unsalted butter

2 shallots or 1 small onion, very finely chopped

¼ cup (60ml) dry white wine

1 cup (250ml) heavy cream

salt and freshly ground white or black pepper, to taste

1 Cook the *tortellini* in boiling salted water, as described in step 8, page 117. Drain and transfer to a serving bowl.

2 Use a soft brush or cloth to clean the mushrooms. Cut off any woody tips. Thinly slice the mushrooms; if they are large, halve them first.

3 Warm the butter in a large skillet over medium heat. Add the shallots or onion and sauté until they begin to sweat. Add the mushrooms and sauté until tender, about 5 minutes.

4 Pour in the wine and cook for about 2 minutes to evaporate the alcohol. Stir in the cream and simmer until the sauce thickens, 5 minutes. Remove from the heat and season. Transfer the *tortellini* to the pan, toss with the sauce, and serve.

Caramelle di Zucca e Mela in Burro Fuso

Squash and Apple Caramelle in the Style of Mantua in Cardamom Butter

*Remembering a dish of squash and apple stuffed pasta that I ate in Mantua many years ago, I was inspired to invent this dish. Cardamom is not an aromatic much used in Italian cooking, but I like its soft gingery scent infused in the butter sauce. **Caramelle** ("bonbons") are the perfect shape for this filling, but **tortelli** (see page 57) would also suit. They may be served as a first course followed by roast pork or veal. (See page 20 for illustration.) For **caramelle**-making technique, see page 57.*

KCal 660 P 20g C 74g S 532mg SFA 18g UFA 13g (4)

Tip

The pumpkins and squashes that grow outside the Mediterranean do not always have the same compact, dry properties of the Italian zucca. *If you cannot find firm, sweet squash, use yams or sweet potatoes instead. While they are somewhat sweeter than Italian* zucca, *the recipes for stuffed pasta and gnocchi that use* zucca *are meant to be sweet, a taste that harkens back to the sweet-and-savory tradition of Renaissance cooking.*

INGREDIENTS

1 quantity (1lb/500g) fresh egg pasta (see page 48), unrolled

1 egg white, to seal

salt, to taste

For the stuffing

1lb (500g) firm butternut squash, pumpkin, sweet potatoes, or yams

1½ tbsp freshly grated Parmesan or grana cheese

1 cup (30g) dried apples, finely chopped

2 tbsp apple, quince, or pear preserve

yolk of 1 small egg

1 tbsp butter

2 tsp grated fresh ginger, or ¼ tsp ground cloves or cinnamon

1 tbsp flour

¼ tsp salt

For the sauce

6 tbsp (90g) unsalted butter

6 cardamom pods

1 Preheat the oven to a temperature of 375°F (190°C).

2 To make the filling, place the whole squash or pumpkin slice on the oven rack. If using sweet potatoes or yams, prick them with a fork. Roast until tender, about 1 hour. When they are just cool enough to handle, peel and cube them, then mash fine with a potato ricer or masher.

3 Transfer the puréed squash, sweet potato, or yam to a bowl. Add the Parmesan or grana, dried apple, preserve, egg yolk, butter, chosen spice, flour, and salt, and mix well. Check the seasoning.

4 Roll the dough as described in pages 50–51. Cut the dough into 1 x 3in (2.5 x 7cm) rectangles. paint around the edges with egg white. Place ½ teaspoon of filling in the center of each rectangle, fold the long edges over the top, twist the ends (see page 57), and seal.

5 Leave the *caramelle* to dry as described for *cappellacci* in step 6, opposite. They should not be left for more than one hour before being cooked or frozen (see page 58). If cooking immediately, bring a pan of water to a boil, add 2 tablespoons of salt and cook as described in step 7, opposite.

6 Transfer the *caramelle* to a warm buttered dish. Warm the butter with the cardamom pods, then drizzle the sauce over the *caramelle*, and serve.

Cappellacci Ripieni di Zucca e Amaretti in Burro Fuso

Cappellacci Stuffed with Squash and Amaretti in Butter and Orange Zest Sauce

This is a variation on the delicious pumpkin-stuffed tortelli *of Parma and other Emilian provinces. Italian pumpkins are less watery than other varieties, so you may need to substitute sweet potatoes, yam, or butternut squash, but the butternut should be ripened before picking, making it less watery. While* cappellacci *are one of the traditional shapes for this filling,* ravioli, caramelle, *or* tortelloni *may be made if preferred. A cream sauce is delicious with these* cappellacci, *but they can also be served with melted butter topped lightly with amaretti crumbs, as here. For* tortellini-*making* technique *(*tortellini *are a smaller version of* cappellacci*), see page 57.*

KCal 731 P 21g C 89g S 599mg SFA 16g UFA 17g (4)

INGREDIENTS

1 quantity (1lb/500g) fresh egg pasta (see page 48), unrolled

1 egg white, to seal

salt, to taste

For the filling

1lb (500g) firm butternut squash, pumpkin, sweet potatoes, or yams

1½ tbsp freshly grated Parmesan

zest of 1 orange

1 tbsp candied orange peel, very finely chopped

5 amaretti, about 2½oz (70g), crushed

1 small egg yolk

¼ tsp freshly grated nutmeg

¼ tsp salt

1 tbsp flour

For the sauce

5 tbsp (75g) unsalted butter

4in (10cm) strip of orange zest

3 amaretti, about 1¼oz (35g), crushed

1 Preheat the oven to a temperature of 375°F (190°C).

2 To make the filling, place the whole squash or pumpkin slice on the oven rack. If using sweet potatoes or yams, prick them with a fork. Roast until tender, about 1 hour. When they are just cool enough to handle, peel and cube them, then mash fine with a potato ricer or masher.

3 Transfer the puréed squash, potato, or yam to a bowl. Stir in the Parmesan, orange zest, candied peel, amaretti, egg yolk, nutmeg, salt, and flour. Taste the mixture and adjust the seasoning if necessary.

4 Divide the pasta dough into six portions. Work with only one piece at a time; keep the remainder covered with a bowl (the dough must not dry out). Roll the dough as thin as possible (see pages 50–51). Cut it into 4in (10cm) wide strips. Work with two strips at a time; keep the remainder covered with a slightly damp cloth until ready to use.

5 Use a 3in (7cm) cookie cutter or glass to cut the dough into disks. Form the *cappellacci* as for *tortellini* (see page 57), putting about ½ teaspoon of filling in the center of each disk, using egg white to seal them.

6 Spread the *cappellacci* out to dry on dish towels sprinkled with flour, turning them every few minutes. They should not be left for more than one hour before being cooked, refrigerated, or frozen (see page 58). Check that the filling does not seep through the dough.

7 Bring a large pan of water to a rolling boil. Pick up one of the cloths holding the *cappellacci* and carefully slide the first batch into the water, followed by 2 tablespoons of salt. Cook for 3–5 minutes once the water has returned to a boil, stirring gently. Taste for doneness.

8 Transfer the *cappellacci* with a slotted spoon to a lightly buttered serving dish. Warm the butter with the orange zest, then drizzle it over the *cappellacci*. Scatter with the crushed amaretti, and serve immediately.

Fazzoletti al Forno con Funghi e Prosciutto

Baked Crepes with Mushroom and Ham Stuffing

I sampled a facsimile of this dish while traveling through Tuscany, at the Trattoria Zaira in Chiusi. The* fazzoletti *were filled with heady, intensely flavored wild porcini gathered from the local woods. In the absence of these marvelous mushrooms, substitute other wild mushrooms or combine dried porcini with cultivated mushrooms.

Fazzoletti, *literally meaning "handkerchiefs," are called many other names throughout the Italian regions. They are very similar to French crepes and, likewise, may be filled with all manner of stuffings, both savory, as above, and sweet, or layered with a filling and stacked. The batter must be very thin, almost watery. Using the correct proportion of egg, and cooking over moderate heat will produce an extremely thin but cohesive, light pancake. The Russians, whose crepes take the form of* blini, *say you should be able to see through them, as the holes that form when the pancake cooks make it almost transparent. The first few in the batch may not work out, but the remainder will no doubt be perfect. Makes 16–20 crepes. Serves 4–6.*

KCal 1429 P 51g C 108g S 2026mg SFA 46g UFA 43g (4)

Advance Preparation

The basic fazzoletti *batter can be made a day ahead, or the crepes can be made up to three days in advance. In both cases, the batter or crepes should be tightly covered and stored in the refrigerator. Crepes can also be made several weeks in advance, stacked between layers of waxed paper, wrapped in foil or plastic wrap, transferred to a sealed freezer bag, and frozen for up to several weeks. Stuffed* fazzoletti *can be prepared up to two days in advance of baking and serving, covered, and refrigerated. The baking time may increase by 5–10 minutes if the dish has been cooked from chilled.*

INGREDIENTS

For the fazzoletti

4 extra large eggs

2 cups 2 tbsp (525ml) milk, or more if necessary

pinch of sugar

½ tsp salt

1½ cup (175g) unbleached white flour

vegetable oil for greasing frying pan

For the filling and dressing

½lb (250g) wild mushrooms such as chanterelles, shiitake, or oyster mushrooms, or a combination

10oz (300g) fresh cultivated mushrooms

2 tbsp unsalted butter

1 onion, grated

¼lb (125g) prosciutto or ham, sliced thinly and cut into julienne strips

scant ½ tsp salt

freshly ground black or white pepper, to taste

2 tbsp chopped fresh flat-leaf parsley

1½ quantities béchamel (see page 77)

30g (⅓ cup) freshly grated Parmesan

FOR THE FAZZOLETTI

1 Using a whisk or electric beater on low speed, mix the eggs, milk, sugar, and salt in a bowl. Add the flour, sifting it in gradually while whisking to break up any lumps. If there are still lumps, put the batter through a sieve. It will be extremely thin – almost watery. Cover the bowl and let the batter rest for 30 minutes.

2 Warm about ½ teaspoon of oil in a nonstick 8in (20cm) crepe pan or a shallow skillet with curved sides. Ensure the entire base of the pan is coated. Heat the oil until it is hot enough to make the batter set on contact.

3 Cook the crepes one at a time, using a ladle to pour about 3 tablespoons of batter into the hot pan. Tilt and rotate the pan to spread the batter evenly so that it is as thin as possible and covers the pan.

4 Use a spatula to turn the crepe as soon as it solidifies and tiny holes begin to form throughout, about 1 minute. Cook lightly on the reverse side. The entire cooking should take less than 2 minutes; about 1 minute on the first side, and 30 seconds on the reverse.

5 Transfer the crepes to a plate, stacking them if necessary. Repeat with the remaining batter, adding only enough oil each time to prevent sticking. Cover with a plate or plastic wrap until ready to use.

FOR THE STUFFING

1 Use a soft brush or cloth to clean the mushrooms. Trim off the hard tips, then slice the stalks and caps thinly.

2 Melt the butter in a skillet. Add the onion and sauté until wilted, about 4 minutes. Add the mushrooms, and sauté over medium heat until tender, about 6 minutes, tossing frequently.

3 Stir in the prosciutto or ham, salt, pepper, and parsley, and continue to sauté for another minute. Remove the pan from the heat, moisten the filling with 4 tablespoons of béchamel, and set aside.

4 Preheat the oven to a temperature of 400°F (200°C).

5 Select two 9 x 12in (23 x 30cm) baking dishes. Smear 2–3 tablespoons of béchamel on the base of each dish. Take one of the crepes and spread a tablespoon of béchamel on it. Spoon two tablespoons of the mushroom filling on top.

6 Fold one side of the disk over the filling, then pull the other side over the center to form a neat roll. Place the roll in the baking dish, seam side up. Repeat with the remaining crepes and stuffing. Arrange in a row in the dishes. Spoon the remaining béchamel over the top and sprinkle with Parmesan.

7 Bake the *fazzoletti* until heated through and bubbly, about 10 minutes. Be careful not to overcook them. Remove the dishes from the oven, allow to settle for 10 minutes, then serve.

Crespelle di Spinaci alla Marcella

Spinach Crepes Stuffed with Taglierini

This interesting recipe was created by my Italian colleague, Marcella Falcomer, when she worked for the Four Seasons Restaurant in New York many years ago. Marcella's food is always as beautifully presented as it is delightful to eat, and this dish is no exception. The pale green color of the crespelle *surrounding the creamy white fresh* taglierini *makes a very attractive dish.*

These crespelle *are particularly suitable as a side dish with pot-roasted meat or other gravy-producing meat dishes. For a colorful presentation, serve the* crespelle *on a small bed of strips of red pepper sautéed in butter or olive oil until tender but still a little crunchy. A little more skill is required to make these* crespelle *than the simple plain crepes. The first one or two are bound to crumple in the pan until you get the feel for making them.*

Makes approximately 12 crepes.

KCal 690 P 24g C 56g S 811mg SFA 18g UFA 22g (4)

Advance Preparation

These crespelle *can be prepared up to one day in advance, stuffed, covered tightly with plastic wrap, and refrigerated.*

INGREDIENTS

For the crepes

10oz (300g) frozen spinach, thawed

2 eggs, beaten

¾ cup (175ml) milk

¾ cup (175ml) water

½ tsp salt

¼ tsp freshly ground white pepper

1 cup (125g) all-purpose flour

2 tbsp vegetable oil, plus oil for cooking

For the filling

½ quantity (½lb/250g) fresh egg pasta (see page 48), cut into taglierini (see page 53)

salt, to taste

5 tbsp (75g) unsalted butter at room temperature, plus butter for coating dish

½ cup (60g) freshly grated Parmesan, plus additional for sprinkling

⅛ tsp freshly grated nutmeg

freshly ground white or black pepper, to taste

1 Cook the spinach according to package directions. Drain and squeeze out the excess water, still leaving the spinach somewhat moist. Purée in a food processor, then set aside until cool.

2 Combine the eggs, milk, water, salt, and pepper, and beat well. Beat in the flour, then the oil and spinach, until all the ingredients are incorporated into a cohesive mixture. If using a food processor, combine all the ingredients and engage the motor until the batter achieves an even green color and smooth texture. Chill for up to 1–2 hours.

3 Warm about ½ teaspoon of vegetable oil in a cold, nonstick 8in (20cm) crepe pan, or a shallow skillet with curved sides, over medium heat. Make sure the entire base of the pan is coated. Heat the oil until hot enough to make the batter set when it is poured into the pan.

4 Cook the crepes one at a time, using a ladle to pour as much batter onto the hot surface as will form the thinnest batter possible while still covering the entire pan base. If the batter is too thick to cover the pan easily by tilting, thoroughly mix in more water to achieve the correct consistency: it may take up to ½ cup (125ml) water. Keep the pan hot enough to cook the *crespelle* quickly without burning (cooling the pan will result in sticking).

5 As soon as the crepe solidifies and small holes start to appear, use a spatula to unstick the edges of the crepe all round before turning it. Slide the spatula under the crepe, being sure it does not adhere to the pan surface, and turn. Cook on the reverse side. The entire process should take 3–4 minutes. Transfer the crepes to a warm plate, stacking them if necessary. Repeat with the remaining batter, keeping the pan oiled. When all the crepes are cooked, cover with a plate or plastic wrap.

6 Bring 4 quarts (5 liters) of water to a rolling boil and add the *taglierini* and 1 tablespoon of salt. Stir immediately and cook over high heat until the water returns to a boil. As soon as the pasta floats to the surface, drain immediately. Toss in a bowl with 4 tablespoons of butter, then add the Parmesan, nutmeg, and pepper.

7 Preheat the oven to a temperature of 375°F (190°C).

8 Select a large baking dish and butter it lightly. Fill each of the crepes with some of the *taglierini*, distributing the pasta evenly. Gather opposite sides of the *crespelle* together and secure each one with a toothpick, or roll into a cone. Transfer to the baking dish. Dot with the remaining butter, sprinkle with a little more Parmesan and slide onto the upper rack of the oven. Bake until heated through and lightly golden, 10 minutes. Serve immediately.

PASTA AL FORNO

BAKED PASTA DISHES

IN ITALIAN CULINARY TERMS, the word *pasticcio* refers to a composition of pasta and various other ingredients, including a sauce, placed together in a dish and baked. If only to simplify, I cautiously offer the term "casserole" in translation. If the word conjures up pasty macaroni tossed with frozen vegetables and condensed soup, perish the image. In this chapter are included all manner of *pasticci,* all utilizing fresh ingredients and staples from the Italian pantry. Even my take on tuna noodle casserole, the signature dish of the American 1950s, is made with fresh and genuine ingredients. Many of these dishes are my own concoctions; others are true regional classics.

PIZZOCCHERI AL FORNO CON CAVOLO, FUNGHI, E TALEGGIO
Buckwheat Noodles with Cabbage, Mushrooms, Caraway, and Taleggio

Special Ingredients

Shiitake mushrooms · Chanterelles · Oyster mushrooms · Cabbage · Leeks · Cumin seeds · Taleggio · Pizzoccheri

Preparation

Pizzoccheri (buckwheat noodles) are a characteristic pasta of Valtellina in Lombardy. They are typically baked into a hearty dish that includes potatoes, cabbage, or Swiss chard, and locally made Taleggio cheese. This is a lighter dish that also utilizes wild mushrooms, whose woodsy flavor and creamy texture are adroitly matched to the nutty buckwheat and earthy cabbage. Caraway and cumin, popular flavorings of the northern mountain regions, unify the ingredients perfectly. If leeks are not available, substitute one large onion. Dry pizzoccheri *can be used instead of fresh. If using dry pasta, cook it in the cabbage cooking water for 8–12 minutes, or until* al dente, *then drain and continue as described.*

KCal 588 P 24g C 51g S 926mg SFA 21g UFA 8g (4)

INGREDIENTS

¼lb (125g) fresh wild mushrooms such as cremini, chanterelles, morels, shiitake, or oyster mushrooms

salt, to taste

1½lb (750g) green cabbage, core removed, shredded

½ quantity (½lb/250g) buckwheat pasta (see page 55), cut into short tagliatelle noodles (see pages 37 and 53)

6 tbsp (90g) unsalted butter at room temperature

3 large leeks, including 2in (5cm) green tops, well washed and thinly sliced across

1 large garlic clove, very finely chopped

1¼ tsp caraway seeds, ground, plus ½ tsp whole

½ tsp cumin seeds

5½oz (160g) Taleggio, fontina, or bel paese cheese, cut into small dice

¾ cup (175ml) chicken broth (see page 63) or light meat broth (see page 68), or 1 chicken bouillon cube dissolved in ¾ cup (175ml) cabbage cooking water

1 Use a soft brush or cloth to clean the mushrooms. Trim any woody stems. If the mushrooms are large, cut them into halves or quarters, then thinly slice.

2 Preheat the oven to a temperature of 400°F (200°C).

3 Bring a large pan of water to a rolling boil. Add 1½ tablespoons of salt and drop in the shredded cabbage. Cover the pan and allow the water to return to a boil. Uncover and cook for 5 minutes longer. Use a slotted spoon to transfer the cabbage to a bowl and set aside. If using a bouillon cube, ladle off ¾ cup (175ml) of the cooking water and dissolve the cube in it. Set aside until ready to use.

4 Add the buckwheat noodles to the cabbage cooking water in the pan and cover. Bring to a boil and then drain immediately. Rinse the pasta lightly in cold running water to arrest cooking and keep the strands separate; set aside.

5 Meanwhile, warm 4 tablespoons of the butter in a large, preferably nonstick, skillet. Add the mushrooms, leeks, garlic, ground caraway seeds, and cumin. Sauté over medium-low heat until the vegetables are tender but still hold their shape, about 5 minutes.

6 Add the cabbage to the skillet and toss well. Sauté the mixture over medium heat until the flavors marry, tossing frequently, 7–8 minutes. Add ½ teaspoon of salt, or to taste. Remove from the heat.

7 Use a little butter to grease a 10 x 14in (25 x 35cm) baking dish. Put one third of the cabbage mixture on the bottom of the baking dish. Dot with butter and sprinkle a third of the cheese over the top. Spread half the *pizzoccheri* noodles over that. Dot with a little more butter and then scatter with half the remaining cheese. Repeat the process, finishing with cabbage topped with the remaining cheese, butter, and whole caraway seeds.

8 Pour the broth or stock over the casserole. Bake the dish on the upper rack of the oven until bubbly and heated through, about 15 minutes. Do not overcook. Let the dish settle for a few minutes before serving.

Pasticcio di Mafalde, Zucchine, e Funghi ai Due Formaggi

Casserole of Mafalde, Zucchini, and Mushrooms with Two Cheeses

I like to make this** pasticcio **in summertime when zucchini are at their best. Zucchini need to be fresh and young when eaten. Those that weigh much more than ½lb (250g) have lost their sweet flavor and tenderness and contain too many seeds. Eggplants may be substituted for zucchini; prepare them according to instructions for Baked Lasagne with Eggplant and Potatoes alla Serra (see page 135, steps 4–5).

KCal 1000 P 44g C 48g S 1552mg SFA 32g UFA 32g (4)

Advance Preparation

This pasticcio *can be assembled up to three days in advance, covered, and refrigerated. Leftover* pasticcio *reheats well. Cover with foil and place in a preheated medium oven for 20–30 minutes.*

Ingredients

2lb (1kg) tender young zucchini
6oz (175g) cultivated mushrooms
2 tbsp unsalted butter, or 2 tbsp extra-virgin olive oil
⅓ cup (75ml) extra-virgin olive oil, or as needed
1 tsp chopped fresh rosemary, or ½ tsp dried rosemary
salt and freshly ground pepper, to taste
6oz (175g) dried mafalde or lasagne
1 quantity tomato sauce with vegetables (see page 75) or other good, homemade meatless tomato sauce
½lb (250g) mozzarella, shredded
¼lb (125g) aged or young pecorino, grated or shredded, or ¼lb (125g) freshly grated Parmesan

For the topping

2 extra large eggs, lightly beaten
2 tbsp milk or heavy cream
2 tbsp freshly grated Parmesan

1. Trim the ends of the zucchini and then cut lengthwise into very thin ⅛in (2.5mm) slices.

2. Use a soft brush or cloth to clean the mushrooms. Trim the hard tips off the stems, then thinly slice the caps and stems. Gently warm the butter or oil in a skillet. Add the mushrooms, turn the heat to high, and sauté, stirring frequently, until tender, about 6 minutes. Remove from the heat and let cool.

3. Preheat the oven to a temperature of 375°F (190°C).

4. Combine the ⅓ cup (75ml) of olive oil, the salt, rosemary, and pepper. Brush the zucchini slices on both sides with the mixture and place them on two baking sheets. Bake until tender and lightly colored, about 30 minutes. Remove from the oven and allow to cool slightly.

5 Meanwhile, bring 4 quarts (5 liters) of water to a rapid boil. Add 1½ tablespoons of salt and the *mafalde*. Cook over high heat, stirring frequently, until not quite *al dente*, about 10 minutes. Drain the noodles and rinse in cold water; drain again and lay flat on waxed paper.

6 Raise the oven temperature to 400°F (200°C).

7 Smear the bottom of a 9 x 12in (23 x 30cm) baking dish with a little tomato sauce. Combine the mozzarella and pecorino in a bowl. Layer half the zucchini slices over the sauce. Smear them with a thin layer of sauce, then sprinkle with about a quarter of the cheese.

8 Place a single layer of *mafalde* noodles on top of the cheese, arranging them close together, side by side, not on top of one another. Spread a layer of sauce over the noodles, then sprinkle with one third of the remaining cheese. Arrange the remaining zucchini on top, then make another layer of sauce, cheese, pasta, sauce, and cheese.

9 To make the topping, stir together the eggs, milk or cream, and Parmesan. Pour the mixture evenly over the *pasticcio*. Bake in the middle of the oven until the top is golden and the *pasticcio* is bubbling, about 20 minutes. Remove from the oven and allow to settle for 10 minutes before cutting into squares. Serve hot.

Maccheroni al Forno con Funghi

Baked Macaroni with Mushrooms

This classic baked macaroni dish was Sunday fare when I was growing up. It is a mushroom lover's delight, as any kind of mushroom, cultivated or wild, can be included. In the traditional version, fresh porcini are used, sometimes combined with dried porcini. As the former are not easily found, the dried porcini are really essential here. I sometimes add half a tin of drained chopped anchovies to the pan, which provides even more depth of flavor.

This pasta dish usually precedes a roast of veal or lamb, though it would also make a fine introduction to a course of any type of fowl or game. Any medium pasta cut may be used, though lumache, rigatoni, fusilli, *or* conchiglie *are traditional.*

(See page 22 for illustration.)

KCal 852 P 21g C 123g S 735mg SFA 11g UFA 20g (4)

INGREDIENTS

½ cup (30g) dried porcini

¾lb (375g) fresh wild or cultivated mushrooms, or a combination

5 tbsp (75ml) olive oil

1 garlic clove, bruised

freshly ground black pepper, to taste

4 tbsp unsalted butter

½ cup (60g) fresh fine white bread crumbs, lightly toasted

1 tsp salt, or to taste

1lb (500g) lumache, rigatoni, fusilli, or conchiglie

2 tbsp chopped fresh flat-leaf parsley

1 Soak the porcini in 2 cups (450ml) warm water for 30 minutes, then drain. Squeeze dry, retaining the soaking liquid, rinse if necessary and squeeze dry. Strain the liquid through paper towels and set aside. Finely chop the porcini.

2 Use a soft brush or cloth to clean the fresh mushrooms. Separate the stems from the caps, discarding any tough stems, then finely chop the mushrooms.

3 Preheat the oven to a temperature of 450°F (230°C).

4 Gently heat 1 tablespoon of olive oil and add the rehydrated porcini. Sauté for 2–3 minutes, stirring. Add the strained liquid to the pan and simmer over very low heat for about 25 minutes, or until the liquid is reduced to about 1 cup (250ml) of sauce. Set aside.

5 Heat 3 tablespoons of olive oil in a separate pan with the bruised garlic, pressing on it with a spoon when it begins to soften to extract the juice. Remove the garlic when golden. Add the chopped fresh mushrooms and stir over medium-low heat until tender, about 12 minutes. Stir in the *porcini* and their liquid and season with pepper.

6 Meanwhile, heat 2 tablespoons of butter and the remaining olive oil. Stir in the bread crumbs. Sauté until lightly golden, tossing to brown them evenly.

7 Bring 4 quarts (5 liters) of water to a boil and add the pasta and 1½ tablespoons of salt. Cook until a shade firmer than *al dente*, then drain, leaving it quite wet. Turn it into a baking dish, while still dripping wet and hot, and toss in the remaining butter, the parsley, and the mushroom mixture.

8 Spread the bread crumb mixture evenly on top. Bake for just 5 minutes in the preheated oven, and serve.

PENNE RIGATE CON RICOTTA AL FORNO ALL'AMENDOLARA

Baked Penne Rigate with Tomato Sauce, Ricotta, and Mozzarella, Amendolara Style

Another delicious recipe in the southern Italian tradition from my friend and well-known cooking teacher, Anna Amendolara Nurse. Because southern Italian pasta-tomato-and-cheese combinations have become so familiar, this recipe is a real crowd-pleaser. However, the use of a freshly made tomato sauce and Italian cheeses makes all the difference in the flavor of the dish. As this recipe is meatless, it makes a good choice for holiday celebrations when meat is eschewed, and is also a natural for the vegetarian pasta lover. Serves 6.

KCal 832 P 42g C 65g S 1110mg SFA 21g UFA 23g (6)

INGREDIENTS

- 1½ cups (350ml) simple tomato sauce (see page 74), fresh tomato sauce (see page 75), tomato sauce with vegetables (see page 75), or other homemade meatless sauce
- 1lb (500g) penne rigate or ziti
- salt, to taste
- 1kg (2lb) ricotta
- ½lb (250g) mozzarella, shredded
- ½ cup (60g) freshly grated pecorino
- 2 large eggs, beaten
- ½ cup (20g) chopped fresh flat-leaf parsley
- freshly ground pepper, to taste

1 Preheat the oven to a temperature of 375°F (190°C).

2 Spoon half the tomato sauce onto the bottom of a 9 x 13in (23 x 32.5cm) baking dish.

3 Bring 4 quarts (5 liters) of water to a rolling boil. Add the *penne* and 1½ tablespoons of salt and cook until not quite *al dente*.

4 Meanwhile, combine and blend the ricotta, mozzarella, half the pecorino, eggs, parsley, and pepper in a large bowl. Check the seasoning.

5 When the pasta is ready, drain and toss in the bowl with the ricotta mixture. Transfer the pasta to the baking dish and spread out evenly. Top with the remaining tomato sauce and sprinkle with the rest of the pecorino cheese. Bake on the upper rack of the oven until bubbly, 20–25 minutes.

ADVANCE PREPARATION

This dish can be prepared a day or two in advance of baking and serving, covered tightly, and refrigerated. The baking time may increase by 5–10 minutes if the dish has been cooked from chilled.

BUCATINI AL FORNO ALL'AMENDOLARA

Baked Bucatini with Chicken and Tomatoes, Amendolara Style

I cannot resist Anna Amendolara's tasty, earthy Apulian dishes, and so inevitably a few make their way into this book. Bucatini *are preferable in this recipe, but* fusilli lunghi *(long* fusilli*),* perciatelli, *or* penne *may be substituted. (See page 22 for illustration.)*

KCal 943 P 61g C 81g S 734mg SFA 9g UFA 31g (4)

INGREDIENTS

- 1½lb (750g) mature, sweet plum tomatoes, cored and seeded, or 7 canned drained tomatoes, seeded
- 3½lb (1.75kg) chicken, cut up, rinsed, and patted dry
- 2 large garlic cloves, cut into slivers
- ½ cup (20g) coarsely chopped fresh flat-leaf parsley
- salt and freshly ground black pepper, to taste
- ⅓ cup (75ml) extra-virgin olive oil
- ¾lb (375g) bucatini
- ⅓ cup (30g) freshly grated pecorino
- 2 cups (450ml) simple tomato sauce (see page 74), fresh tomato sauce (see page 75), or tomato sauce with vegetables (see page 75)

1 Preheat the oven to a temperature of 400°F (200°C).

2 Crush four or five of the tomatoes in your hands and scatter them in a 10 x 14in (25 x 35cm) baking dish. Place the chicken pieces over the tomatoes, skin-side down. Crush the remaining tomatoes and scatter them over the chicken.

3 Tuck the garlic slivers in between the chicken pieces. Scatter the parsley, salt, and pepper over the top then drizzle over the oil. Bake until the chicken is browned on one side, about 30 minutes, then turn and brown the other side, 30–45 minutes. If it starts to dry out, add a little water.

4 Meanwhile, bring 4 quarts (5 liters) of water to a boil. Add the *bucatini* and 1 teaspoon of salt. Stir and cook until not quite *al dente*. Drain and set aside.

5 Remove the chicken from the oven and spread the *bucatini* on top. Sprinkle with pecorino and plenty of pepper. Cover with sauce and bake until heated through and bubbly, 10–15 minutes.

ADVANCE PREPARATION

This dish can be prepared a day or two in advance of baking and serving, covered tightly, and refrigerated. The baking time may increase by 5–10 minutes if the dish has been cooked from chilled.

Conchiglioni al Forno con Ricotta e Spinaci in Salsa Aurora

Baked Pasta Shells with Ricotta, Spinach, and Pine Nut Filling with a Creamy Tomato Sauce

Large pasta* conchiglioni *shells are a popular shape for stuffing and baking, but* lumaconi *("large snails") will also do nicely. The creamy ricotta filling includes spinach, which gives a flavor boost, and chopped pine nuts. ***(See page 23 for illustration.)***

KCal 1242 P 52g C 81g S 1489mg SFA 45g UFA 31g (4)

Preparing Tomato Sauce

Pass the cooled tomato pulp through a food mill placed over a clean pan, pressing out as much pulp as possible.

The resulting sauce will be smooth, light but substantial

INGREDIENTS

½lb (250g) conchiglioni (giant pasta shells)

salt, to taste

3 tbsp fine semolina

2oz (60g) mozzarella, shredded

For the sauce

4lb (2kg) fresh peeled or canned drained plum tomatoes, seeded and crushed or mashed

¼ cup (15g) chopped fresh basil

4 tbsp unsalted butter

½ cup (125ml) heavy cream

¾ tsp salt, or to taste

freshly ground white or black pepper, to taste

For the filling

1½lb (750g) fresh spinach, washed and stems removed

2 tbsp unsalted butter

2lb (1kg) ricotta

⅓ cup (45g) pine nuts

2 egg yolks

2 tbsp freshly grated Parmesan

2 tbsp chopped fresh flat-leaf parsley

½ tsp salt

pinch of freshly grated nutmeg

freshly ground white pepper, to taste

1 For the sauce, simmer the tomatoes in an uncovered pan over medium-low heat until thickened, about 1 hour, stirring occasionally. Remove the pan from the heat and let cool slightly. Pass the tomatoes through a food mill (see left) or press through a strong wire-mesh sieve. The yield will be about 2½ cups (600ml).

2 To make the filling, place the spinach in a pan with just the water clinging to the leaves after washing. Cover and cook until wilted and tender. Let cool then squeeze out the water and finely chop.

3 Melt the butter in a skillet. Add the spinach, sauté for 1 minute, then allow to cool slightly. In a bowl, blend the ricotta with the cooked spinach and other filling ingredients.

4 Bring 4 quarts (5 liters) of water to a boil. Add the *conchiglioni* and 2 tablespoons of salt. Stir and cook until about half-cooked. Drain the pasta and rinse in cold water; drain again thoroughly.

5 Preheat the oven to a temperature of 350°F (180°C).

6 Meanwhile, bring the tomato sauce to a simmer. Stir in the basil, butter, cream, and salt, and heat through. Add pepper. Smear a large baking dish with a little of the tomato sauce.

7 Using a teaspoon, fill each of the shells with some of the ricotta mixture until plump. Sprinkle a little semolina over each to seal. Place the filled shells in the baking dish. Spoon the sauce over the shells, keeping any excess back.

8 Sprinkle the mozzarella over the top, then cover the dish with foil. Bake until bubbly and heated through, adding extra sauce if needed, 30–40 minutes. Remove from the oven and allow to settle for 10 minutes before serving hot.

Advance Preparation

This dish can be prepared up to three days in advance of baking and serving, covered tightly, and refrigerated. Baking time may increase by 5–10 minutes if the dish has been cooked from chilled.

Pennette al Forno con Cavolo e Fontina

Baked Pennette with Cabbage and Fontina

Here is a completely meatless, tasty pasticcio. The flavors of cumin and fontina are in the northern Italian tradition, but this dish is an invention of my mother's. I have found it to be a big hit with vegetarians because it includes several fresh vegetables – fennel, onion, and cabbage, as well as pasta, making it a true one-pot meal.

While the original version was made with the ordinary compact green cabbage, there is no reason why other varieties couldn't be substituted, such as savoy or the various lovely oriental cabbages that have become more widely available. The elongated, celery-shaped varieties will not do well, however. One or two thinly sliced cooked potatoes can be added for a heartier version. Medium-sized pasta shells or a similar short macaroni cut, such as fusilli or broken up ziti, may be substituted for pennette.

(See page 22 for illustration.)

KCal 587 P 25g C 61g S 886mg SFA 13g UFA 12g (4)

INGREDIENTS
1 large fennel bulb
salt, to taste
3 tbsp olive oil
1 large onion, cut into quarters and thinly sliced
1 large garlic clove, very finely chopped
1½ lb (750g) green cabbage, finely shredded
1 tsp crushed fennel seeds
½ tsp cumin seeds
1 tbsp red wine vinegar
½ cup (125ml) tomato sauce passato
½lb (250g) pennette
freshly ground black pepper, to taste
butter for coating dish
7oz (200g) fontina, or substitute Monterey Jack, thinly sliced or shredded

1 Trim the tough bottom off the fennel. Cut off the stalks and feathery leaves. Chop 2 tablespoons of the tender fronds and set aside; reserve the remainder for some other use. Trim any blemishes from the fennel bulbs, then cut them lengthwise into quarters and slice very thin.

2 Bring enough water to cover the fennel to a boil. Add 1 teaspoon of salt and the chopped fennel. Bring to a boil and cook until tender, about 10 minutes. Drain, reserving a cup of the cooking water.

3 Preheat the oven to a temperature of 400°F (200°C).

4 Warm the olive oil in a large skillet over medium-low heat. Add the onion and garlic, and sauté gently until softened, about 5 minutes. Add the fennel and cabbage, and stir well. Cover and cook, stirring occasionally, until the vegetables are softened, 12–15 minutes.

5 Add the fennel seeds, cumin seeds, and vinegar, and mix well. Stir in the tomato passato and 3 tablespoons of the fennel cooking water. Cover partially and cook for an additional 10 minutes.

6 Meanwhile, bring 4 quarts (5 liters) of water to a rolling boil. Add 1½ tablespoons of salt and the *pennette*, stir immediately, and cook over high heat, stirring occasionally to prevent the pasta sticking together. Cook until not quite *al dente*, then drain and add to the skillet with the fennel and cabbage. Toss well, then taste for salt and add pepper to taste.

7 Butter a 9 x 12in (23 x 30cm) baking dish. Pour the fennel, cabbage, and pasta mixture into the dish. Top with the cheese. Cover with foil and bake for 15 minutes, or until heated through. Uncover and bake until lightly golden, about 5 minutes. Remove from the oven, garnish with fennel fronds, and serve.

Advance Preparation

The entire casserole can be assembled up to two days in advance, covered, and refrigerated. The cooking time may increase by 5–10 minutes if the dish has been cooked from chilled.

Tagliatelle al Forno con Tonno

Baked Tagliatelle with Tuna, Tomato, and Sour Cream

The popular version of this dish might be called "tuna noodle casserole," a dish I associate with school dining halls. This, my mother's creation, is nothing like that. I happen to love tuna sauce for pasta, and it works exceptionally well in this baked dish. The light tomato sauce combined with the sour cream ensures the pasta stays perfectly moist as it bakes.

KCal 905 P 42g C 53g S 856mg SFA 24g UFA 33g (4)

Advance Preparation

This dish can be prepared up to two days in advance of baking and serving, covered tightly, and refrigerated. The baking time may increase by 5–10 minutes if the dish has been cooked from chilled.

INGREDIENTS

1 quantity simple tomato sauce (see page 74) or tomato sauce with vegetables (see page 75)

2 x 6½oz (190g) cans high-quality tuna packed in olive oil, drained and flaked

salt, to taste

¾lb (375g) fresh egg pasta (see page 48), cut into tagliatelle (see page 53) or dried tagliatelle

2½ cups (500g) sour cream

1 Bring the tomato sauce to a simmer and stir in the tuna. Simmer for 3–4 minutes to marry the flavors, then remove from the heat and set aside.

2 Bring 4 quarts (5 liters) of water to a rolling boil. Add 1 tablespoon of salt and the pasta. Half-cook the fresh or dried pasta, referring to the instructions for cooking pasta on pages 58–59, or package directions. When the pasta nears the end of its cooking time, ladle ⅓ cup (90ml) of the cooking water into the sour cream and blend; set aside. Drain the pasta then rinse in cool water to separate the strands and set aside.

3 Preheat the oven to a temperature of 400°F (200°C).

4 Pour one third of the tomato sauce on the bottom of a 9 x 12in (23 x 30cm) baking dish. Arrange half the *tagliatelle* over it. Smear half the thinned sour cream over the pasta, then cover with the second third of the tomato sauce. Spread the remaining *tagliatelle* over the sauce, cover with the rest of the sour cream, and finish with the tomato sauce, using a spatula to blend them together slightly.

5 Cover the dish with foil and bake in the middle of the oven for 10 minutes. Remove the foil and continue to bake until bubbly, about 5 more minutes. Remove the dish from the oven, allow it to settle, and serve hot or warm.

Pasticcio di Tagliatelle con Ragù, Salsiccie, e Besciamella

Pasticcio of Tagliatelle with Ragù, Sausages, and Béchamel

Fresh or dried tagliatelle *can be used in this recipe, though fresh* tagliatelle *make a more delicate dish. The Southern-style Ragù made with pork is a favorite of mine and I like to use it in this* pasticcio *to emphasize the flavor of fennel. If preferred, another tomato-based sauce could be substituted, such as any of the other* ragù*, or Tomato Sauce with Wild Mushrooms and Red Wine (see page 76). The addition of béchamel softens the tomato flavor and keeps the pasta moist as it bakes.*

KCal 593 P 24g C 43g S 1133mg SFA 14g UFA 21g (4)

INGREDIENTS

1 tbsp olive oil

¼lb (125g) sweet Italian sausages

½ quantity (½lb/250g) fresh egg pasta (see page 48), cut into tagliatelle (see page 53) or dried tagliatelle

salt, to taste

½ quantity southern-style ragù (see page 74)

½ quantity béchamel (see page 77)

¼ cup (30g) freshly grated Parmesan

1 Warm the olive oil in a skillet. Add the sausages and sauté gently until browned all over and cooked through, about 10 minutes. Drain on paper towels and allow to cool. Cut into thin diagonal slices; set aside.

2 Bring 4 quarts (5 liters) of water to a boil. Add the *tagliatelle* and 1 tablespoon of salt. Stir occasionally to prevent the strands sticking. Half-cook the fresh or dried pasta, referring to cooking instructions on pages 58–59, or package directions. Drain and, while the *tagliatelle* are still dripping slightly, toss with the hot *ragù* and set aside.

3 Preheat the oven to a temperature of 400°F (200°C).

4 Select a 9 x 12in (23 x 30cm) baking dish. Place half the sauced *tagliatelle* in the dish, then cover with 4 tablespoons of béchamel. Scatter some of the sliced sausages over that, and then sprinkle with some of the Parmesan. Repeat the process with a second layer of ingredients, but finish with a layer of béchamel.

5 Bake the *pasticcio* in the middle of the oven until hot and bubbling, about 20 minutes. Remove and allow it to settle for 10 minutes before serving.

Advance Preparation

This dish can be prepared up to three days in advance of baking, covered tightly, and refrigerated. The baking time may increase by 5–10 minutes if the dish has been cooked from chilled.

Ravioli Gratinati

Gratin of Ravioli with Ricotta and Spinach Filling

This dish is made with traditional ricotta and spinach-filled ravioli *(see page 112), but other shapes can be used, as long as the fillings and the sauces are compatible. It's a good, elegant ahead-of-time dish because once the* ravioli *are cooked, they can be sauced and layered with béchamel to keep them moist, then covered and refrigerated for up to three days before baking.*

KCal 1134 P 53g C 56g S 1516mg SFA 40g UFA 34g (4)

INGREDIENTS

1 quantity classic ravioli with ricotta and spinach filling (see page 112)

2–3 tbsp unsalted butter, melted

1 quantity simple tomato sauce (see page 74) or tomato sauce with vegetables (see page 75)

1 quantity béchamel (see page 77)

½ cup (60g) freshly grated Parmesan

1 Cook the *ravioli* as directed, then drain and place on a broad, shallow dish. Drizzle with a little melted butter to prevent them sticking to each other.

2 Preheat the oven to a temperature of 400°F (200°C).

3 Select a baking dish large enough to accommodate the *ravioli* in two layers. Smear a few tablespoons of the tomato sauce on the bottom, then place a layer of *ravioli* over the sauce. Anoint the *ravioli* with just enough tomato sauce to moisten them. Over that, spoon a thin layer of béchamel. Sprinkle with some of the Parmesan. Repeat with the second layer, ending with a layer of béchamel sprinkled with Parmesan.

4 Bake the *ravioli* on the upper rack of the oven until heated through and bubbly, about 20 minutes. Remove from the oven and allow to settle for 10 minutes. Serve hot or warm.

FRITTATA DI PASTA CON MOZZARELLA

Pasta Frittata Stuffed with Mozzarella

The Italians rarely eat leftovers as leftovers, but instead transform them into entirely new dishes. A typical example is this dish, made by folding leftover sauced pasta into a frittata. *While the dish begins cooking in the skillet, it is finished off under the broiler or in the oven to give a golden-brown baked top. I think the dish is improved by inserting a layer of mozzarella in the center. This recipe is best made with strand pasta, such as* spaghetti *or* tagliatelle, *that has been combined with a tomato sauce. Serve it for lunch, as a snack, or as an* antipasto.

KCal 338 P 24g C 9g S 632mg SFA 11g UFA 10g (4)

INGREDIENTS

6 eggs

3 tbsp finely chopped fresh flat-leaf parsley,

⅓ cup (45g) freshly grated Parmesan

½ tsp salt

freshly ground pepper, to taste

6oz (175g) cooked and sauced spaghetti or tagliatelle, cut into small pieces

1 tbsp unsalted butter, melted and mixed with 1 tsp olive oil

¼lb (125g) mozzarella, shredded

1 Beat the eggs with the parsley, Parmesan, salt, pepper, and pasta.

2 Heat the butter and oil in a 10in (25cm) all-metal omelet pan. Add half the egg mixture and cover it with the mozzarella. Pour over the rest of the egg mixture. Cook gently on one side for 10 minutes over medium-low heat, rotating the pan to heat it evenly.

3 Meanwhile, preheat the broiler. Place the *frittata* 6in (15cm) from the broiler flame for 7–10 minutes, or until golden. Test with a toothpick to make sure it is cooked. If it doesn't come out clean, put the *frittata* back under the broiler. If the *frittata* is already browned but runny inside, transfer to an oven preheated to 450°F (230°C) and bake until the center is cooked.

4 Let the *frittata* settle for 5–10 minutes, then invert it onto a serving dish. Cut into wedges, and serve warm or at room temperature.

PASTA AL FORNO PER LE FESTE

FESTIVE BAKED PASTA DISHES

MOLDED OR LAYERED AND BAKED pasta dishes are one of the oldest type of pasta in the Italian kitchen. There are many references to them in accounts of lavish Renaissance feasting. Now, as then, typical ingredients, such as chicken livers, capon, sausages, tiny meatballs, sweetbreads, and mushrooms, are combined with pasta and a sauce and baked. The sauce, usually béchamel, tomato, a *ragù*, or eggs beaten with Parmesan, moistens and unifies the various components. Included in this diverse family are the *timpano* or *sformato*, "molded" pasta, and *timballo*, or "drum," sometimes made with a pastry crust, and baked *lasagne*. This chapter features baked dishes of a particularly festive nature.

Lasagne al Forno con Gamberi e Spinaci

Baked Lasagne with Shrimp and Spinach

There are numerous traditional recipes for lasagne *in Italy. Few contain seafood, but this type of baked dish is an ideal vehicle for fish and shellfish. I created this* lasagne *variation when I had some fresh spinach and shrimp on hand, with very successful results. Despite the use of both béchamel and a small quantity of tomato sauce, the dish is quite light. Fresh pasta is best for this splendid and delicate* lasagne.

KCal 807 P 49g C 52g S 1749mg SFA 25g UFA 19g (4)

INGREDIENTS

½ quantity (½lb/250g) fresh egg pasta (see page 48), unrolled

salt, to taste

For the filling and dressing

2lb (1kg) fresh spinach, washed and stems removed

1lb (500g) fresh raw shrimp, washed and shelled

4 tbsp unsalted butter

1 large onion, very finely chopped

½ tsp salt, or to taste

freshly ground white or black pepper, to taste

½ cup (125ml) plain tomato sauce, such as simple tomato sauce (see page 74)

1 quantity béchamel (see page 77), flavored with nutmeg

½ cup (60g) freshly grated Parmesan

1 Roll the pasta as thin as possible (see pages 50–51). With a knife or fluted pastry wheel, cut the sheets of pasta into 3½ x 4½in (8 x 11cm) rectangles and let them rest on dry dish towels for at least 15 minutes.

2 Meanwhile, bring 4 quarts (5 liters) of water to a rolling boil. Add 1½ tablespoons of salt and slip in the pasta, two or three pieces at a time, and cook for a total of 1 minute. Retrieve with a slotted spoon and immediately immerse in a bowl of cold water (do not put ice in the water as it will make holes in the pasta). Lay the strips on a damp dish towel and finish cooking and cooling all the pasta in the same manner. Do not overlap them. Pat dry.

3 Place the spinach in a large, deep, lidded pan with no water except the drops still clinging to the leaves after washing. Steam the spinach until tender, tossing occasionally for even cooking, 5–10 minutes. Remove from the heat, drain, and leave until cool enough to handle. Using your hands, squeeze out most of the excess water. Finely chop the spinach and set aside.

4 Using a small knife, make a slit down the back of each shrimp and remove the dark intestinal vein. Rinse well under cold running water, pat dry, then finely chop and set aside.

5 Warm the butter in a skillet and add the onion. Sauté over medium heat until wilted, about 4 minutes. Add the shrimp and sauté quickly just until they turn pink, stirring to cook evenly. Remove the pan from the heat and stir in the chopped spinach, salt, and pepper.

6 Preheat the oven to a temperature of 400°F (200°C).

7 Combine the tomato sauce and the béchamel. Select a 10 x 14in (25 x 35cm) baking dish. Smear a very thin layer of sauce on the bottom of the baking dish. Carefully place a layer of the *lasagne* noodles over the sauce, making them touch without overlapping, and covering the entire surface area.

8 Smear a thin layer of sauce over the *lasagne*. Spoon some of the spinach-shrimp mixture over it. Over that, scatter some of the grated Parmesan. Lay down another layer of *lasagne*, making sure there are no gaps and no overlapping. Repeat the process of layering, ending with a layer of *lasagne* topped with béchamel sauce and a sprinkling of Parmesan.

9 Slip the dish onto the middle oven rack. Bake until the sauce forms a light golden crust, about 20 minutes. Do not overcook. Remove the dish from the oven and leave to settle for 10 minutes. Cut into squares, and serve hot.

Advance Preparation

This dish can be prepared one day in advance of baking and serving, covered tightly, and refrigerated. The baking time may increase by 5–10 minutes if the dish has been cooked from chilled.

Lasagne al Forno alla Marcella

Baked Lasagne Stuffed with Spinach and Artichokes

My colleague Marcella Falcomer spent years as an apprentice in some of Milan's most celebrated restaurants. She brought her gift for cooking and her fine Italian training to New York, where she has cooked for some of the city's four-star restaurants. She has shown me many unusual dishes that she has created herself, combining her gift for cooking with an unmistakable Italian style. This dish is one of her creations. (See page 24 for illustration.)

KCal 902 P 42g C 54g S 1622mg SFA 35g UFA 20g (4)

INGREDIENTS
salt, to taste
½ quantity (½lb/250g) fresh egg pasta (see page 48), cut into lasagne sheets (see step 1, page 133)
For the filling
2lb (1kg) fresh spinach, washed and stems removed
3 medium artichokes, about 7oz (200g) each
5 tbsp (75g) unsalted butter, plus butter for dish
freshly ground black pepper, to taste
1 quantity béchamel (see page 77)
1lb (500g) ricotta
½ cup (60g) freshly grated Parmesan

1 Bring 4 quarts (5 liters) of water to a rolling boil. Add 1½ tablespoons of salt, slip in the *lasagne*, two or three pieces at a time, and cook for a total of 1 minute. Retrieve them with a slotted spoon and immediately immerse in a bowl of cold water (do not put ice in the water as it will make holes in the pasta). Lay the strips on a damp dish towel and finish cooking and cooling all the pasta in the same manner. Do not overlap them. Pat dry.

2 Place the spinach in a large, deep, lidded pan with no water except the drops still clinging to the leaves after washing. Steam the spinach over medium heat until tender, tossing occasionally for even cooking, 5–10 minutes. Remove from the heat, drain, and leave until cool enough to handle. Using your hands, squeeze out most of the excess water. Finely chop the spinach and set aside.

3 Trim the artichokes (see page 101), then put into water acidulated with vinegar or lemon juice to prevent browning. When all of the artichokes have been trimmed, drain them. Place each artichoke half cut-side down and cut lengthwise into ¼in (5mm) thick slices.

4 Combine 1 tablespoon of butter, 1 cup (250ml) water, and ½ teaspoon of salt and pepper in a pan and add the artichokes. Cover and simmer until tender, 4–8 minutes, depending on their freshness. Remove the pan from the heat, drain thoroughly, and then set the artichokes aside to cool.

5 Chop the cooled artichokes together with the spinach until well minced. Warm 1 tablespoon of butter in a pan, and add the artichoke–spinach mixture, stirring until well-incorporated; set aside.

6 Preheat the oven to a temperature of 375°F (190°C).

7 Melt the remaining butter in a small pan and set aside. Butter a 10 x 14in (25 x 35cm) baking dish. Spread a thin layer of béchamel on the bottom of the dish. Place a layer of *lasagne* noodles over the sauce, making them touch without overlapping, and covering the entire dish. Spread a thin layer of béchamel over that, then some artichoke–spinach mixture.

8 Spoon over a layer of ricotta and then some of the grated Parmesan. Make another layer of *lasagne*, ensuring there are no gaps and no overlapping. Repeat the process of layering, ending with *lasagne* topped with béchamel and melted butter.

9 Slip the dish onto the middle rack of the oven. Bake until the béchamel sauce forms a light golden crust, about 20 minutes. Immediately remove the dish from the oven. Allow it to settle for 10 minutes, then cut into squares, and serve hot.

Advance Preparation

This dish can be prepared up to three days in advance of baking and serving, covered tightly, and refrigerated. The baking time may increase by 5–10 minutes if the dish has been cooked from chilled.

Lasagne al Forno con Melanzane e Patate alla Serra

Baked Lasagne with Eggplant and Potatoes, Serra Style

My dear friends Valerie and Elio Serra gave me this recipe, which originated with their family in the Veneto. In the original version, the eggplant was breaded and deep-fried. In Valerie's version, the eggplant slices are brushed with olive oil and rosemary and then baked before being assembled with the other ingredients in the casserole. This method makes the dish a great deal lighter without any compromise in flavor. The eggplant should be fairly small and as fresh as possible, which makes salting and draining unnecessary before cooking. Valerie often uses dried* lasagne *for a quick baked dish, but fresh* lasagne *noodles work well too.

KCal 909 P 29g C 89g S 924mg SFA 15g UFA 34g (4)

Advance Preparation

This dish can be prepared up to three days in advance of baking and serving, covered tightly, and refrigerated. The baking time may increase by 5–10 minutes if the dish has been cooked from chilled.

INGREDIENTS

10oz (300g) dried lasagne noodles

salt, to taste

For the sauce

4 tbsp extra-virgin olive oil

1 onion, finely chopped

2lb 3oz (1kg 90g) canned drained tomatoes, seeded and crushed

8 large fresh basil leaves, torn into very small pieces

salt and freshly ground black pepper, to taste

For the filling

7 medium new potatoes, peeled and very thinly sliced

1 purple or white eggplant, about ¾lb (375g)

⅓ cup (75ml) olive oil

1 tsp chopped fresh rosemary, or ½ tsp dried rosemary

⅙ tsp salt

freshly ground pepper, to taste

6oz (175g) fontina, cut into very small dice

⅓ cup (45g) freshly grated pecorino or Parmesan

1 To make the sauce, warm the olive oil in a pan. Add the onion and sauté until wilted, about 4 minutes. Add the tomatoes, basil, and salt and pepper to taste. Cook over medium heat, stirring frequently, for about 30 minutes. Remove from the heat. The sauce should not be very thick as liquid is needed to keep the baked dish moist.

2 Meanwhile, soak the sliced potatoes in cold water for 2 minutes to remove excess starch. Drain, then pat dry with paper towels and set aside.

3 Preheat the oven to a temperature of 375°F (190°C).

4 Peel the skin off the eggplant and remove the stem and navel. Cut it in half crosswise and then into thin slices.

5 Combine the olive oil, rosemary, salt, and pepper; brush the eggplant slices on both sides with the mixture. Place them on baking sheets and bake until tender and lightly colored, about 30 minutes. Remove from the oven and allow to cool slightly.

6 Meanwhile, bring 4 quarts (5 liters) of water to a rolling boil. Add the *lasagne*, two or three strips at a time, and 1½ tablespoons of salt and half-cook the pasta, stirring occasionally to prevent sticking. Drain the *lasagne* and rinse in cool water; drain well again.

7 Pour one third of the tomato sauce into a 9 x 12in (23 x 30cm) baking dish. Place half of the *lasagne* over it, using a spoon to moisten it with the sauce. Cover with half the eggplant and half the potatoes, then add a second layer of sauce and half the cheeses. Repeat the layering process, finishing with the remaining sauce and cheeses.

8 Cover the dish with foil, slide it onto the middle rack of the oven, and bake until bubbly and golden, about 45 minutes. Remove from the oven, let settle for 10 minutes, and serve.

Lasagne al Forno con Melanzane e Ragù

Baked Lasagne with Eggplant and Ragù

I am very fond of eggplant, particularly when they are young and not full of large, bitter seeds. Here is a very delicate and delicious* lasagne *I devised for fresh noodles. If small eggplants are not available, be sure to salt and drain larger ones. When selecting eggplant, look for those that have taut, unwrinkled skins and small navels (these are the male vegetable and are less seedy). Fresh eggplant have stems that are still green, not wrinkled and brown.
(See page 24 for illustration.)

KCal 983 P 43g C 54g S 1111mg SFA 31g UFA 32g (4)

Advance Preparation

This dish can be prepared up to three days in advance of baking and serving, covered tightly, and refrigerated. The baking time may increase by 5–10 minutes if the dish has been cooked from chilled.

INGREDIENTS

- ½ quantity (½lb/250g) fresh egg pasta (see page 48), cut into lasagne sheets (see step 1, page 133)
- 2 or 3 young eggplants, total weight 1½–2lb (750g–1kg), washed, and stems and navels trimmed
- extra-virgin olive oil for brushing eggplants
- salt and freshly ground pepper, to taste
- 2 cups (500ml) béchamel (see page 77)
- 2½ cups (600ml) bolognese sauce (see page 73), southern-style ragù (see page 74) or Tuscan ragù (see page 72)
- 60g (2oz) freshly grated Parmesan

1 Blanch the fresh *lasagne* as described in step 2, page 133.

2 Preheat the oven to a temperature of 375°F (190°C).

3 Cut the eggplants into ⅛in (2.5mm) thick disks. Cut each slice in half. Mix enough olive oil to cover the eggplant with a pinch of salt and pepper. Brush the slices on both sides. Place on baking sheets and bake until golden, 20–30 minutes. Allow to cool slightly.

4 Raise the oven temperature to 400°F (200°C). Spread a thin layer of béchamel on the bottom of a 10 x 14in (25 x 35cm) baking dish. Place a layer of *lasagne* over the sauce, making them touch without overlapping.

5 Spread a thin layer of *ragù* over the *lasagne.* Scatter some Parmesan on top. Over that, arrange some of the eggplant slices and another thin layer of béchamel. Make a second layer of *lasagne.* Repeat the process of layering, ending with *lasagne* topped with béchamel and Parmesan.

6 Bake until the béchamel forms a light golden crust, about 20 minutes. Allow to settle for 10 minutes before serving.

Lasagne Semplici al Forno con Salsiccia

Simple Baked Lasagne with Sausage

Here is a simple* lasagne *in comparison to the more elaborate versions often made for holidays or special occasions. Dried or fresh* lasagne *noodles can be used, of either spinach or egg variety.

KCal 1744 P 69g C 126g S 2524mg SFA 44g UFA 62g (4)

Advance Preparation

This dish can be prepared up to three days in advance of baking and serving, covered tightly, and refrigerated. The baking time may increase by 5–10 minutes if the dish has been cooked from chilled.

INGREDIENTS

- 1lb (500g) dried lasagne noodles
- salt, to taste

For the filling

- 2½ cups (625g) canned tomatoes in passato, seeded
- ½ cup (175g) tomato paste dissolved in 1 cup (250ml) water
- ⅓ cup (75ml) extra-virgin olive oil
- 1 small onion, very finely chopped
- 1 large garlic clove, very finely chopped
- 1 tbsp chopped fresh basil
- ½ tsp chopped fresh marjoram, or ¼ tsp dried marjoram
- ¾ tsp salt
- 1½lb (750g) sweet Italian sausage meat, crumbled
- 1lb (500g) ricotta
- ⅛ tsp freshly grated nutmeg
- ½lb (250g) mozzarella, shredded
- ¼ cup (30g) freshly grated Parmesan

1 Blanch the dried *lasagne* as described in step 6, page 135, reserving ¼ cup (60ml) of the cooking water for thinning the ricotta.

2 Preheat the oven to a temperature of 375°F (190°C).

3 Liquefy the tomatoes with the passato and the paste mixture in a food processor. Warm 4 tablespoons of the olive oil in a pan and sauté the onion and garlic until soft. Add the tomato mixture, herbs, and salt. Simmer gently until thickened, about 30 minutes. Heat the remaining oil in a skillet and fry the sausage until golden.

4 Blend the ricotta, cooking water, and nutmeg. Smear tomato sauce on the bottom of a 8 x 12in (20 x 30cm) baking dish. Cover with a layer of *lasagne*. Spoon some sauce over, then make layers of sausage, ricotta, and mozzarella. Repeat the layers, topping the mozzarella with Parmesan. Bake in the middle of the preheated oven for 25 minutes. Allow to settle for 10 minutes before serving.

TIMBALLO DI PASTA CON POLPETTINE

Timballo of Pasta with Meatballs in Short-Crust Pastry

Pasta encased in a pastry "drum" was a dish of the nobility in Renaissance times. The crust was traditionally sweet, but I prefer unsweetened pastry. It is best baked immediately after assembly. ***(See page 25 for illustration.)***

KCal 788 P 44g C 87g S 1252mg SFA 14g UFA 15g (4)

INGREDIENTS

For the sauced pasta filling

salt, to taste

¾lb (375g) short ziti, penne, or other medium tubular macaroni

½ quantity béchamel (see page 77)

½ cup (60g) freshly grated Parmesan

1½ cups (350ml) ragù or tomato sauce (any of those in pages 71–75 is suitable)

For the meatballs

2 slices stale white bread, crusts removed, cubed

4 tbsp milk or stock for soaking bread

¾lb (375g) ground beef, or a combination of ground beef and pork

1oz (30g) prosciutto, sliced and coarsely chopped

½ small onion, coarsely grated

1 tbsp freshly grated Parmesan

1 tbsp chopped fresh flat-leaf parsley

¾ tsp salt

freshly ground black pepper, to taste

1 egg white, beaten

vegetable oil for frying meatballs

flour for dredging meatballs

For the pastry crust

4½ cups (560g) unbleached white flour, chilled

1 tsp salt, plus an extra pinch

¾lb (375g) unsalted butter, chilled, or equal amounts of butter and lard, chilled

⅔ cup (150ml) ice water

2 eggs, beaten

unsalted butter and flour for coating pan

1 egg, separated, for brushing crust

FOR THE PASTRY

1 Mix the flour and the teaspoon of salt. Cut the butter into the flour with two knives, a pastry cutter, or in a food processor on low speed, until thumbnail-sized pieces are formed. They should be no smaller.

2 Mix the ice water into the beaten eggs. Slowly add the liquid to the flour mixture and stir by hand until the dough holds together when pinched. If there is too much liquid for the dough, do not use it all. If you are using a food processor, engage it for only 5 seconds (do not allow the dough to form a ball).

3 Quickly gather up the dough with your hands into two balls, making one about twice the size of the other. For a proper flaky crust it is important not to overwork the dough. Press each ball into a thick disk and wrap loosely in plastic wrap. Chill for 2 hours.

FOR THE MEATBALLS

1 Combine the ingredients for the meatballs in a bowl. Shape the mixture into balls about the size of large olives.

2 Heat the oil for frying the meatballs in a pan. When it is hot enough to make the meatballs sizzle, dredge them lightly in flour and slip them into the pan. Fry until browned and cooked through, turning occasionally, about 8 minutes. Drain on paper towels.

TO ASSEMBLE

1 Preheat the oven to a temperature of 375°F (190°C).

2 Roll the pastry disks on a floured surface until about ⅛in (2.5mm) thick. The larger disk should line the bottom and sides of an 8in (20cm) springform pan; the smaller disk will form the lid. Work quickly to avoid overworking the dough.

3 Butter the springform pan and dust with flour. Roll the larger disk around a rolling pin and transfer to the pan. Unroll it gently, centering it over the pan. Gently push the pastry into the bottom of the pan to shape it, taking care not to tear it. Do not trim the excess dough (it should join the pastry lid later).

4 Brush the inside of the pie crust with egg white and allow to dry. (This will help prevent the bottom from becoming soggy.) Combine the remaining egg white with the yolk and a pinch of salt and set aside for glazing the outside crust.

5 Bring 3 quarts (3.75 liters) of water to a boil. Add 1½ tablespoons of salt and the pasta. Cook until not quite *al dente* (it should be firm). Drain the pasta, taking care not to overdrain, and toss with the béchamel and Parmesan. Combine this with the meatballs and chosen sauce.

6 Turn the sauced pasta and meatballs into the pastry casing. Drape the second pastry disk over a rolling pin and center it over the *timballo*. It should rest evenly on top of the pan. Crimp the edges of the top and bottom crust together with your fingers; do not allow the crust to overlap the edges of the pan. Cut off any excess pastry and reserve the scraps.

7 Cut a small hole in the center of the top pie crust and roll out the scraps of pastry. Cut them into a decorative flower. Place the "flower" over the hole, leaving vents for steam to escape.

8 Brush the entire crust with the egg wash, taking care not to touch the edges of the pan. Bake the *timballo* in the preheated oven for 1 hour, or until golden. Remove and let stand for about 10 minutes. Carefully remove the pan ring and present the *timballo* whole at the table. Cut into slices, and serve.

Timpano di Tagliatelle con Salsa di Vitello

Timpano of Egg Noodles with Veal, Lemon, and Sage Sauce

Here is a really lovely, elegant dish in which cooked* tagliatelle *are combined with béchamel sauce, then baked in a mold. The result is a savory noodle* budino, *pudding of sorts, in the shape of a ring. Some of the sauce is placed in the middle; the remainder is served on the side. Depending on the accompanying sauce, the* timpano *can be made with dried or fresh egg noodles, spinach noodles, or other flavored noodles, though I prefer to use fresh pasta because it retains its moisture and produces a more delicate end result.

KCal 1225 P 78g C 84g S 812mg SFA 31g UFA 27g (4)

INGREDIENTS
1 quantity béchamel (see page 77)
salt and freshly ground pepper, to taste
½ small onion, grated
butter, to coat mold
5 tbsp bread crumbs for coating mold
salt, to taste
1 quantity (1lb/500g) fresh egg pasta (see page 48), cut into tagliatelle (see page 53)
For the veal sauce
2lb (1kg) veal scaloppine, pounded very thin
flour for dredging
salt and freshly ground pepper, to taste
3oz (90g) unsalted butter
2 tbsp extra-virgin olive oil
1 cup (250ml) dry white wine
16 fresh sage leaves, chopped, plus additional for garnish, or 1 tsp dried crumbled sage
2 tbsp freshly squeezed lemon juice
1½ cups (350ml) light meat broth (see page 68)

1 Warm the béchamel. Add salt and pepper to taste and the onion. Continue stirring until the sauce is just thick enough to coat a spoon lightly.

2 Preheat the oven to a temperature of 375°F (190°C).

3 Prepare a mold with a hole in the center (see step 1, opposite).

4 Bring 4 quarts (5 liters) of water to a boil. Add 1½ tablespoons of salt and the *tagliatelle*. Stir frequently to prevent the noodles sticking together. Cook until the *tagliatelle* are slightly undercooked, then drain, taking care not to overdrain (the pasta should still be dripping a little). Toss the noodles with the béchamel sauce and transfer them to the mold.

5 Bake the mold in the preheated oven for 25–30 minutes, or until the top is golden. Remove it from the oven and allow to settle for 10 minutes. Carefully unmold the *timpano* (see step 2, opposite) onto a large serving platter.

6 While the *timpano* is baking, cut the veal into pieces about 2 x 3in (5 x 7cm) each. Place the flour on a plate and season with salt and pepper. Heat half the butter and half the olive oil in a large skillet. Dredge as many pieces of the veal in the flour as will fit comfortably in the pan – do not flour all the meat at once as the flour coating will become soggy as it rests.

7 Sauté the veal pieces in batches for 1–2 minutes on each side, until golden on the outside but still pink inside (they must have space to sauté properly). Transfer to a plate. Add the remaining oil and butter to the pan and sauté the rest of the veal. Take care not to overcook the scaloppine, or they will toughen. Transfer to a plate.

8 Add the wine to the pan with the meat drippings and allow to evaporate over medium heat, about 3 minutes. Add the sage, lemon juice, and broth. Simmer for 2 minutes, then check the seasoning. Return the veal to the skillet and warm through in the sauce. Remove the sauce from the heat.

9 Arrange the veal sauce in the unmolded *timpano* (see step 3, opposite). Garnish with sage leaves if available, and serve the sauce on the side.

MAKING A TIMPANO

1 Use soft butter to grease the mold, then sprinkle it generously with bread crumbs, tilting the pan to coat it evenly.

2 If using a springform mold, release the spring. Using a cloth, gently lift the hot pan off the timpano *and allow to drop onto the plate.*

3 Spoon as much veal and sauce as will fit into the middle of the mold and surround the ring with the remainder.

Fresh *tagliatelle* noodles remain moist after baking

Cannelloni al Forno con Pollo e Funghi

Cannelloni with Chicken and Mushroom Stuffing in Béchamel Sauce

There are both fresh and dried forms of* cannelloni, *"large reeds" or tubes, which are filled with savory stuffings, moistened with a sauce or sauces, and baked. This filling has a very delicate flavor and is perfect with* cannelloni *or* fazzoletti *(see page 120). (See page 24 for illustration.)

KCal 945 P 50g C 68g S 1245mg SFA 27g UFA 24g (4)

INGREDIENTS

½lb (250g) dried cannelloni or ½ quantity (½lb/250g) fresh egg pasta (see page 48), rolled as thinly as possible (see pages 52–53) and cut into 3½ x 4½in (8 x 11cm) cannelloni wrappers

salt, to taste

For the filling and dressing

½lb (250g) wild or cultivated mushrooms

4 tbsp unsalted butter

3 shallots or 1 small onion, very finely chopped

3 boneless chicken breasts, minced

2oz (60g) thinly sliced prosciutto, ham, or mortadella, chopped

⅓ tsp ground cloves

salt and freshly ground white or black pepper, to taste

1 egg and 1 egg yolk, beaten

1 quantity béchamel (see page 77)

1 cup (250ml) simple tomato sauce (see page 74) or tomato sauce with vegetables (see page 75), puréed

¼ cup (30g) freshly grated Parmesan

1 To make the filling, use a soft brush or cloth to remove any dirt clinging to the mushrooms. Slice off and discard the hard tips. Thinly slice the caps, then chop them.

2 Melt the butter in a skillet. Add the shallots or onion, and sauté gently until wilted. Add the mushrooms, minced chicken, prosciutto, ham or mortadella, cloves, salt, and pepper. Sauté gently until the chicken is lightly colored, stirring frequently, about 5 minutes. Remove from the heat and allow to cool.

3 Preheat the oven to a temperature of 400°F (200°C).

4 Blend the egg and egg yolk and 3 tablespoons of béchamel sauce with the chicken mixture.

5 Bring 4 quarts (5 liters) of water to a rolling boil. Add the dried *cannelloni* and 1½ tablespoons of salt. Half-cook the pasta, stirring occasionally to prevent sticking. If using fresh *cannelloni* wrappers, blanch them briefly in the boiling water, then drain and rinse in cool water. Let cool on damp dish towels. Pat with a dry dish towel.

6 Smear 2–3 tablespoons of tomato sauce on the bottom of a baking dish. Push 1–2 tablespoons of filling into the *cannelloni* tubes, or fill the fresh *cannelloni* wrappers as shown below. Arrange them side by side in a single layer in the dish.

7 Spoon the remaining tomato sauce over the *cannelloni* and spoon béchamel over that. Sprinkle with Parmesan.

8 Bake the *cannelloni* in the middle of the oven until bubbly and golden, about 15 minutes. Allow to settle for 10 minutes before serving.

Stuffing Cannelloni

1 Place 2 generous tablespoons of filling along the short end of each fresh pasta rectangle, covering a third of the area.

2 Roll up each rectangle, starting at the filled end, to make a secure bundle. Place in the baking dish in a single layer.

The two sauces keep the pasta moist

Cannelloni al Forno con Carne di Vitello e Funghi

Baked Fresh Cannelloni with Veal and Mushroom Stuffing

This is a dish I enjoyed in Bologna, where cannelloni are always made with delicate fresh egg pasta. Veal is used more frequently than beef in meat stuffings – a reflection of the Italian penchant for the delicate, tender meat of younger animals and the necessity of slaughtering cattle at an early age due to a lack of pasturage.

Veal is not so popular outside Italy and people often ask if they can make this type of filling with chicken. While veal is subtle in taste, chicken is bland in comparison so the amount of mortadella or prosciutto should be increased proportionally. Ground turkey, which has more flavor than chicken, is another possible substitute. However, to experience the authentic flavor of this fine stuffing, use veal. This cannelloni filling includes a small quantity of potato purée, which I like to add to give more body and a smoother texture. Makes about 24 cannelloni; enough for 4 as a substantial first course.

KCal 856 P 50g C 46g S 1917mg SFA 25g UFA 25g (4)

INGREDIENTS

½ quantity (½lb/250g) fresh egg pasta (see page 48), rolled as thinly as possible (see pages 52–53) and cut into 8 x 11cm (3½ x 4½in) cannelloni wrappers

salt, to taste

For the filling

1 small boiling potato, about ¼lb (125g), scrubbed

5 tbsp (75g) unsalted butter

3 large shallots or 1 onion, very finely chopped

1lb (500g) high-quality ground veal

3oz (90g) thinly sliced mortadella or prosciutto, chopped

⅓ tsp ground cloves

¼ tsp freshly ground nutmeg

10oz (300g) mushrooms, cleaned, quartered, and very thinly sliced

¾ tsp salt, or to taste

4 tbsp dry white wine

⅓ cup (45g) freshly grated Parmesan

¼ tsp freshly ground white pepper

1 egg and 1 egg yolk, beaten

For the dressing

1 cup (250ml) simple tomato sauce (see page 74), puréed, or tomato sauce with vegetables (see page 75), puréed

½ quantity béchamel (see page 77)

1 To make the filling, boil the whole potato until tender. Drain and when cool enough to handle but still warm, peel and mash in a potato ricer (for best results) or with a masher.

2 Warm the butter in a large skillet and add the shallots or onion. Sauté until wilted, about 4 minutes, then add the veal, mortadella or prosciutto, cloves, nutmeg, mushrooms, and salt. Sauté the mixture over medium-low heat until the veal is barely pink, 4–5 minutes, using a wooden spoon to break up the meat. Do not let the meat get hard and brown.

3 Stir in the wine and allow to evaporate, about 1 minute. Remove from the heat and blend in the mashed potato, grated Parmesan, and pepper. Allow to cool slightly, then blend in the egg and egg yolk.

4 Blanch the fresh *cannelloni* wrappers as described in step 5, opposite.

5 Put 2 generous tablespoons of the filling along the short end of each rectangle, covering a third of the area. Roll up each rectangle, starting at the filled end, as shown opposite.

6 Preheat the oven to a temperature of 400°F (200°C).

7 Select a large rectangular baking dish. Heat the tomato and béchamel sauces separately, using a whisk to beat the béchamel to remove any lumps.

8 Smear a very thin layer of béchamel on the bottom of the baking dish. Place the *cannelloni* in the dish, seam-side up and side by side without overlapping. Smear with a layer of tomato sauce and over that spread a layer of béchamel. (You may have some sauce left over.)

9 Slip the dish onto the middle rack of the oven. Bake until heated through and bubbly, about 10 minutes. Do not overcook. Let settle for 10 minutes before serving.

GNOCCHI

GNOCCHI AND DUMPLINGS

IN COLLOQUIAL ITALIAN, *GNOCCO* refers to a person whose personality is similar to that of a "lump." In culinary terms it refers to dumplings whose composition is varied. There are other types of *gnocchi* besides those that are formed into dumplings, then boiled and served with a sauce, or cooked and eaten in broth. The Roman kitchen produces a hardened porridge of semolina, eggs, milk, and cheese, which is baked with butter and cheese. Those found in Sardinia are made of hardened cornmeal polenta, or semolina mush, formed into disks and baked with a tomato sauce and sheep milk cheese. The various types of *gnocchi* found in the Italian kitchen are represented in this chapter.

GNOCCHI DI RICOTTA
Ricotta Spoon Gnocchi with Tomato Sauce

Gnocchi di Ricotta

Ricotta Spoon Gnocchi with Tomato Sauce

I have found people to be intimidated by the prospect of making these lovely gnocchi, perhaps as the ratio of ricotta to flour is high and it would seem that they would fall apart. In fact, they are easy to make, as long as the ricotta is dry (see below). A fresh or fruity tomato sauce goes best with them. Stir a generous amount of basil into the cooked sauce, and perhaps a little good extra-virgin olive oil.

KCal 638 P 31g C 28g S 786mg SFA 21g UFA 21g (4)

Tip

Ricotta varies greatly in consistency. If using soft, runny ricotta, drain it before use so that the gnocchi do not absorb too much flour and become heavy. The day before you plan to make the gnocchi, or up to two days before, place the ricotta in a sieve suspended over a bowl. Cover and refrigerate overnight until it has a firm consistency.

INGREDIENTS

salt, to taste

2lb (1kg) ricotta, drained if necessary (see Tip, left)

¼ cup (30g) freshly grated Parmesan, plus extra to serve

3 tbsp chopped fresh flat-leaf parsley,

¼ tsp freshly grated nutmeg

¾ cup (90g) plain flour, or more if necessary

To serve

1 quantity fresh tomato sauce (see page 75) or tomato sauce with vegetables (see page 75)

8 large basil leaves, torn into very small pieces, plus extra for garnish

1–2 tbsp extra-virgin olive oil (optional)

1 Bring 4 quarts (5 liters) of water to a boil in a large pan then add 2 tablespoons of salt.

2 Meanwhile, thoroughly blend the ricotta, Parmesan, parsley, nutmeg, 1 teaspoon of salt, and the flour in a bowl.

3 Using two teaspoons, take enough of the mixture to make a dumpling approximately the size of a walnut.

4 Drop the dumpling into the boiling water. When it floats to the surface, 30–45 seconds, retrieve it with a slotted spoon. If the dumpling holds together, proceed to make *gnocchi* out of the rest of the dough, dropping in only as many at a time as you can easily retrieve. If the first *gnocco* is too soft, add as much flour as is needed to make the mixture firm, but take care that it does not become heavy.

5 Transfer the cooked *gnocchi* to a large plate. Do not pile them up, but arrange in one layer.

6 While the *gnocchi* are cooking, warm the sauce. Remove it from the heat and stir in the basil and olive oil, if using. Spoon the sauce over the *gnocchi*, garnish with basil, and sprinkle with Parmesan.

Gnocchi di Ricotta e Spinaci

Ricotta and Spinach Spoon Gnocchi

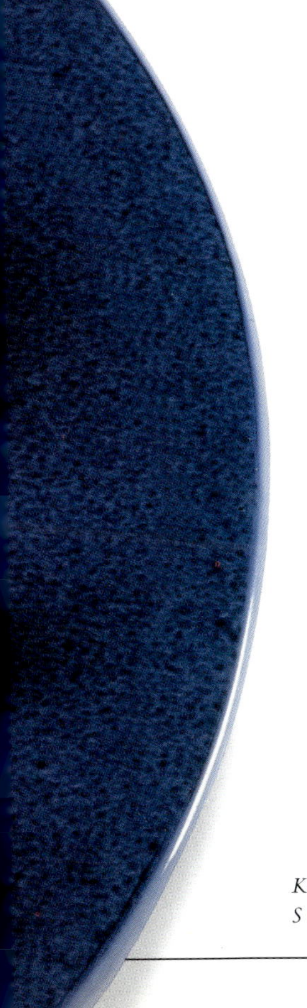

KCal 375 P 31g C 18g S 1567mg SFA 11g UFA 8g (4)

INGREDIENTS

4lb (2kg) fresh spinach, washed and stems removed

1lb (500g) ricotta, drained (see Tip, above)

4 tbsp finely grated onion

¼ cup (30g) freshly grated Parmesan, plus extra to serve

¼ cup (30g) all-purpose flour, or more if necessary

⅓ tsp freshly grated nutmeg

salt, to taste

4 large egg whites

freshly ground white or black pepper, to taste

1 Place the spinach in a large pan with no water except the drops still clinging to the leaves after washing. Cover and steam until tender, tossing occasionally but replacing the lid, about 5–10 minutes. Remove from the heat, drain, and leave until cool enough to handle. Squeeze out as much water from the spinach as possible. Chop the spinach very finely and set aside.

2 Use a wooden spoon to combine the ricotta, spinach, 1 teaspoon of salt, and the other ingredients. Bring 4 quarts (5 liters) of water to a boil in a large pan. Add 2 tablespoons of salt.

3 Using two teaspoons, take enough of the mixture to make a dumpling approximately the size of a walnut.

4 Drop the dumpling into the boiling water. When it floats to the surface, 30–45 seconds, retrieve it with a slotted spoon. If the dumpling holds together, proceed to make *gnocchi* out of the rest of the dough, dropping in only as many at a time as you can easily retrieve. If the first *gnocco* is too soft, add as much flour as is needed to make the mixture firm, but take care that it does not become heavy.

5 Transfer the cooked *gnocchi* to a large, warm plate, arranging them in one layer. Sprinkle with Parmesan, and serve.

GNOCCHI DI PATATE CON PESTO ALLA SILVANA

Potato Gnocchi with Pesto, Silvana Style

***Many recipes for potato** gnocchi **include eggs, or egg whites, and even baking powder. While eggs help to bind the dough, they add more moisture to the mixture, making it necessary to use additional flour. Egg also gives** gnocchi **an unappealing bouncy quality. While it is impossible to give an exact recipe for potato** gnocchi **as the amount of flour needed depends on the moisture content of the potatoes, there is one hard and fast rule: the less flour, the lighter the** gnocchi.*

KCal 609 P 13g C 58g S 827mg SFA 11g UFA 25g (4)

PREPARING GNOCCHI

1 Roll the dough into a rope about ¾in (1.5cm) thick. For smaller gnocchi (gnocchetti), *roll it into ropes ½in (1cm) thick. Cut the rope into ¾in (1.5cm) pieces, or ½in (1cm) pieces if making* gnocchetti. *Take each piece of dough and roll it into a ball.*

2 Taking the dough ball between thumb and forefinger, drag it along the ridges of a wooden butter paddle or over the medium-sized holes of a grater, pushing your thumb into it as you do so. A concave dumpling will result (the hollow makes them light and allows even cooking).

INGREDIENTS

For the gnocchi

1½lb (750g) boiling or baking potatoes of uniform size

approximately 1 cup (125g) all-purpose flour, plus additional as needed

salt, to taste

⅛ tsp freshly ground white pepper

To serve

1 quantity basil pesto, Silvana style (see page 107)

freshly grated Parmesan

1 Preheat the oven to a temperature of 400°F (200°C).

2 Place the potatoes on a baking sheet and cook until tender, 45 minutes–1 hour, depending on size. Meanwhile, line three baking sheets with dish towels.

3 Measure the flour onto a large pastry board or work surface. Make a well in the center. When the potatoes are cool enough to handle but still warm, lift off their skins with a paring knife. They must still be warm when combined with the flour. Pass the potatoes through a ricer directly into the well of flour (or mash by hand and add to the flour). Evenly sprinkle 1 teaspoon of salt and the pepper over the mashed potatoes.

4 Incorporate the flour into the potatoes, drawing the flour in as you work to form a uniform, tender dough. The amount of flour absorbed will depend on the moisture content of the potatoes so work it in gradually. Do not overwork the dough; it should be quite soft without being at all sticky.

5 Knead the dough lightly for 5 minutes. Cut into four parts. Work with one quarter at a time and keep the remainder covered and refrigerated until ready to use (but no longer than 30 minutes). Form the *gnocchi* as shown left. If the mixture becomes a little sticky, dust the ropes and the paddle or grater with flour. If the dough is too sticky altogether, form it into a ball again and knead in a little more flour before proceeding.

6 Transfer the *gnocchi* to the baking sheets, arranging them in a single layer. The uncooked *gnocchi* can be refrigerated for up to 3 hours, if desired.

7 Spread a little of the *pesto* on the bottom of a shallow serving dish, or grease with butter, and keep warm.

8 Bring 4 quarts (5 liters) of water to a boil in a large pan and add 2 tablespoons of salt. Pick up one of the cloths holding the *gnocchi* and slide the contents into the water. Stir with a wooden spoon. As soon as the *gnocchi* float to the surface, scoop out with a slotted spoon and let drain in a colander for 2–3 minutes. Repeat with the remaining batches.

9 Transfer the *gnocchi* to the serving dish, arranging them in a single layer. Take a few teaspoons of the cooking water and mix it into the *pesto* to give it a creamy consistency. Spoon the *pesto* over the *gnocchi* and scatter Parmesan lightly over the top. Serve immediately.

TIP

Because the ideal is to introduce as little flour as possible, the potatoes should be fairly old; recently harvested potatoes are higher in water content. Baking is the driest cooking method, although the potatoes may be boiled or steamed in their skins. It is best to use a potato ricer to mash the cooked potatoes. A hand-masher or fork does not remove lumps as effectively, while a food processor makes cooked potatoes gluey.

ADVANCE PREPARATION

Once completed, the baking sheets full of gnocchi *can be covered with foil or waxed paper and refrigerated for up to 3 hours. For longer storage, cook the* gnocchi *as directed, then place in a single layer in the freezer until frozen solid, which will take several hours. Frozen* gnocchi *can be transferred to a plastic bag or container and frozen for up to one month. To reheat, drop directly into boiling salted water, cook until they float to the surface, and serve as directed.*

GNOCCHI DI PATATE CON RAGÙ DI MANZO

Potato Gnocchi with Beef Ragù

Potato gnocchi *are often served with a tomato sauce or meat sauce. I particularly like this beef* ragù *with the flavor of the* gnocchi*. It is a spontaneous creation of my mother's that almost harkens back to the meat sauces of the eighteenth century.*

The ragù *of those times and up until the 1900s did not make use of tomatoes, but there was a great reliance upon cinnamon, nutmeg, and other spices. The meat was often cut into small pieces or shredded rather than ground, which gave the sauce the feeling of an* intingolo*, a light stew. This contemporary* ragù*, lightly scented with cloves, is very much in that genre. It is also lovely with homemade* pappardelle *(see page 52), or even dried macaroni cuts, such as* gnocchetti *and* cavatelli*.*

KCal 669 P 52g C 72g S 1101mg SFA 6g UFA 14g (4)

INGREDIENTS

1 quantity potato gnocchi (see opposite)

For the ragù

3 tbsp extra-virgin olive oil
¼ cup (30g) flour for dredging
¼ tsp ground cloves
¼ tsp freshly ground black pepper
1½lb (750g) beef chuck steak or chuck roast, trimmed and diced
1 large onion, very finely chopped
2 carrots, chopped
2 celery ribs with leaves, chopped
1 cup (250g) tomatoes, peeled, seeded, and crushed
2 cups (500ml) freshly made beef stock, or 1 beef bouillon cube dissolved in 2 cups (500ml) water
1 large bay leaf
salt, to taste

1 To make the *ragù*, warm the oil in a heavy-based skillet or casserole. Meanwhile, place the flour on a plate and mix in the ground cloves and pepper.

2 Dry the meat well with paper towels and dredge it lightly in the seasoned flour. Add the meat to the pan and sauté over medium heat until browned on both sides, about 10 minutes.

3 Add the onion, carrots, and celery, and reduce the heat to medium-low. Stir, then add the tomatoes, half the beef stock or bouillon cube dissolved in water, and the bay leaf. Partially cover and simmer over low heat until the meat is fork-tender, about 50 minutes, stirring occasionally to prevent sticking. Add the remaining cup of stock as needed to prevent the sauce drying out.

4 Meanwhile, cook the *gnocchi* as directed in step 8, opposite. Stir ½ teaspoon salt, or to taste, into the *ragù* and add more pepper, according to taste. Drain the *gnocchi* and toss with the *ragù*.

GNOCCHI DI PATATE CON SALSA DI SPINACI

Potato Gnocchi with Spinach Sauce

Traditional sauces for potato gnocchi *include* pesto*, simple tomato sauces, and* Gorgonzola *sauce. The combination of potato* gnocchi *and spinach sauce is not at all traditional. However, I find this sauce eminently suitable for* gnocchi*, which beg for sauces with big flavors. Once the ingredients are prepared, the sauce is simple to make, so it is best to make and cook the* gnocchi *first, then keep them warm until ready to dress. This sauce also works well with* fettuccine *or* tagliatelle*.*

KCal 861 P 18g C 63g S 1145mg SFA 38g UFA 20g (4)

INGREDIENTS

1 quantity potato gnocchi (see opposite)

For the sauce

1lb (500g) fresh spinach, washed and stems removed
4 tbsp unsalted butter
1 onion, grated or minced
1½ cups (350ml) heavy cream
pinch of freshly grated nutmeg
salt, to taste
½ cup (60g) freshly grated Parmesan, plus extra to serve
freshly ground white pepper, to taste

1 Place the spinach in a large pan with no water except the drops still clinging to the leaves after washing. Cover and steam over medium heat until tender, stirring occasionally but replacing the lid, 4–5 minutes. Remove from the heat, drain and leave until cool enough to handle. Squeeze out the excess water then chop the spinach and set aside.

2 Warm the butter in a broad skillet and add the onion. Sauté over medium heat until translucent, about 4 minutes. Add the spinach, toss it with the onion, and cook for another minute.

3 Add the cream, nutmeg, and ⅓ teaspoon of salt, and allow the sauce to come to a simmer. Stir in the Parmesan, check the seasoning, and remove the sauce from the heat.

4 Meanwhile, cook the *gnocchi* as directed in step 8, opposite. Drain the *gnocchi* and toss with the sauce. Serve with additional Parmesan at the table.

Gnocchetti con Pomodoro e Mozzarella

Potato Gnocchetti with Tomato and Mozzarella

Many years ago I went on a holiday to the Amalfi Coast. We were taken by my aunt's friends to a small trattoria in the hills of Capo di Sorrento. I don't recall its name, but it was set underneath the terrace of a hillside home. Perhaps it is no longer there, but though I was some seventeen years old then, I have never forgotten the remarkable flavor of the gnocchi. They were lightly covered with a sauce made from tomatoes that grew on the vines at our feet. Locally made mozzarella was dotted sparingly on top.

KCal 559 P 20g C 62g S 1119mg SFA 8g UFA 18g (4)

INGREDIENTS

1 quantity potato gnocchetti (see page 144)

olive oil, to grease

To serve

1 quantity fresh tomato sauce (see page 75), substituting fresh basil for parsley

6oz (175g) freshly made mozzarella

1 Make the *gnocchetti* as directed on page 144. Transfer to baking sheets lined with dish towels. Lightly grease a baking dish with warm olive oil.

2 Bring 4 quarts (5 liters) of water to a boil in a large pan and add 2 tablespoons of salt. Pick up one of the cloths holding the *gnocchetti* and slide the contents into the water. Stir with a wooden spoon. As soon as the *gnocchetti* float to the surface, scoop out with a slotted spoon and let drain in a colander for 2–3 minutes. Repeat with the remaining batches. Arrange the drained *gnocchetti* in the baking dish in a single layer.

3 Preheat the oven to a temperature of 450°F (230°C).

4 Cover the *gnocchetti* lightly with the sauce and scatter the mozzarella on top. Slide the dish onto the upper rack of the oven and bake just until the mozzarella begins to melt, about 5 minutes. Serve immediately.

Gnocchi di Spinaci alla Marcella

Spinach Gnocchi, Marcella's Way

Here is another of Marcella Falcomer's dishes that I have enjoyed. These are unlike the spinach spoon dumplings on page 143, and rather more like classic potato* gnocchi*, except for the addition of a little ricotta and spinach. Be careful to remove all the spinach stems, which gives a creamier spinach purée. If using frozen spinach, choose a premium brand, which usually excludes the stems. Marcella dresses these delightful* gnocchi *with a very simple tomato sauce into which she stirs a tablespoon or two of butter just before serving, making the sauce silky and naturally sweet. (See page 27 for illustration.)

KCal 491 P 18g C 53g S 1153mg SFA 14g UFA 8g (4)

Advance Preparation

The baking sheets full of gnocchi *can be covered with foil or waxed paper and refrigerated for up to 3 hours. For longer storage, cook the* gnocchi *as directed, then place in a single layer in the freezer until frozen solid, which will take several hours. Frozen* gnocchi *can be transferred to a plastic bag or container and frozen for up to one month. To reheat, drop them directly into boiling salted water, cook until they float to the surface and serve as directed.*

INGREDIENTS
For the gnocchi
½lb (250g) boiling potatoes, washed and dried
1lb (500g) fresh spinach, well washed and stems removed, or 10oz (300g) frozen spinach
¼lb (125g) ricotta, drained (see Tip, page 143)
¼ cup (30g) freshly grated Parmesan
1 egg
⅛ tsp freshly grated nutmeg
½ tsp salt, or to taste
⅛ tsp freshly ground white or black pepper
1½ cups (175g) all-purpose flour
To serve
1 quantity fresh tomato sauce (see page 75), simple tomato sauce (see page 74), or tomato sauce with vegetables (see page 75), made with unsalted butter instead of olive oil
1 tbsp unsalted butter
2 tsp chopped fresh flat-leaf parsley, or 6–8 large fresh basil leaves, torn into small pieces
freshly grated Parmesan

1 Preheat the oven to a temperature of 400°F (200°C).

2 Bake the potatoes until tender, 45 minutes–1 hour, depending on size. Alternatively, steam until tender (see Tip, page 144). Line three baking sheets with clean dish towels and set aside.

3 Place the spinach in a pan with no water except the drops still clinging to the leaves after washing. Cover and steam until tender, tossing it occasionally but replacing the lid, about 5–10 minutes. If using frozen spinach, cook according to package directions. Remove from the heat, drain, and leave until cool enough to handle. Squeeze out as much water as possible, then chop the spinach very finely or purée in a food processor. Set aside.

4 When the potatoes are cool enough to handle but still warm, peel them and pass through a potato ricer, or finely mash with a potato masher or fork. In a large bowl, thoroughly combine the puréed potato, chopped spinach, ricotta, Parmesan, egg, nutmeg, ½ teaspoon of salt, and pepper.

5 Pour the flour onto a large pastry board. Make a well in the center. Place the spinach mixture in the well. Draw in the flour gradually to form a dough, taking care not to overwork it. The dough should be soft, smooth, and slightly sticky. Keep adding flour until the mixture is dry enough to handle but not hard. The amount of flour needed will depend upon the water content of the ingredients, but bear in mind that the less flour used, the lighter the *gnocchi*.

6 Form the *gnocchi* as described on page 144. Transfer to the baking sheets, arranging them in a single layer. The uncooked *gnocchi* can be refrigerated, if desired (see Advance Preparation, left).

7 Cover the bottom of a large serving dish with a thin layer of the tomato sauce and keep it warm.

8 Bring 4 quarts (5 liters) of water to a boil in a large pan. Add 1½ tablespoons of salt. Pick up one of the cloths holding the *gnocchi* and slide the contents into the water. Stir with a wooden spoon. As soon as the *gnocchi* float to the surface, scoop them out and let drain in a colander. Transfer to the serving dish. Repeat with the remaining batches. The *gnocchi* can be frozen at this point, if desired (see Advance Preparation, left).

9 Meanwhile, warm the tomato sauce and stir in the butter. Allow the sauce to simmer for 5 minutes. Remove from the heat and stir in the parsley or basil; set aside. Spoon the sauce over the *gnocchi*, scatter Parmesan lightly over the top, and serve immediately.

GNOCCHI DI PATATE DOLCI AL GORGONZOLA

Sweet Potato Gnocchi with Gorgonzola Sauce

Many foods were introduced to Italy after the voyages to the "New World." Among these were the sweet potato and various squashes. It seems intrinsic to the Italian character to embrace foreign ideas and then turn them into something entirely new. In Britain, the new-found potato was boiled and in Germany it was roasted; in Italy it was transformed into gnocchi. Similarly, squashes and pumpkins were transformed into delicious gnocchi such as these.

I have always dressed these gnocchi with an almond sauce or the classic sage butter sauce (see Variation), but while in Parma several years ago with a group of food journalists, I tried pumpkin gnocchi with Gorgonzola sauce in La Greppia, a delightful restaurant in the city center. We all found it to be a delightful combination, the tangy sauce acting as a perfect foil to the sweetness of the little dumplings. Again, I have substituted sweet potatoes for the traditional Italian pumpkin (see Tip, page 118).

KCal 812 P 22g C 65g S 1282mg SFA 33g UFA 18g (4)

INGREDIENTS

For the gnocchi

1½lb (750g) sweet potatoes or yams of uniform size

1 tbsp unsalted butter

2 tbsp freshly grated Parmesan

salt, to taste

⅛ tsp finely ground white pepper

approximately 1 cup (125g) flour, plus additional as needed

To serve

1 quantity Gorgonzola sauce (see page 77)

1 Preheat the oven to a temperature of 375°F (180°C).

2 Prick the sweet potatoes or yams with a fork. Place them directly on the oven rack and roast until tender, about 1 hour. When they are cool enough to handle, peel and cube them. Meanwhile, line three baking sheets with clean, dry dish towels.

3 Warm the butter, preferably in a nonstick pan. Add the sweet potato or yam. Cook over low heat, stirring frequently to evaporate excess moisture, about 8 minutes. Allow to cool slightly. Use a potato ricer, masher, or fork to mash the potato or yam finely while still warm. Do not use a food processor.

4 Transfer the puréed potato to a bowl. Blend in the Parmesan, ½ teaspoon of salt, and freshly ground pepper. Pour the flour onto a large pastry board and make a well in the center. Put the warm sweet potato in the well. Draw in the flour gradually to form a dough, taking care not to overwork it. The dough should be uniform and soft, but not sticky – add a little more flour if needed.

5 Form the *gnocchi* as described on page 144. If the *gnocchi* mixture becomes sticky, dust the butter paddle or grater with flour.

6 Transfer the *gnocchi* to the baking sheets, arranging them in a single layer. The uncooked *gnocchi* can be refrigerated for up to 3 hours, if desired.

7 Bring 4 quarts (5 liters) of water to a boil in a large pan. Add 2 tablespoons of salt. Pick up one of the cloths holding the *gnocchi* and slide the contents into the water. Stir with a wooden spoon. As soon as the *gnocchi* float to the surface, scoop them out with a slotted spoon and let drain in a colander.

8 Transfer the *gnocchi* to a serving dish, arranging them in a single layer. Repeat with the remaining batches. The *gnocchi* can be frozen at this point (see Advance Preparation, page 147). Meanwhile, warm the sauce. Spoon the sauce over the *gnocchi*, and serve.

VARIATION

To make sage sauce, melt ¼lb (125g) of butter in a double boiler or heavy-based pan. Drop in 5–6 fresh large sage leaves and stir. Allow the sage to infuse in the butter for 4–5 minutes. Stir in ¾ cup (175ml) of heavy cream and simmer until the sauce thickens, about 2 minutes. Remove the pan from the heat and stir in ¾ cup (90g) freshly grated Parmesan. Remove the sage leaves. Drizzle the sauce over the gnocchi, *and sprinkle with Parmesan.*

Gnocchi di Semolino alla Romana

Semolina Gnocchi, Roman Style

It is puzzling as to why this dish and the following are called gnocchi, *for they have virtually nothing in common with potato* gnocchi. *I suspect it is just their rather lumpish shape that accounts for the nomenclature. This is a classic Roman dish, which predates potato* gnocchi *by many centuries, and is typically made in spring or during the Easter holidays.*

The semolina is cooked into a kind of porridge, like polenta, then spread out to set on an oiled surface. The gnocchi *are stamped out from the set mixture of semolina, eggs, and cheese, layered in a casserole, and baked. It is a delicious and delicate dish, and really worth the effort, which I believe is relatively little as far as the* gnocchi *tribe goes. Some Italians like to mix the milk with meat broth to give the* gnocchi *added flavor, and this makes them somewhat lighter. I like both variations.*
(See page 26 for illustration.)

INGREDIENTS

4 cups (1 liter) milk, or a mixture of milk and light meat broth (see page 68) or other tasty broth

1½ cups (250g) fine semolina

1 tsp salt

5 tbsp (75g) unsalted butter, softened, plus butter to coat baking dish

1 cup (125g) freshly grated Parmesan

¼ tsp freshly grated nutmeg

1 extra large egg, beaten

1 Preheat the oven to a temperature of 450°F (230°C).

2 Lightly oil a pastry board or chopping board. Generously butter an 11 x 14in (28 x 35cm) baking dish. Have a jug of cold water ready next to the board.

3 Pour the milk or milk/broth mixture into a deep pan. Using a whisk, stir in the semolina and salt *"a pioggia"* (literally, "like rain"), little by little, to prevent lumps forming. Turn on the heat and stir continuously with the whisk until the semolina begins to pull away easily from the sides of the pan, about 20 minutes. Remove the semolina from the heat but keep stirring.

4 Whisk in 4 tablespoons of butter, half the Parmesan, the nutmeg, and finally the egg. Blend all the ingredients well, whipping fast with the whisk to prevent the egg setting in the hot semolina.

5 Now, using a large rubber spatula to guide the semolina, pour the mixture onto the oiled pastry board or cutting board. Take the spatula or spoon and dip it in the cold water. Use it to spread the semolina evenly to a thickness of about ¼in (5mm). Let set, about 15 minutes.

6 Using a 2½in (6cm) wide glass or cookie cutter, cut disks out of the hardened semolina. If preferred, cut the semolina into squares.

7 Arrange the semolina disks in the baking dish in neat overlapping rows. Melt the remaining butter. Sprinkle the rest of the Parmesan on top, then drizzle with butter. Bake the dish on the upper rack of the oven until bubbly and golden. Let rest for 10 minutes before serving.

Gnocchi di Semolino con Ragù alla Sarda

Semolina Gnocchi with Ragù in the Style of Sardinia

These polenta-style gnocchi, *typically found in Sardinia, are in the same family as those above. Corn polenta can also be used in place of semolina. This is much like a dish called* pasticciata di polenta *that I learned from my mother, the only difference being that in my mother's variation, the polenta is cut into squares not disks. The same can be done here, if preferred. It is an uncomplicated dish with roots in the peasant kitchen. The only elaboration is the sauce, which can be a simple tomato-meat sauce or a more complex* ragù *(see pages 71–73).*

KCal 972 P 65g C 73g S 2235mg SFA 23g UFA 14g (4)

INGREDIENTS

butter for coating baking dish

4 cups (1 liter) milk

1½ cups (250g) fine semolina

½ tsp salt

1 quantity of any ragù (see pages 71–73)

½lb (250g) semi-soft Sardinian pecorino, Tuscan caciotta, or Manchego cheese, diced

1 Preheat the oven to a temperature of 450°F (230°C).

2 Lightly oil a pastry board or chopping board. Generously butter an 11 x 14in (28 x 35cm) baking dish. Have a cup of cold water ready next to the board. Warm the sauce and, while it is simmering, make the *gnocchi.*

3 Pour the milk into a deep, ample saucepan. Using a whisk, stir in the semolina and salt as described in steps 3–4, above.

4 Pour the semolina as described in step 5, above, and let cool. Cut the hardened semolina into disks or squares (see step 6, above).

5 Place a layer of semolina disks in the baking dish. Cover with a layer of *ragù,* then with a layer of pecorino. Place the remaining disks on top. Finish with a layer of sauce and a final sprinkling of pecorino. Bake the dish on the upper rack of the oven until the top is bubbly and golden. Remove and let rest for 10 minutes before serving.

CANÈDERLI

Bread Dumplings with Prosciutto and Herbs in Meat Broth, Trentino-Alto Adige Style

Bread dumplings, called canèderli, tirolerknödel, *and* gnocchi di pane *among other things, are a specialty of the northern regions of Trentino-Alto Adige and neighboring Friuli-Venezia Giulia, whose cultures and cuisines have been largely influenced by the Teutons, Austrians, and Slavs. These dumplings are a terrific way to use up old bread.* Speck, *the smoked, cured pork-leg sausage of Alto Adige is traditionally used in* canèderli, *but it can be hard to come by outside Italy. Substitute* prosciutto crudo, *Italian* salame, *or a combination of both.*

Served in a rich, homemade broth of meat or poultry, the dish is humble but splendid. It is essential that the bread be substantial, such as good Italian bread. It mustn't be cottony sliced white bread or the airy so-called Italian loaves that have no crumb to speak of. Note that the bread should be stale, that is, dried out somewhat; toasted bread or soft, fresh bread will not suffice.
(See illustration opposite.)

INGREDIENTS

½lb (250g) stale bread (weight with crusts removed), plus extra as necessary
4 eggs and 1 egg white, beaten
¼ tsp freshly grated nutmeg
½ tsp salt, or to taste
1 cup (250ml) milk
3 tbsp unsalted butter
1 large onion, very finely chopped
2oz (60g) prosciutto, sliced and chopped
2oz (60g) Italian salami, chopped
4 tbsp all-purpose flour
2 tbsp chopped fresh flat-leaf parsley
2 tbsp chopped fresh chives or scallion tops
freshly ground black or white pepper, to taste
1 quantity light meat broth (see page 68)
freshly grated Parmesan, to serve

1 Finely shred the bread with your hands. Combine the eggs and egg white, nutmeg, salt, and milk in a bowl. Add the bread to the bowl and allow it to soak until the liquid is absorbed by the bread and it is thoroughly dampened. If the resulting pulp is too liquid, add more shredded bread until a cohesive, workable consistency is achieved. Use your hands to combine the bread with the egg mixture.

2 Meanwhile, warm the butter in a skillet. Add the onion and sauté over medium-low heat until softened thoroughly, about 6 minutes. Add the prosciutto and salami. Continue to sauté to marry the flavors, about 2 minutes. Stir the contents of the skillet into the egg and bread mixture, along with the flour, parsley, chives, or scallion tops, and pepper to taste.

3 Warm the broth in a large saucepan, keeping the lid on partially to prevent excessive evaporation.

4 Using your hands, form a little of the mixture into a walnut-sized ball. Drop it into the boiling broth. If it holds its shape, form the remaining mixture into balls the size of a small tangerine. If the mixture does not hold together well, add a little more flour before attempting to form the dumplings.

5 Slip the dumplings into the simmering broth all at once and cook until they float to the surface. Remove the pan from the heat when they are done and serve the dumplings, pouring over some of the broth, with freshly grated Parmesan.

VARIATION

In Trentino-Alto Adige, similar dumplings, called schwarteknödel, *made of stale rye bread, are typical. These are also cooked in meat broth, but they are typically served "dry" with sauerkraut, or alongside roasted meats. To make them, substitute stale rye for wheat bread, and lean pancetta for speck or prosciutto. Substitute 1 small very finely chopped leek for the scallion tops, add a small clove of very finely chopped garlic, and omit the nutmeg. Proceed as for the main recipe.*

Ricette Regionali

REGIONAL RECIPES

ITALIAN ANTHROPOLOGISTS HAVE FOUND that there are as many as two thousand types of pasta made throughout the twenty Italian regions. Cooking styles have developed independently in each of the regions, touched by the cultures of successions of inhabitants and conquerors. There have also been hordes of individual foreigners who have fallen in love with Italy and stayed, leaving their own indelible mark. This regional diversity shows itself as much in pasta dishes as in every other aspect of the Italian kitchen. Some of these dishes remain treasures of their places of origin, but it is remarkable that others, such as *lasagne alla bolognese*, have caught the fancy of restaurant chefs and stepped over their regional borders. Their inclusion here serves as a reminder that popular, hybrid, and sadly lackluster, internationalized versions have evolved from more delectable recipes that are well worth reviving.

Pasta e Fasioi
Pasta and Beans in the Style of the Veneto

PASTA E FASIOI

Pasta and Beans in the Style of the Veneto

Pasta is not an important food in the cuisine of the Veneto with the exception of a few dishes. One of these is a genre of pasta and bean dish, **pasta e fagioli,** ***or in the dialect of the Veneto,*** **pasta e fasioi,** ***which the Veneto people make with a degree of refinement perhaps unmatched anywhere else in Italy. One of the things that makes Venetian bean dishes so good is the quality of the beans. In this dish, a type of plump, meaty, and tender pinkish-brown bean from Lamon in Friuli is used. As they are not available outside of Italy, I have substituted*** **borlotti** ***or even pinto beans with excellent results.***

KCal 861 P 47g C 108g S 1107mg SFA 9g UFA 17g (4)

INGREDIENTS

- *2½ cups (500g) dried borlotti or pinto beans, preferably soaked overnight*
- *1 tbsp extra-virgin olive oil*
- *2oz (60g) salt pork back, or 2 tbsp extra-virgin olive oil and 2 tbsp butter*
- *1 large garlic clove, very finely chopped*
- *1 small carrot, chopped*
- *1 small onion, chopped*
- *1 celery rib with leaves, chopped*
- *3 bay leaves*
- *½lb (250g) ham steak, rinsed well and diced*
- *6oz (175g) fresh egg pasta (see page 48), cut into tagliatelle (see page 53) or dried tagliatelle, fettuccine, or nidi ("nests"), broken up into 2in (5cm) lengths*
- *salt, to taste*
- *½ tsp freshly ground black pepper*

1 Drain and rinse the beans in cold water until the water runs clear. Set aside.

2 Warm the olive oil and salt pork or olive oil mixed with butter in a large wide pan. Add the garlic, carrot, onion, celery, and bay leaves and sauté over medium or medium-low heat until the vegetables are tender, about 10 minutes, stirring occasionally so they cook evenly.

3 Stir in half the diced ham, then add the beans. Continue to sauté for 10 minutes to marry the flavors. Pour in 8 cups (2 liters) of cold water and bring to a boil. Reduce to a simmer and cook over low heat until the beans are tender, 1 hour–1 hour 15 minutes.

4 Fifteen minutes before the beans have finished cooking, bring 10 cups (2.75 liters) of water to a rolling boil. Add the pasta to the pan with 1 tablespoon of salt. Half-cook the pasta, stirring occasionally as it boils to prevent sticking; about 1 minute for fresh pasta and 4 minutes for dried.

5 Drain the pasta and add it to the beans with the remaining ham. Simmer for 1–2 minutes, or until the pasta is almost done. Add 1½ teaspoons salt, or to taste, and the pepper.

LASAGNE ALLA BOLOGNESE

Lasagne in the Style of Bologna

KCal 1325 P 67g C 82g S 1377mg SFA 42g UFA 33g (4)

INGREDIENTS

- *1½ quantities bolognese sauce (see page 73)*
- *1 quantity (1lb/500g) spinach pasta (see page 54), or ½ quantity (½lb/250g) each spinach pasta and fresh egg pasta (see page 48), unrolled*
- *1 quantity béchamel (see page 77)*
- *1¼ cups (150g) freshly grated Parmesan*

1 Simmer the bolognese sauce while you roll the pasta out as thinly as possible (see pages 50–51). Cut the sheets into 3½ x 4½in (8 x 11cm) rectangles. Let dry for at least 15 minutes.

2 Preheat the oven to a temperature of 375°F (190°C).

3 Select an 8 x 11in (20 x 28cm) baking dish. Precook the *lasagne* (see step 6, page 135). Spread a thin layer of bolognese sauce on the bottom of the dish. Put a layer of *lasagne* on top, making them touch without overlapping. Spread a layer of bolognese sauce over this. Follow with a thin layer of béchamel. Sprinkle Parmesan over it. Repeat the process, until all the ingredients are used (hold back a little of the bolognese sauce if there is too much). Finish with béchamel sprinkled with Parmesan.

4 Cook on the upper oven rack until bubbly and golden, 20–25 minutes. Let settle for 10 minutes before serving.

ADVANCE PREPARATION

Lasagne alla Bolognese can be prepared one day in advance of baking and serving, covered tightly, and refrigerated. The baking time may increase by 5–10 minutes if the dish has been cooked from chilled.

SCHIAFFETTONI

Baked Rigatoni Stuffed with Pork in the Style of Calabria

Another recipe from Carlo Benevidas of the New York restaurant I Trulli, this one originating in Calabria. Large pasta shells or lumaconi ("big snails") can be substituted for rigatoni.

KCal 1246 P 80g C 99g S 1784mg SFA 17g UFA 40g (4)

INGREDIENTS
1lb (500g) rigatoni
salt, to taste
4 tbsp extra-virgin olive oil
1 small onion, chopped
2oz (60g) thick-cut pancetta or prosciutto, minced
½ small carrot, very finely chopped
1 celery rib with leaves, very finely chopped
¼ cup (15g) coarsely chopped fresh flat-leaf parsley
2lb (1kg) lean ground pork
freshly ground black pepper, to taste
2 small bay leaves or 1 large one
4 tbsp chicken or meat stock or broth
½ cup (60g) freshly grated pecorino
¼ cup (30g) freshly grated Parmesan
For the sauce
1 quantity simple tomato sauce (see page 74), fresh tomato sauce (see page 75), or tomato sauce with vegetables (see page 75)

1 Bring 4 quarts (5 liters) of water to a boil. Add the *rigatoni* and 1½ tablespoons of salt. Cook the pasta until half-tender, about 7 minutes. Drain in a colander, then cool under cold running water. Drain well and set aside.

2 Prepare the stuffing. Warm the olive oil in a skillet and add the onion. Sauté until wilted, about 4 minutes. Add the pancetta or prosciutto, carrot, celery, and parsley, stirring until coated with oil.

3 Add the pork, 1 teaspoon of salt, the pepper, and bay leaves. Use a fork to break up the meat and toss it. Add the stock or broth. Sauté gently, stirring frequently, until the meat is tender and the flavors marry, 25 minutes.

4 Take the pan off the heat and remove the bay leaves. Allow the mixture to cool and then grind it very fine in a meat grinder or food processor. Add half the pecorino and all the Parmesan to the mixture and work in thoroughly.

5 Preheat the oven to a temperature of 375°F (190°C).

6 Select a large baking dish. Spread several tablespoons of tomato sauce on the bottom of the dish. Use a tiny spoon or a pastry bag fitted with the largest nozzle to stuff the *rigatoni.*

7 Arrange the *rigatoni* in the baking dish, placing them side by side. Spoon a layer of sauce over the top and sprinkle with some of the remaining pecorino. Continue layering in this sequence until all the *rigatoni* are arranged, finishing with sauce sprinkled with pecorino.

8 Bake the *schiaffettoni* in the middle of the oven until heated through and bubbly, 10–20 minutes. Allow to settle for a minute or two before serving.

Rigatoni alla Fiorentina

Rigatoni with Long-Simmered Meat Sauce in the Style of Florence

This lovely aromatic meat sauce is called* stracotto *in Italian, which means long-cooked. It is a specialty of Florence, where it is usually made with beef. I like to use pork for* stracotto*, too, as it enhances the flavor of meat sauces. This sauce is usually served with* rigatoni*, but other macaroni cuts such as* penne*,* lumache *(medium-sized pasta shells),* fusilli*,* gnocchi*, and* penne mezzanine *can also be used.

KCal 986 P 51g C 140g S 704mg SFA 12g UFA 11g (4)

INGREDIENTS

- *½oz (15g) dried porcini*
- *4 tbsp unsalted butter*
- *1oz (30g) pancetta, finely chopped*
- *1 small onion, very finely chopped*
- *1 celery rib with leaves, very finely chopped*
- *1 small carrot, very finely chopped*
- *3 tbsp very finely chopped fresh flat-leaf parsley*
- *½lb (250g) boneless beef chuck, fat trimmed, cut into ½in (1cm) dice*
- *½lb (250g) boneless pork chop, fat trimmed and cut into ½in (1cm) dice*
- *⅛ tsp ground cloves*
- *1 tbsp flour*
- *¾ cup (175ml) beef stock*
- *⅔ cup (150ml) good dry red wine*
- *salt, to taste*
- *1in (2.5cm) strip lemon zest (no pith)*
- *freshly ground pepper, to taste*
- *1lb (500g) rigatoni*

1 Soak the porcini for 30 minutes in 1 cup (250ml) warm water. Drain, reserving the liquid, and chop the porcini. Strain the liquid through paper towels.

2 Melt the butter in a large skillet. Add the pancetta and allow it to color lightly, about 4 minutes. Add the onion, celery, carrot, and porcini. Increase the heat to medium and sauté until lightly colored, about 5 minutes.

3 Stir in the parsley. Add the meat and reduce the heat to medium-low. Sauté until lightly browned all over, about 5 minutes. Stir in the cloves and flour. Pour in the porcini liquid, beef stock, and wine, and season to taste with salt.

4 Twist the lemon zest to release its oil and add to the sauce. Stir, then cover and simmer at the lowest possible heat for 2½–3 hours, stirring occasionally. The meat should disintegrate into the sauce. If the sauce is not thick enough, remove the cover and allow it to evaporate very gently. If it seems too thick, moisten it with a little stock. Add pepper to taste.

5 Bring 4 quarts (5 liters) of water to a boil. Add the *rigatoni* and 1½ tablespoons of salt and stir immediately. Cook until *al dente*. Drain, toss with the sauce in the pan, and serve piping hot.

Cecatelli di Ricotta

Ricotta Cecatelli in the Style of Apulia

I met Apulian-born Nicola Marzovilla on a trip to Lecce in Apulia. He led me to discover some of the best food the city's restaurants had to offer, but then I discovered that his own restaurant in New York, I Trulli, served some of the interesting local dishes I had found in Apulia. I Trulli's chef, Carlo Benevidas, gave me this recipe for the traditional handmade pasta of the Capitanata ("captaincy" or northern province) of Apulia.* Cecatelli *are a variation of the more popular* cavatelli *of Apulia, but ricotta rather than hot water is combined with the flour in this pasta.

KCal 556 P 19g C 56g S 674mg SFA 11g UFA 18g (4)

INGREDIENTS

- *2 cups (250g) all-purpose flour*
- *salt, to taste*
- *1lb (500g) ricotta, drained if necessary* *(see Tip, page 143)*

For the sauce

- *1 quantity simple tomato sauce* *(see page 74)* *or fresh tomato sauce* *(see page 75)**, made with basil instead of parsley*
- *freshly grated pecorino, to serve*

1 Pour the flour into a mound and add 1 teaspoon of salt. Make a well in the center and place the ricotta in the well. Use your hands to work the flour into the ricotta to form a uniform dough. It should be soft and elastic but not sticky. Cover with a bowl and let rest for 5 minutes.

2 Line four baking sheets with dish towels dusted with flour. Cut the dough into four parts. Roll each piece out into ½in (1cm) thick ropes, using more flour if they become sticky. Cut the ropes into 1¼in (3cm) lengths. Take each piece and gently press down on it with two fingers (not using the little finger or thumb), dragging it toward you to form a little spiral. Push it away to a floured part of the work top then transfer to the sheets.

3 Warm the sauce. Bring 4 quarts (5 liters) of water to a boil. Pour the *cecatelli* into the water and add 2 tablespoons of salt. When the *cecatelli* float to the surface, scoop them out and transfer to a warm platter. Top with sauce, sprinkle with pecorino, and serve.

SPAGHETTI CON TONNO ALLA MOLISANA

Spaghetti with Tuna in the Style of Molise

This is an adaptation of a recipe given to me by Michele DiFilippo, an Italian chef whose origins are in the Molise region. It is really a summer dish because it is made with fresh vine-ripened tomatoes, though canned plum tomatoes may be substituted. Olive oil-preserved canned tuna of the Italian variety is superior in flavor to other types of canned tuna, but if it is not available, use other tuna packed in oil.

KCal 705 P 30g C 106g S 653mg SFA 3g UFA 15g (4)

INGREDIENTS
3 tbsp extra-virgin olive oil
2 large garlic cloves, very finely chopped
1 onion, very finely chopped
½ cup (125ml) dry white wine
3lb (1.5kg) fresh, mature vine-ripened plum tomatoes, peeled, seeded, and coarsely chopped, or 1¼lb (625g) drained canned tomatoes, seeded and chopped
salt, to taste
6½oz (190g) canned tuna in olive oil, drained and flaked
small handful (about 2 tbsp) of fresh basil leaves, torn into very small pieces
2 tbsp chopped fresh flat-leaf parsley
½ tsp chopped fresh oregano, or ¼ tsp dried oregano
½ tsp freshly ground white or black pepper
1lb (500g) spaghetti

1 Warm the oil in a pan and add the garlic and onion. Sauté over medium-low heat until softened, about 5 minutes.

2 Stir in the wine and cook, stirring constantly, until the alcohol is evaporated, about 3 minutes. Add the tomatoes and ½ teaspoon of salt and simmer, uncovered, until the sauce is thickened, about 15 minutes.

3 Add the tuna to the pan and cook for 5 minutes. Stir in the basil, parsley, oregano, and pepper and then remove the sauce from the heat.

4 Meanwhile, bring 4 quarts (5 liters) of water to a boil. Add the *spaghetti* and 1½ tablespoons of salt. Stir immediately and cook until *al dente*. Drain, combine with the sauce, and serve.

CURLIGIONIS 'E PATATA

Ravioli with Potato, Mint, and Pecorino Filling in the Style of Sardinia

These delicious and unusual ravioli ***are peculiar to the island of Sardinia, which produces some of the best pecorino cheese in the world. The potato filling is flavored with two types of pecorino –*** viscidu, ***a dry, sour salted cheese, and aged pecorino of the kind that is exported abroad. As*** viscidu ***is not available outside Sardinia, I have substituted feta, which is similar in flavor. Beef fat, which offers a great deal of flavor to the filling, is traditionally used for sautéing the onions for the filling, but extra-virgin olive oil may be substituted.*** Curligionis 'e patata ***are served simply with grated pecorino, or with tomato sauce, such as Simple Tomato Sauce (see page 74) or Fresh Tomato Sauce (see page 75).***

KCal 713 P 27g C 81g S 1117mg SFA 12g UFA 19g (4)

INGREDIENTS
1 quantity (1lb/500g) fresh egg pasta (see page 48), unrolled
beaten egg, to seal
butter, to coat dish and brush ravioli
For the filling
1lb (500g) boiling potatoes, scrubbed but unpeeled
3 tbsp beef fat or extra-virgin olive oil
1 onion, very finely chopped
1 large garlic clove, very finely chopped
2 tbsp finely chopped fresh mint
2oz (60g) feta cheese, very finely crumbled
6 tbsp freshly grated pecorino sardo or pecorino romano, plus extra to serve
¼ tsp freshly ground pepper
1 tsp salt

1 To make the filling, place the potatoes in a pan with cold water to cover. Bring to a boil, then cook until soft, about 25 minutes. Drain and when cool enough to handle, peel them. Pass the potatoes through a potato ricer into a bowl, or mash them very fine.

2 Melt and warm the beef fat or oil in a small skillet, and add the onion and garlic. Sauté over medium-low heat until very soft, about 6 minutes, stirring occasionally. Transfer the onion and garlic to the bowl with the potato.

3 Add the remaining filling ingredients to the bowl. Using your hands or a wooden spoon, work the mixture well to distribute the ingredients evenly. Check the seasoning.

4 Roll out the pasta according to directions on pages 50–51, and stuff the *ravioli* as shown on page 56.

5 Butter a large serving dish. Melt a little additional butter to use for brushing the cooked *ravioli*.

6 Cook the *ravioli* as described on page 111, step 6, then transfer to the serving dish. If you are layering them, drizzle a little butter over to prevent sticking. Serve the *ravioli* hot or warm, passing the grated pecorino at the table.

Ravioli Pusteresi

Rye-Flour Ravioli in the Style of Trentino-Alto Adige with a Butter and Crumb Sauce

Also known as turteln, *these unusual* ravioli *from the north are not found elsewhere. Traditionally, they are made entirely out of rye flour, but I have found the rye flour produced outside Italy tricky to work with because of its low gluten content. Consequently, I suggest a blend of rye and all-purpose flour. For* ravioli-*making technique, see page 56.*

KCal 715 P 26g C 60g S 966mg SFA 26g UFA 15g (4)

INGREDIENTS

For the pasta

1 cup (125g) rye flour

1 cup (125g) all-purpose flour

1 extra large egg, plus 1 egg white to seal

2 tsp melted butter

2 tbsp milk at room temperature

salt, to taste

For the filling

2 cups (500g) ricotta, drained if necessary (see Tip, page 143)

½ tsp cumin seeds

2 tbsp finely chopped chives or scallion tops

1 egg yolk

½ cup (60g) freshly grated pecorino

To serve

6 tbsp (90g) unsalted butter, plus extra for brushing

3 tbsp bread crumbs

salt and freshly ground pepper, to taste

1 Make the pasta according to directions for fresh pasta on pages 48–51, rolling it as thin as possible and using all-purpose flour to dust the dough as you work.

2 Combine the ricotta with the other filling ingredients in a bowl.

3 Form the *ravioli* as described in steps 3–7, page 112. Butter a large shallow serving dish. Melt a little additional butter for brushing the cooked *ravioli*.

4 Cook the *ravioli* as described in step 8, page 112. Use a slotted spoon to transfer them to the dish. If you are layering them, drizzle a little melted butter over them.

5 To make the sauce, melt the butter in a pan, add the bread crumbs, and turn them in the butter until golden. Spoon over the *ravioli*, season with salt and pepper, and serve.

Tortelli di Zucca

Tortelli Stuffed with Squash in the Style of Lombardy

Pasta is not a focus of Lombardy as it is in most of the central and southern Italian regions. However, a number of superb pasta dishes have evolved that reflect the refinement and delicacy of the cooking in this area. Tortelli alla zucca, *pasta stuffed with pumpkin, is one of the signature dishes of Lombardy, and of Mantua in particular. As with the other pasta dishes in this book that traditionally use pumpkin, ripe, firm butternut squash or sweet potatoes or yams are suggested as a substitute (see Tip, page 118). This delicious rendition of* tortelli di zucca *is made by Marcella Falcomer, a native of the region. Serve with butter and Parmesan or with a light tomato sauce. For* tortelli-*making technique, see page 57.*

KCal 833 P 31g C 78g S 984mg SFA 24g UFA 21g (4)

INGREDIENTS

1 quantity (1lb/500g) fresh egg pasta (see page 48), unrolled

1 egg white, to seal

salt, to taste

For the filling

2lb (1kg) butternut squash, sweet potatoes, or yam

1½ tbsp unsalted butter, melted

3oz (90g) good mortadella, very finely chopped

3 tbsp freshly grated Parmesan

2 tsp chopped fresh flat-leaf parsley

⅛ tsp freshly grated nutmeg

1 egg yolk

salt and freshly ground pepper, to taste

To serve

6 tbsp (90g) unsalted butter, plus extra for brushing

1oz (30g) Parmesan, cut into fine shavings or grated

1 Preheat the oven to a temperature of 375°F (190°C).

2 To make the filling, bake the squash, sweet potatoes, or yams as described for Caramelle, steps 1–2, page 118. Peel and cube them when still warm.

3 Warm the butter in a nonstick pan. Add the squash, sweet potato, or yam. Cook gently, stirring frequently, for about 8 minutes. Allow to cool slightly then mash fine using a potato ricer or hand masher. Transfer the pulp to a bowl and add the mortadella, Parmesan, parsley, nutmeg, and egg yolk. Season with salt and pepper.

4 Roll the pasta dough as thin as possible (see pages 50–51). Form the *tortelli* as described on page 57, and spread out to dry for a few minutes. Butter a warm serving dish.

5 Cook the *tortelli* as described in step 8, page 112, then transfer to the serving dish. Melt the butter, drizzle it over the *tortelli*, and scatter with Parmesan.

Crostoli

Fried Sweet Pasta with Grappa in the Style of Friuli-Venezia Giulia

I have offered a recipe for sweet ribbon-shaped pastries called frappe *in my book "Classic Italian Cooking," but this recipe, which was given to me by my colleague, pastry wizard Marcella Falcomer, is somewhat different. Unlike the fried sweet pastry ribbons of other regions, also called* cenci, sfrappole, *and* cartadatte, crostoli *are formed into what looks like a roll of ribbon. The dough contains grappa, rather than the more usual marsala or wine, and this makes the* crostoli *lighter. The low sugar content also helps to ensure that the pastry absorbs little oil when fried. The dough is made in much the same way as fresh pasta, on a pasta machine (sse pages 50-51). A long-handled two-pronged fork is essential for forming the rolled ribbons. (See illustration opposite.)*

KCal 337 P 5g C 54g S 25mg SFA 1g UFA 9g (6)

INGREDIENTS
1¼ cups (200g) all-purpose flour
2 eggs
2 tsp sugar
2 tsp vegetable oil, plus extra for frying
2 tbsp grappa, Cognac, or whisky
superfine sugar or granulated sugar for sprinkling
confectioners' sugar or raisin sauce (see page 161) to serve

1 Pour the flour onto a pastry board or work surface. Make a well in the center, then add the eggs, sugar, 2 teaspoons of vegetable oil, and the grappa or other spirit. Use a fork to incorporate the wet mixture into the flour, as you would for making pasta dough (see page 48).

2 Continue to work the dough as for pasta, until you have a smooth, elastic ball of dough. Wrap the dough in plastic wrap and let it rest for 2 hours at room temperature or overnight in the refrigerator.

3 Cut the dough into six pieces. Work with one piece at a time, keeping the remainder wrapped in plastic wrap. Pass each piece of dough through the rollers of the pasta machine at each setting to make the thinnest strip possible.

4 Using a fluted pastry wheel, cut the dough strip into ribbons 1in (2.5cm) wide and 12in (30cm) long.

5 Heat the oil for deep-frying the *crostoli* in a deep pan. It should be hot enough to make the dough sizzle upon contact.

6 Take one ribbon of dough at a time and drop only 1in (2.5cm) of it into the hot oil. Take the long-handled fork and roll the frying tip of the dough ribbon onto it, twirling the fork to allow the end to attach onto the fork's tines. Continue to roll the ribbon around the fork, twirling it as you would thread around a spool.

7 When the dough ribbon is completely rolled around the fork, shake the fork to release the roll and loosen it so that the hot oil can get in between the coils of the dough and cook it evenly. The end shape should resemble a loose roll of ribbon. As soon as it turns a light golden color, turn it over and cook on the other side. When golden, lift it out and drain on paper towels. Repeat with the remaining dough. Sprinkle the *crostoli* with sugar while hot.

8 Allow the *crostoli* to cool, then sprinkle with confectioners' sugar, or drizzle with raisin sauce, if preferred.

Tagliatelle con le Noci

Tagliatelle with Sugar, Cinnamon, and Hazelnuts in the Style of Umbria

An unusual recipe from Umbria, these sweet tagliatelle *are served on Christmas Eve. Sweetened cocoa powder may or may not be added. After the pasta is cooked and combined with the sauce, it is allowed to cool to room temperature before serving.*

KCal 971 P 23g C 90g S 607mg SFA 24g UFA 32g (4)

INGREDIENTS
1 cup (125g) hazelnuts
¼lb (125g) fresh unseasoned bread crumbs, lightly toasted
zest of 1 lemon
1 tsp cinnamon
1 quantity (1lb/500g) fresh egg pasta (see page 48), cut into tagliatelle (see page 53)
salt, to taste
10 tbsp (150g) unsalted butter, melted
2 tbsp superfine or granulated sugar
2 tbsp sweetened cocoa powder, optional

1 Preheat the oven to a temperature of 350°F (180°C).

2 Sprinkle the hazelnuts with water, place in a roasting pan and lightly toast them, 12–15 minutes. Pour the hot nuts onto a dish towel, then rub in the cloth to remove the skins. Coarsely grind the nuts in a food processor. Combine the nuts, breadcrumbs, lemon zest, and cinnamon.

3 Bring 4 quarts (5 liters) of water to a boil. Add the pasta and 1½ tablespoons of salt. Cook for about 30 seconds. Drain, but while it is still dripping slightly, return it to the pan, add the nut mixture, pour over the melted butter and sugar, and toss well. Sprinkle with sweetened cocoa powder, if desired. Serve at room temperature.

CALCIUNI

Sweet Fried Chestnut Ravioli in the Style of Calabria

When I first began writing a food column for a group of metropolitan New York newspapers, a co-worker offered me his mother's recipe for these sweet chestnut ravioli, called calciuni or "little trousers" in dialect. The signora, Carmela Genovese, was an immigrant from Calabria, and her son had fond memories of her making these traditional Calabrese sweets.

Canned or puréed chestnuts can be used. The weight of fresh chestnuts is a little more to compensate for the shells and any nuts that have to be discarded. The cooked weight should be 10oz (300g). The pastry contains no sugar, but the abundant sugar or honey that decorates the ravioli provides sweetness. *For ravioli-making technique, see page 56.*

KCal 618 P 8g C 84g S 91mg SFA 12g UFA 16g (4)

INGREDIENTS
For the filling
¾lb (375g) fresh chestnuts, or 10oz (300g) drained canned whole or puréed chestnuts
2 tbsp strong black coffee (liquid, not powder)
1oz (30g) good-quality dark chocolate
2 tbsp sweet sherry
3 tbsp sugar, or to taste
¼ tsp ground cinnamon
For the dough
1 cup (125g) unbleached all-purpose flour
2 tbsp unsalted butter, chilled
1 egg, lightly beaten
2 tbsp sugar
pinch of salt
1 tbsp water
1 beaten egg, to seal
vegetable oil for frying
honey for drizzling, or confectioners' sugar for dusting

1 If using fresh chestnuts, place them in a bowl with warm water to cover. Let soak for about 30 minutes. Use a small knife to score an X shape on the flat side of each chestnut, avoiding penetrating the chestnut itself.

2 Place the chestnuts in a pan with water to cover. Bring to a boil, then reduce the heat. Simmer, partially covered, for 40 minutes–1 hour from the boiling point, or until tender. Add more water to the pan if it evaporates below the level of the chestnuts.

3 Remove the chestnuts from the heat, drain, and cover with fresh boiling water. Peel them, letting them soak until each one is done (peeling is easy if the chestnuts are kept warm). If the inner skin cannot be easily removed, reboil the chestnuts briefly. Purée in a food mill, potato ricer, or food processor.

4 Pour the coffee into a pan and melt the chocolate in it. Add the puréed chestnuts and other filling ingredients, blending well. The consistency should be like that of mashed potatoes. Add a little more sherry if the mixture is too dry. Taste for sugar and add more if necessary.

5 To make the dough by hand, place the flour in a bowl and cut the butter into small pieces directly into the flour. Rub the butter into the flour until the mixture forms small pea shapes.

6 Pile the flour–butter mixture onto a board. Make a well in the center and put the egg and remaining dough ingredients into the well. Stir carefully with a fork, in one direction, until the liquid is incorporated into the flour and forms a soft dough. When you can no longer mix with the fork, knead with your hands.

7 Scrape any dried bits of dough off the board to prevent them getting into the dough, which should be smooth, uniform, and elastic. If the dough is too soft, knead in a little more flour. If it is too stiff, wet your hands with water as you knead. Knead for about 10 minutes. To make the dough in a food processor, follow the procedure for pasta (see Tip, page 49), adding the sugar to the egg mixture. Cover the dough with a clean towel and leave to rest for 30 minutes.

8 Cut the ball of dough in half. Work with one piece at a time; keep the other half covered with a slightly damp cloth. Roll the dough as thinly as possible (see pages 50–51). Cut the dough into 12in (30cm) long strips. Place a rounded teaspoon of filling at 2in (5cm) intervals along the dough strip and seal and form as for *ravioli* (see page 56).

9 Pour the oil into a deep skillet to a depth of 2in (5cm), and heat until hot enough to make a piece of dough sizzle upon contact. Deep-fry the *ravioli* a few at a time until golden, turning them so they cook evenly. Remove with a slotted spoon and drain on paper towels. Layer the *ravioli* on a plate. Drizzle honey over each layer or sprinkle generously with confectioners' sugar. Serve hot or at room temperature.

Torta Dolce di Spaghetti con Salsa d'Uva Secca

Neapolitan Sweet Spaghetti Pie with Raisin Sauce

Pasta is sometimes used for sweet dishes in Italian cooking, including soufflés and puddings, as in this Neapolitan recipe, given to me by Anna Salerno. In the* cucina povera*, the poor Italian kitchen, the dish was typically made on Easter Sunday. While it is traditional to eat it plain, I serve it with my paternal grandmother's raisin sauce. She served it drizzled over sweet ribbonlike fried pastry (*cartadatte *in Apulia), very similar to the* crostoli *on page 158. The original recipe did not include port (*vino santo *can also be used), but it does add depth and interest.
Makes about 2 cups (500ml).

KCal 1134 P 18g C 218g S 467mg SFA 6g UFA 11g (4)

Advance Preparation

This dish can be prepared a day or two in advance of baking and serving, covered tightly, and refrigerated. The baking time may increase by 5–10 minutes if the dish is cooked from chilled.

INGREDIENTS
For the pie
½lb (250g) very thin spaghetti, broken up
2 tbsp vegetable oil for pasta water
1½ tbsp coarse salt
3 large eggs
½ cup (125g) sugar
juice and grated zest of 1 orange
⅓ cup (60g) sultanas
1 tbsp grated pecorino or Parmesan
1 tbsp melted unsalted butter, plus extra to coat
For the sauce
1lb (500g) raisins
3 cups (750ml) water
1 cup (250ml) port
½ tsp each ground cloves and cinnamon
½ cup (170g) honey

FOR THE SAUCE

1 Gently boil the raisins in the water for 1 hour in a covered pan, reducing the heat once the liquid starts to simmer.

2 Put the boiled raisins through a food mill or press through a sieve. Approximately 2 cups (500ml) of pulpy, syruplike sauce will be produced.

3 Return the raisin sauce to the pan and add the port, cloves or cinnamon, and honey. Simmer gently for 30 minutes, stirring occasionally. Cool before serving.

FOR THE PIE

1 Preheat the oven to a temperature of 350°F (180°C).

2 Bring 4 quarts (5 liters) of water to a boil. Add the broken *spaghetti*, oil, and salt. Stir with a fork, and cook over high heat until tender but not mushy.

3 Meanwhile, combine the remaining ingredients, except the melted butter, in a large bowl. Drain the *spaghetti*, rinse with cold water, and drain again. Mix the *spaghetti* into the egg batter.

4 Transfer the mixture to an 8 x 11in (20 x 28cm) buttered dish and drizzle with melted butter. Bake for 45 minutes, or until golden. Check the pie during the last 15 minutes to prevent overcooking. Serve warm with raisin sauce, if desired.

Pantry

THE SINGLE MOST important factor in the success of cooking is the quality of ingredients. I learned this lesson from my mother, who loved to linger at the produce stands in the market, picking and choosing each vegetable carefully, or mulling over what to cook for dinner. But there were also times when she had to put something together quickly for unexpected visitors. On such occasions she inevitably created a quick pasta dish using what was on hand. Thus, at an early age, I learned that a well-stocked pantry always includes the essential ingredients described here.

Other indispensable pantry ingredients

Unbleached all-purpose flour, dried pasta, mozzarella, mascarpone, unsalted butter, heavy cream, Gorgonzola, green and white peppercorns, buckwheat flour, celery, onions.

00 flour, highly refined white flour, is ideal for fresh pasta

Choose large, free-range eggs for fresh pasta.

A good extra-virgin olive oil is essential for sauces

Rosemary is popular in meat sauces, and is one of the few herbs that dries well

Anchovies in olive oil melt into sauces

Dried porcini lend an inimitable flavor and aroma

Tuna from the belly (ventresca) *of the fish and packed in olive oil has the best texture and flavor*

Young tender spinach is used chopped in ravioli fillings and in gnocchi and sauces

Canned plum tomatoes and concentrated tomato paste are invaluable

Semolina flour is used for Roman gnocchi

Prosciutto crudo and pancetta are superb in ragù and stuffed pasta

Basil, garlic, and pine nuts are three of the essential ingredients of pesto, and of course have endless uses individually in Italian cuisine

Fresh ricotta is a classic ingredient in sauces and fresh pasta stuffings

Parmesan (parmigiano reggiano) and pecorino (below) should be used freshly grated

Fresh flat-leaf parsley is irreplaceable in Italian cooking

Glossary

Al dente Literally "to the tooth," this expression refers to the ideal firm texture of properly cooked dried pasta. Fresh pasta can never be cooked *al dente* as it is too soft.

Battuto A combination of chopped raw vegetables for sautéing – typically carrots, celery, onion and/or garlic, and parsley – that is the foundation of many Italian sauces and other dishes.

Maccheroni An old-fashioned term referring to dried pasta, particularly in use in southern Italy. Also refers to tubular pasta.

Pastasciutta Literally "dry pasta," meaning fresh or dried pasta with sauce (as opposed to a soup or a baked pasta dish).

Pasticcio A baked dish of pasta and other ingredients, moistened with one or more sauces.

Ragù A complex meat sauce that may or may not contain tomato.

Salsa Tomato sauce or other type of sauce flavored with a fairly wide variety of ingredients.

Soffritto This refers to a *battuto* when it is sautéed and wilted.

Sugo A simple tomato sauce or other type of sauce comprised of relatively few ingredients.

Grind black pepper just before using to attain its full strength and clarity of aroma

Dried red chilis (peperoncini) *are crushed and used in southern-style dishes*

Saffron strands or powder are a prized aromatic

Black and green olives should be bought with pits and preserved in olive oil

Capers should be very small and compact

INDEX

Figures in **bold** refer to page numbers with illustrations

A

B

C

Q·R

S

T

V•W•Z

USEFUL ADDRESSES

Mail-order sources for Italian cooking equipment and provisions

BALDUCCI'S
Mail-Order Department
42 26 13th Street
Long Island City, NY 11101
(800) BALDUCCI
Comprehensive line of Italian specialty foods, breads, desserts, sauces, fresh produce, meats, and seafood. Catalog available.

BRIDGE KITCHENWARE CORP.
214 East 52nd Street
New York, NY 10022
1-800-BRIDGE K
Complete line of high-quality professional and home cookware, utensils, and equipment.

DEAN & DELUCA
Mail-Order Department
560 Broadway
New York, NY 10012
(212) 431-1691
(800) 221-7714
Kitchen equipment; Italian specialty foods. Catalog available.

LAMALLE KITCHENWARE
36 West 25th Street
New York, NY 10016
(212) 242-0750
Complete line of professional cookware. Call for catalog.

THE MOZZARELLA COMPANY
2944 Elm Street
Dallas, TX 75226
(214) 741-4072/
(800) 798-2954
Large variety of fresh and aged cheeses; sun-dried tomatoes; imported olive oils and balsamic vinegar. Cheeses shipped overnight.

G.B. RATTO INTERNATIONAL GROCER
821 Washington Street
Oakland, CA 94607
(800) 228-3515 (in CA),
(800) 325-3483
Italian specialty foods, large assortment of grains, flours, herbs, and spices. Catalog available.

THE SANDY MUSH HERB NURSERY
Route 2
Surrett Cove Road
Leicester, NC 28748
(704) 683-2014
Live herbs and herb seeds shipped. Illustrated catalog, information about growing and drying herbs, recipes.

VIVANDE PORTA VIA
2125 Fillmore Street
San Francisco, CA 94115
(415) 346-4430
Imported Italian seeds for hard-to-find Italian vegetable varieties; Italian specialty foods.

ACKNOWLEDGMENTS

I wish to thank the following people for their kindness in allowing me to reproduce their recipes and for help with my research: Marcella Falcomer, Valerie and Elio Serra, Anna Amendolara Nurse, Flavia Destefanis, Paolo Destefanis, Stephen Schmidt, Nicola Marzovilla and I Trulli Restaurant, Mario Randazzo and La Manda Restaurant, Massimo Iacono and Professor Folco Portinari of the University of Turin. Also thanks to La Molisana pasta for the supply of excellent pasta with which to test recipes. I am grateful to those who helped me with historical and art research, especially Eva Agnesi of Imperia, Liguria. Special thanks go to my mother, Giustina Ghisu della Croce and Alexander Barakov for the many long hours spent at my side assisting in the development and testing of recipes and also to Alexander Barakov for his assistance with research and editing; and always to Flavia Destefanis for her counsel in Italian. I am most grateful to my extraordinary editor, Lorna Damms, Helen Diplock, the art editor, and the marvelous staff at Dorling Kindersley, photographers Ian O'Leary and Dave King, and home economist Oona van den Berg, for a job superbly done. Thanks also to Richard Bowditch and Eileen Brady-Nelson for their photography. I would also like to acknowledge the following books and publications, which were helpful in my research: *Bartolemeo Pinelli 1781-1835 e il suo tempo,* Maurizio Fagiolo and Maurizio Marini, Centro Iniziative Culturali, Pantheo, Roma, 1983; *Buffo,* Anthony Caputo, Wayne State Publishers, Indiana, 1978; *La Cucina Futuristica,* F.T. Marinetti, English Translation, Bedford Arts Publishers, San Francisco, 1989; *Domenico Tiepolo: The Punchinello Drawings,* Adelheid Gealt and James Byam Shaw, George Braziller, Inc., New York, 1986; *Gli Italiani a Tavola,* Felice Cúnsolo, U. Mursia 7C., Milano; *The Italian Comedy,* Pierre Louis Duchartre, Dover, New York, 1966; *I Maccheroni,* Alberto Consiglio, Newton Compton Editori, Roma, 1973; *Pasta Classica: The Art of Italian Pasta Cooking,* Julia della Croce, Chronicle Books, San Francisco, 1987; *Portrait of Pasta,* Anna del Conte, Paddington Press, London, 1976.

DK would like to thank Jasmine Challis for the nutritional breakdowns; Jenny Stacey for additional home economics; Tim Ridley; Emma Brogi for assisting Ian O'Leary; and Emy Manby for design help. Thanks also to Sue Henderson for assisting Oona van den Berg; Flavia Destefanis for checking the Italian; William Dane at Newark Public Library, New Jersey.

Picture credits

Jacket photograph of author by Eileen Brady-Nelson.

Photograph of author on page 6 by Richard Bowditch.

Page 6, bottom left, and page 7, bottom. Julia della Croce (private collection).

Page 7, top. Tiepolo illustration, from a print by Georg Friedrich Schmidt. Courtesy of Newark Public Library.

Page 8. Flavia Destefanis (private collection).

All other photographs by Ian O'Leary, except pages 30–43 by Dave King and pages 46–47 by Tim Ridley.